Gender, Social Inequalities, and Aging

THE GENDER LENS SERIES

Series Editors

Judith A. Howard
University of Washington

Barbara Risman
North Carolina State University

Joey Sprague
University of Kansas

The Gender Lens Series has been conceptualized as a way of encouraging the development of a sociological understanding of gender. A "gender lens" means working to make gender visible in social phenomena; asking if, how, and why social processes, standards, and opportunities differ systematically for women and men. It also means recognizing that gender inequality is inextricably braided with other systems of inequality. The Gender Lens series is committed to social change directed toward eradicating these inequalities. Originally published by Sage Publications and Pine Forge Press, all Gender Lens books are now available from AltaMira Press.

BOOKS IN THE SERIES

Gender, Social Inequalities, and Aging

Toni M. Calasanti
and
Kathleen F. Slevin

ALTAMIRA
PRESS

A Division of Rowman and Littlefield Publishers, Inc.
Walnut Creek • Lanham • New York • Oxford

AltaMira Press
A Division of Rowman & Littlefield Publishers, Inc.
1630 North Main Street, #367
Walnut Creek, CA 94596
http://www.altamirapress.com

Rowman & Littlefield Publishers, Inc.
4720 Boston Way
Lanham, MD 20706

12 Hid's Copse Road
Cumnor Hill, Oxford OX2 9JJ, England

British Library Cataloguing in Publication Information Available

Library of Congress Cataloging-in-Publication Data

Calasanti, Toni M.
   Gender, social inequalities, and aging / Toni M. Calasanti, Kathleen F. Slevin.
      p. cm. — (Gender lens)
   Includes bibliographical references and index.
   ISBN 0-7591-0185-X (cloth : alk. paper) — ISBN 0-7591-0186-8 (pbk. : alk. paper)
   1. Aging—Sex differences. 2. Aged—Social conditions. 3. Aged—Sexual behavior. 4. Aged—Economic conditions. 5. Ageism. 6. Feminist theory. I. Slevin, Kathleen F., 1947– II. Title. III. Series.

HQ1061 .C28 2001
305.26—dc21

2001022919

Printed in the United States of America

♾™ The paper used in this publication meets the minimum requirements of American National Standard for Information Sciences—Permanence of Paper for Printed Library Materials, ANSI/NISO Z39.48–1992.

CONTENTS

ACKNOWLEDGMENTS

We thank the editors of this series who had the wisdom to see the need for this book. As feminist scholars we are committed to approaching the study of aging and old age through a critical and feminist lens. Thus, writing this book provided us the opportunity to explore areas and topics that we consider underdeveloped or ignored in the study of old age. Our dedication to the book and to each other as colleagues and friends of more than a decade provided a solid foundation as we weathered the predictable struggles that accompany co-authorship. Living at disparate ends of a large state requires a four-and-a-half-hour drive to work together. With the demands of full-time teaching, other academic duties, and mothering of two active children each, getting together to brainstorm and to do the things that cannot be done via phone or e-mail sometimes pushed us to our limits.

The finished product is a testimony to our commitment to the project and to each other. We are fortunate to have many friends and colleagues who provided us help and support. Our editors, Barbara Risman and Judy Howard, deserve special mention. What you read bears the mark of their expertise. In addition to insightful comments on each chapter, they provided emotional support. Their timing with a special push or a word of praise proved impeccable. In all the ways that our own feminism helped us to support each other, Barbara's and Judy's feminism helped us bring this project to closure and ensured that the end product is better for their involvement.

To Neal King, Toni's partner, we owe thanks for two years of service as critic-on-demand. He read drafts—sometimes several—of every chapter; and during our marathon sessions together, made himself available around the clock—editing, commenting and arguing, cooking for us, and seeing to our every need. His gestures of support and caring provide us a deeper appreciation for the feminist men in our lives.

Other colleagues and friends were very generous and supportive of us, both intellectually and personally. We acknowledge them alphabetically: David Aday, Alicia Almada, Jennifer Bickham Mendez, Rosemary Blieszner, Bill Fletcher, Joe Hendricks, Matt McAllister, Tom Linneman, Gul Ozyegin, and Ray Wingrove. Their many sources of help included reading various drafts and giving insightful comments; providing us key references for perspectives that ultimately shaped our thinking in important ways; lending us support and inspiration during times of self-doubt. Our graduate students also provided valuable help in a variety of ways and we appreciate their contributions to the final product. Jill Behnke worked with Kate; and Rosemary Ellis, Maureen Clark, John Wilkins, Steve Poulson, and Janet Arnado all provided Toni with various kinds of help. In addition, we want to thank Brenda Husser and Missy Graham for their help, and the Center for Gerontology at Virginia Tech for supporting some of Toni's research.

Both of us have parents—Ann and Tony Calasanti and Rose and Francie Woods—who are facing many of the issues we discuss in this book. We appreciate what we have learned first-hand from them about survival, resistance, and dignity.

We also thank Bob Yeomans, Kate's husband, for his love, patience, and support. Completing this manuscript required that we intensely focus on our goal and, as a result, those near and dear to us, including our children, Annamarie and Marisa (Toni) and Conor and Sarah (Kate), endured our absences—mentally and physically.

Finally, the recognition of the support and love of many people in no way implies that they are responsible for the ideas expressed herein. As authors, we are proud of the perspectives and insights we offer to you and we take full responsibility for them.

Picture a small college town full of university faculty who write books. Two of them enjoy lunch and chat about their various projects. "Oh, you're writing a book! That's wonderful? What is it about?"

"Gender and aging."

"Oh. Hmm. Check, please!"

Though the unguarded may blurt out "How depressing," real-life colleagues mostly give us awkward silences while they grope, often in vain, for congratulatory lines. We try to fill these painful pauses by assuring them that we understand what a difficult topic this must be to imagine or relate to. Sometimes we hear platitudes about the importance of this unexciting field of study. In any case, people switch topics quickly and move on to less repulsive ground.

So common has this awkward conversation become, in fact, that we often truncate it ourselves—answering quickly and moving on. On only one occasion did we pursue the topic and demonstrate to the questioners (who seemed attentive) how important and interesting this work is for us all. While successful, this was time-consuming and exhausting.

We open the book with this example because it tells us how people view old age in this society. They often greet it in contradictory fashion: as a very important issue, given that we are an "aging society," but also with a sort of denial. Even professionals within our discipline assure us that the topic we study is important but not the stuff of "real" sociology. The subjects of our work, the old, seem to hold little value for most people, and so the study of old age carries low prestige as well.

Despite the negativity involved, the importance of aging and old age in our lives is beyond dispute. Even if we wanted to escape the topics, it would be impossible in today's world. Daily, if not hourly, we are exposed to a barrage of commentary and advice in multiple media that draw our attention to age. Consider the simple fact that television shows are deftly programmed and marketed to attract audiences of different ages, as are the age-specific advertisements that accompany such programming. Their negative images about old age abound—youth is equated with beauty, strength, and productivity. By contrast, the messages about old age and aging convey passivity and weakness; growing old is to be avoided, fought, denied, and disguised.

People have grown ever more concerned with the aging of the population, both nationally and globally, and worry about the "burden" that the old present. Natural and social scientists advance careers by presenting old age as a "problem" to be "solved." Furthermore, in a culture that covets youth, "experts" who help us "age successfully" can attain the status of gurus. Indeed, one might argue that "aging well" has become a growing national, if not Western, obsession—particularly given the baby boom generation's increasing attention to growing old.

What has gender to do with all of this? Certainly it shapes the social organization of aging and affects how people and their larger social systems treat the old. Yet most Western societies at this point in time stigmatize all old people, women and men. Witness, in the United States for instance, the growing boom in elective plastic surgery for affluent, middle-aged men—stereotypically the domain of affluent, aging women. Clearly these men, despite their more privileged position on the gender hierarchy, do not feel immune to pressures to maintain youthful faces and bodies as they grow old.

Whether at the individual or structural level, gender remains a powerful force—an organizing principle—that shapes our social world, including our constructions of old age. But other systems of inequality also intersect with aging and gender to shape experiences. That is, while gender organizes every aspect of our lives, it intersects with other hierarchies of class, race and ethnicity, and sexuality. Thus, old people share the reality of aging bodies and the stigma of old age; but men and women who are poor, who are members of racial or ethnic minorities, who are gay or lesbian experience these differently from those of majority populations.

A Gender Lens

The perspective that we take in this book is rooted in feminist theories. While gender studies have influenced work in many disciplines, including our own in sociology, feminist perspectives remain little used in gerontology, even in research focused on old women (Hooyman 1999). While we are not the first or only scholars of aging to use a feminist framework,[1] we hope that our discussion moves the field one step closer toward a revisioning of old age through a more dynamic and inclusive framework.

We explain our perspective more thoroughly in chapters 1 and 2, but here we want to highlight what we mean by a *gender lens* approach to old age. It draws on a feminist framework that requires us to explore old age and its intersections with gender, race and ethnicity, class, and sexual orientation. We recognize that we must include all of these crosscutting relations of power (Baca Zinn and Thornton Dill 1996; Collins 1990), that we cannot speak of gender as if it were shaped by the power relations between men and women alone. Our approach is also relational. This means that we realize that men and women gain identities and power in relation to one another (Glenn 1999); that we must look at *gender relations* in order to understand how both men and women age. As a result, this book is not about old age as a "woman's issue," nor is it about simply looking at women who are old (though we may begin with their experiences). Instead, it is about how men's and women's experiences of old age are shaped in relation to one another. Similarly, examining the influence of race and ethnicity implies that we must include majority as well as minority racial status in our analyses. The privileged position of one group relies on the disadvantaged position of another.

Importantly, then, our gender lens challenges all of us to acknowledge a key point for this book: that we all, not just the old, have *age*. Ultimately, we will explore the ways in which these age relations underlie our approaches to old age and our ageism. Finally, our gender lens allows us to see that sources of oppression can also be sources of resistance and strength (Calasanti and Zajicek 1997; Slevin and Wingrove 1998). We will show that some of the ways in which women are disadvantaged relative to men, or

---

[1] We realize that there are many different feminist theories. But for simplicity, we speak of a singular feminist approach. Readers who are interested in learning about the variety of feminisms and how they may examine old women might begin with Collette Browne's (1998) book.

Blacks relative to Whites, also give each group different strategies or resources for meeting the challenges of old age. Importantly, these advantages are often hidden when we do not begin with the experiences of more oppressed groups.

Thus, our approach encompasses an analytical framework for understanding old age that incorporates multiple perspectives and realities at both the individual and structural levels. That is, a relational approach emphasizes and embeds notions of diversity into its analyses. Using perspectives that differ from those of the majority allows us to uncover realities that might otherwise remain hidden because privilege and oppression are linked. Consider, for example, the male bias reflected in the common idea that paid work matters most to men and that retirement represents a loss of status. Such an assumption reinforces a mindset that hinders us from exploring work as more than paid productive activity, a perspective that would allow us to inquire into the ways in which "retirement" may be very different for women who engage in significant unpaid labor in the home. In addition it obscures the importance of such important parts of male retirees' lives as family. Similarly, consider the race, gender, and class bias present in the persistent myth that older Black American women resist retirement because only paid labor provides status and meaning in their lives (Jackson 1988). The assumption that Black American women must work for pay in order to give meaning to their lives suggests a panoply of biases, among them the notion that paid labor in old age is a choice and not a financial necessity. In addition, it implies a monolithic image of African American women that ignores the class advantages that accrue, for example, to professional women (Slevin and Wingrove 1998). Further, when we concentrate on retirement as an event shaped by a clearly defined time at which one enters and exits the labor force, we do so from a "majority" perspective, one that ignores an inherent gender, class, and racial/ethnic bias (Calasanti 1993; R. Gibson 1987). Similarly, when scholars focus on the experiences of some racial/ethnic minority groups, or on those whose sexual orientation is different from the majority, new notions of family emerge and debunk the assumptions that spouse and children are the only or the most important informal supports in later life (Dorfman et al. 1995).

Using a gender lens approach presents its own set of challenges, and we next present some of the important issues that we had to deal with in writing a book of this kind. In particular, a number of conceptual concerns come to the fore when trying to explore race/ethnicity and sexuality in old age. Below, we discuss the difficulties in each of these areas as well as some background material that will underlie our discussions. We hope readers will bear these concerns in mind as we review the research available throughout this book. We depend on such research but must remain critical of what it does not tell us.

Race/Ethnicity

One experiences old age differently depending on how one's gender intersects with race and ethnicity. For example, patterns of discrimination experienced by Black Americans cannot be explained by allusions to gender or class alone (Wilkinson 1995). We must examine and differentiate among old members of racial/ethnic groups. In fundamental ways, the lives of old Native Americans, Asian Americans, or African Americans differ from those of old White Americans.

However, we should first offer some cautionary notes, which we hope readers will bear in mind throughout. First, racial/ethnic diversity has only recently gained the interest of (predominantly White) social scientists. As a result, the field of aging, like so many others, lacks research on nondominant groups. Our reports in this book remain severely restricted by the paucity of research, especially in relation to American Indians. Apart from the general lack of research, the diversity among this group by nation and location (reservation versus urban, for example) is tremendous (John 1999; Antonucci and Cantor 1994). As a result, much of what we will discuss is suggestive, based as it is on a very small number of studies.

Second, as the discussion of American Indians implies, the research available does not often reflect the tremendous diversity within racial/ethnic groups. The understanding that Whites differ from one another on the basis of such factors as social class is often forgotten when the focus switches to racial and ethnic minority groups. Membership in a racial/ethnic minority group—being Black, for instance—tends to be of overriding importance to researchers, and all members of this group become homogenized. As a result, studies that focus on lower-class Blacks—the most often-researched group of Blacks—are taken to apply to the entire group (Antonucci and Cantor 1994).

Diversity within groups is based on more than class, sexuality, or gender, and in ways we generally do not explore in this book. As with American Indians, very culturally diverse groups are often lumped together under the rubric of, say, African Americans or Asian Americans. This situation is often beyond researchers' control. For instance, in analyzing secondary sources such as Census data, researchers are restricted to using the racial and ethnic categories used to collect the information. In addition, some research designs require large enough numbers of a particular group in order to do analysis. As a result, groups such as Puerto Ricans, Cubans, and Mexican Americans may be put together to form a larger category designated "Latinos."

Consequently, we can report little research on racial and ethnic minority groups with any certainty. Historic and cultural differences are critical but generally unexplored. A group designated as African American may include Blacks who do not have roots in Africa; they could be recent immigrants or they could be fifth-generation Americans. Asian Americans can be from as diverse backgrounds as Japan, China, or Korea. Although many of the latter are influenced by Confucianism and its norms of filial piety, they are diverse as well in terms of history of immigration and country of origin (Lockery 1992). And in many instances, Indians, Nepalese, and others are also included in this category.

Depending on when they arrived in the United States, each group also faced particular immigration and socioeconomic conditions that influenced their status in the wider society (Amott and Matthaei 1996). More recent immigrants diverge widely in terms of ethnic and class composition from those who immigrated before 1965 (Glenn 1999). Such differences not only influence the financial wherewithal one has when entering old age, for example, but also the ability of different groups to enact cultural proscriptions concerning old age in instances where they might want to do so.

The conditions of immigration also influence the age and sex composition of groups of elderly as well (Siegel 1999). For instance, laws that restricted the immigration of Asian women meant that many of the old Chinese men never married and are thus without typical forms of support in old age (Amott and Matthaei 1996). This also means that the sex ratio—the number of women to men—among the Chinese is not as skewed as is the case among other racial and ethnic groups. Among present-day elderly Asians, the bulk are likely to be Chinese, then Japanese and Filipino; new immigrants include Indians, Vietnamese, and Koreans (Siegel 1999).

Similarly, those who are often referred to as "Hispanic" or "Latino/a" vary widely in terms of country of origin and subsequent cultures. What the federal government has designated as "Hispanic," for instance, combines groups that differ not only in class but in terms of their racial designation by the majority. As Glenn (1999, 30) notes, the U.S. government considers Mexicans White even though people perceive them to be "Brown," whereas Puerto Ricans are seen to be Black despite very different designations in Puerto Rico. Cubans may be seen as White in part because the immigrants after the Cuban revolutions were the more light-skinned, upper- and middle-class Cubans, however, more recent immigrants have not had the same social standing as those who were a part of the 1960 refugee movement (Siegel 1999).

Length of time in the United States also varies widely. Some of Spanish origin, for example, have been in the United States for more than three hundred years (Magilvy et al. 2000); some Mexicans were literally colonized in 1848 as a result of the war with Mexico while others are much more recent immigrants (Amott and Matthaei 1996). Still others are Puerto Rican, which involves an entirely different relationship with the United States and may involve a back-and-forth sort of migration; and others may come from any number of Central or South American countries.

Research differentiating among Hispanic groups is sparse. Most commonly, groups are examined together and referred to as either Hispanic or Latino/a. When research does not break them down into smaller groups, then, we adopt the term used in the particular study as it is often impossible for us to distinguish the different ethnic groups represented.

Sexual Preference

Throughout the book we will also take note of similarities and differences wrought by sexual preference, when possible. Studies examining sexuality are quite scarce (Berger and Kelly 1996), even more so than are studies on race and ethnicity. Researchers of aging tend to assume that everyone is heterosexual or that any difference has no consequence, while scholars of sexuality tend to focus on the young. Still, a small number of studies have revealed issues important to examining sexual preference in relation to old age.

Understanding diversity of sexuality among the old is fraught with difficulty. First, sexual orientation is not a static entity. As a result, many who might presently define themselves as gay, lesbian, bisexual, or heterosexual might not have done so earlier in life. Second, some old people might not want to identify themselves as gay or lesbian for fear of negative consequences. Accurately estimating their numbers, then, or having the opportunity to learn about their lives, can be difficult. Despite myths to the contrary, we cannot assume sexual orientation on the basis of marital history or the presence of children. Researchers estimate that one in five gay men and one in three lesbians report having been in a heterosexual marriage; about half of these marriages resulted in children (Allen and Demo 1995). Third, among those presently old, others may never have adopted an *identity* as gay or lesbian. Shenk and Fullmer (1996), for example, show that some lifelong companions appear to not ever identify themselves as "lesbians."

Forming any identity is a social process, one in which multiple power relations come into play. First, some identities would never come to the fore at all as they would have no social relevance ("freckled" or "blue-eyed," for instance). Second, people might prefer to bypass stigmatized identities as well. If identifying oneself as a gay man leads others to assume that one is "feminine" or "unnatural," then men who do not see themselves in these ways are likely to avoid calling themselves homosexual and may not even see themselves as gay. Both of these contexts would help explain why old gays and lesbians might not have adopted a self-identity as homosexual. Old lesbians may be even less likely to self-identify than gay men because of the interaction of heterosexism with sexism (Fullmer, Shenk, and Eastland 1999). Contemporary old women grew up in an era in which women were not supposed to be overtly sexual at all, much less so deviant as to be lesbian.

These considerations reveal the special importance of attending to cohort differences among gay men and lesbians. A cohort refers to a group of people born at a particular time who therefore share experiences that may differentiate them from those born at another time (Kimmel 1995). As implied by the discussion above, gay men and women who are presently old often had their sexual coming of age during a time in which homosexuality was not only the basis for flagrant discrimination and but was also considered an example of individual deviance. The 1969 Stonewall rebellion, in which a police raid on a gay bar precipitated gay insurgence against oppressive police practices, "represented a paradigm shift that made possible the development of the current lesbian and gay community" (Kimmel 1995, 291). As one old gay man stated,

> "[B]ack in 1948 to 1950 . . . there wasn't as yet in the minds of my fellow Queers, let alone the American society at large, even the beginnings of such as concept as that of a GAY IDENTITY. Everywhere we were constantly being told . . . that we were heteros who occasionally performed nasty acts. . . . *But we were HETEROS, we were just exactly the same as everybody else (except when we perversely insisted on performing those degenerate and WHOLLY ILLEGAL acts)."*
>
> The tremendous leap forward in consciousness that was the Stonewall Rebellion changed the pronoun in Gay identity from "I" to "WE." (Hay 1990, 5, in Kimmel 1995, 291)

Many gays and lesbians who claimed this identity in the aftermath of this rebellion have seen, not only the decline in police harassment, but also the growth of community as the veil of secrecy has lifted (Kimmel 1995).

These different "identity cohorts" (Rosenfeld 1999) are further complicated by the timing of coming out and other variations in life courses. Recent research among lesbians and, in particular, gay men has found that marital histories and the presence/absence of children are important. Having been married often means that gays and lesbians acquire their same-sex preference identification later in life and thus begin learning "appropriate" dating behavior later. The downside of "'doing at 48 what most people do at 23'" is that such individuals have difficulty fitting into and feeling a part of either straight or gay communities (Herdt, Beeler, and Rawls 1997, 240). Similarly, gay men with children also report difficulties in forming bonds and feeling a part of a community. They feel different both from straight men and from gay men who either do not understand the obligations that parenthood may present or may not be able to relate to this often-important aspect of their lives (Herdt, Beeler, and Rawls 1997).

These considerations reveal the special importance of considering both cohort differences and the life course when looking at old gays, lesbians, and bisexuals. That is, the process of sexual identification shapes the lives of nonheterosexuals in critical ways. At the same time, the diversity by race/ethnicity, gender, and class has only begun to be examined as samples drawn from therapeutic populations have tended to be White, middle-class men (Herdt, Beeler, and Rawls 1997; Boxer 1997).

A Note on Language—("Old")

The words we use do more than signify what we intend—they also often represent unspoken opinions and values. Throughout this book, we refer to those over sixty-five as "old." We specify why more fully in chapter 2, when we discuss the ageism within gerontology. But we address a few points here at the outset.

People can object that the term "old" both reifies a socially constructed process of aging and treats a diverse population as though they were all the same. That is, it sets boundaries around and makes solid what is fluid and amorphous. It creates the impression that socially constructed age categories, like old, have a natural basis, and can somehow be clearly differentiated from, say, "middle age." For this reason, and because of the negative meanings attached to "old," many authors use the term "old*er*."

We acknowledge and agree that "old" is a reified category, but also point out that all categories share this reified status. Racial categories and the two sexes are socially created as well; yet no one suggests that we refer to Blacks as "darker" or women as "more female." People voice few objections to the use of "young" or "youth."

All such designations reify; but they do not all make people equally uncomfortable. "Old" carries a unique stigma. The discomfort you may feel in reading or hearing the term reveals our cultural values, including those of gerontologists. Indeed, not so long ago the term Black carried only negative connotations; and many shuddered at its use. However, activists have successfully reclaimed this term by using it while demanding respect for their communities. The message was clear. While racial and ethnic groups may be similar in some respects, they are also different; those differences do not justify scorn and in fact should be valued. We use "old" in this activist manner—to naturalize and neutralize it. Just as "young" or "middle aged" carry both positive and negative connotations, we hope to show the same for "old" and reclaim its use. By using it in relation to all experiences discussed in this book, we hope to underscore the valuable similarities and differences between the old and other age groups, as well as among the old, and to bring the positive connotations back into the word.

Overview of the Book

To help simplify our discussion of gender and aging we take a few liberties that some might find objectionable. First, we tend to lump together the related but different fields, social gerontology and the sociology of aging. Second, while our perspective is one of multiple oppressions, in the book we focus primarily on gender. We may also speak of a particular social location, such as class, by itself, in order to talk about particular effects; but we do understand that these locations are multiple.

Finally, we wish to show how a gender lens would affect our vision of the old. That is, we examine the ways in which attention to power relations allows us to understand diverse experiences of old age and transforms research on aging. Our attention to power relations keeps two insights front and center: First, old people are diverse, but in relational ways; and second, no matter how diverse, the old are also bound together by their age. In this sense they are all influenced by ageism, albeit in similar and different ways that result from lifelong processes related to the intersections of social inequalities. This understanding forms the thread that underlies our discussion in each chapter.

To discuss the multiple facets of old age in one book is a daunting task, one that, ultimately, we do not undertake. That is, we do not try to cover the entire terrain of old age. Rather, with each topic we discuss, we explore how these power relations influence the diverse experiences of old age. We apply the gender lens to specific substantive areas only, but without the belief that these topics are the most important, much less exhaustive; they simply represent some vital aspects of the lives of the old.

In chapter one, we begin by looking at the ways in which age is socially constructed and shaped by multiple social locations—gender, race/ethnicity, class, and sexuality. We also establish that ageism toward the old is pervasive, not only in our society but also in the very scholarship that examines notions of old age and aging. In chapter 2 we explore how mainstream theories in both sociology and gerontology conceive of gender and other social inequalities. We discuss the various ways in which theories tend to be based on the experiences of White, middle-class, heterosexual men. Such theories often view gender narrowly and ignore feminist scholarship. We explore, too, other implicit biases of dominant perspectives in gerontology, including notions of "aging successfully" and "productive aging," and then contrast these with our own approach to examining gender and old age. We discuss gender as a social relation, and we delve into the ways that race/ethnicity, class, and sexual orientation intersect with gender and old age.

Our bodies change throughout our lives, from infancy onward, and certainly as we grow old. Thus, in chapter 3 we focus on the body as a critical marker of old age. We show how ageism intersects with sexism and other hierarchies to construct the most popular perceptions of aging bodies. We attend especially to the recent emphasis on transforming the body in order to "stop the clock," the mounting pressure to maintain a youthful appearance as one grows old. In chapter 4 we shift focus to explore how people have constructed sex and sexuality and how different forms of inequality create multiple experiences and perspectives of this. An ageist bias permeates scholarship on sexuality such that silence prevails about old people's sexualities, especially those of old women.

Chapters 5 and 6 further our understanding about diverse experiences of work and retirement. Sensitivity to power relations reveals that vulnerability to economic dependence varies tremendously by gender, race/ethnicity, and class; and we discuss this reality in chapter 5. At the same time, a gender lens on work and retirement in chapter 6 reveals that "work" is much broader than paid labor and that, in fact, many retired people are quite involved in both paid and unpaid labor while in their "nonproductive" years. We argue, too, that notable power differences by gender, race, and class influence the freedom to choose whether or not to engage in paid or unpaid work in old age. This discussion on unpaid labor provides a segue into the diversity of informal care work in old age in chapter 7. Here we looked extensively at how gender relations interact with other social locations to shape care work in old age. Our analysis reveals that women are more involved in elder care in old age than are men, both as care workers and as recipients. In addition, the increasing numbers of old women, particularly within racial/ethnic minority groups and the working class, are engaged in custodial grandparenting. Our discussion of care work in later life also highlights the diversity of "families" as we find that the intersections of social hierarchies influences who is considered "family" in the context of care work.

Finally, in chapter 8, we turn the gender lens back on itself, asking how this lens would change were it to take seriously power relations based on age. That is, we examine the ageism and neglect of age relations that underlie both gerontological and feminist approaches. We then speculate on the ways in which a consideration of old women and age relations might change feminist theories themselves. In this way, our sensitivity to power relations takes us full circle, and we conclude with a call to take age relations seriously as one way of undermining ageism and seeing old age as a valuable time of life.

Ultimately, our book does not advocate for an "ideal" way to grow old. Instead, our focus on diversity reveals many ways to age, each tied to lifelong experiences. Rather than prescribe an aging process, we ask whether old people are equally able to have the sort of old age they would prefer. Also, we question the ability of any person to be "old" with the fullest dignity in our present social context. Given our ageist climate, it would be difficult for any old person to be able to claim to be "old" and receive respect for it. This book will offer an extended argument for a sense of value and respect for the old, in all of their diversity.

CHAPTER 1

A Gender Lens on Old Age

It's 11 A.M., her private yoga session is over and she's dressed to the nines in a beige Oscar de la Renta suit. . . . The monogrammed handkerchief with which she occasionally dabs at sniffles is the only sign that she braved a cold rain the night before to attend the Rose Garden dinner-dance at the New York Botanical Garden in the Bronx. Over tea, she sits in the library of her Park Avenue apartment, examining the printout of her daily schedule. There will be lunch at Café Bouloud, a trustees' meeting at the Metropolitan Museum of Art, and in the evening a Louis Armstrong Concert at Carnegie Hall, followed by a benefit dinner where flashes will pop upon her arrival.

(*New York Times*, Living Section, 1, October 8, 2000)

This vignette details the life of a New York woman of considerable privilege. Most readers are likely to be struck not only by the affluence of this socialite's surroundings and activities but also by the sheer number of social occasions she packs into a single day. The description makes clear that she is a member of the upper class and, by that token, we might also assume that she is most likely White. If asked to guess her age, most would probably say forties, fifties, or maybe even sixties. How accurate are our predictions? Well, our hunch on social class and race would be on target, but on age we would be wrong. She is ninety-eight years old. Most of us expect ninety-eight-year-olds to be debilitated and living under another's care. But we do not expect that someone this age, even when she is among society's most elite, would be the focus of paparazzi attention that we assume to be the domain of the young and the youthfully beautiful.

In this chapter, we examine constructions of old age in our society. We explore how our conceptions of age, specifically of "old" age, are socially constructed—shaped by cultural notions, in conjunction with social institutions that shift over time and place, as well as by other characteristics. For instance, over the last century becoming old has increasingly come to be viewed as something that can be cured, controlled, even stopped. Exhortations to defy growing old abound in our popular media. We know that discrimination against society's old is also a reality and we explore ageism in its varied forms. We also pay attention to the ways in which people's social locations shape their experiences of growing and being old. Old people are not all equally disadvantaged or advantaged—as the opening vignette suggests. It would be difficult to see this old woman as oppressed, certainly in relation to a White, working-class, retired woman. Old-age experiences depend on intersections of gender, race, class, and sexual orientation.[1] Examining the importance of these diverse backgrounds to our lives is at the heart of the gender lens approach that we discuss as we conclude the chapter by suggesting ways to improve how old age is studied.

The Social Construction of Old Age

A complex web of social and cultural factors that fluctuate over the globe and over time shape old age, our understanding of it, and our responses to it. Consequently, we need to be sensitive to these contexts as we try to understand the nature of aging experiences (Sokolovsky 1993). Old age is just one of the life stages that societies create, and the number and timing of these stages vary. For instance, prior to the twentieth century there was no term for adolescence. In the past, people arrived at adulthood and its accompanying responsibilities of independence and full-time employment at much earlier ages than in today's Western industrial societies. Today, entire markets, such as those for clothes and entertainment, cater exclusively to teenagers and their leisure time. So it goes for the old. As institutions arise with new services and products to sell, we

---

[1] Of course, experiences of gender, race, ethnicity, class, and sexuality also vary by age. However, because our focus is on old age, we emphasize the intersections of these other power relations on this time of life. We take up the issue of age relations more closely in chapter 8.

reconstruct what it means to be old, and those constructions vary with gender, race and ethnicity, class, and sexual preference.

People create different meanings that they associate with various stages of the life course. Age serves in important ways to distinguish acceptable behavior for different groups. Voting rights, the ability to hold certain offices (one cannot be President of the United States unless one is at least thirty-five years old), the legal right to consume alcohol, the age at which one can collect Social Security benefits as a retired worker—these are all examples of specific, formal age norms in the United States.

Informal rules also illustrate how a society defines what is considered appropriate by age. Thus, we might ask, how might people react to an old woman wearing a miniskirt? There is nothing intrinsically wrong with an old woman wearing a miniskirt, but given the popular equation of youth with attractiveness, especially sexual attractiveness for women, her attire would draw scorn or even disgust from many people. So while there is nothing inherently wrong with older age groups dressing in clothes or adopting punk hairstyles associated with younger groups, the old person may well experience sanction for doing so. Indeed, the Irish sometimes chastise such old people as "mutton dressed as lambs"!

Bodies are key sites for judgments about age (Oberg 1996). As the example of the old woman in a skimpy skirt suggests, how we present our bodies provides symbols that allow others to judge us. By looking at a person's body we immediately, and mostly unconsciously, come to a set of opinions about his or her age, race, sex, social class, and even sexual orientation. Indeed, our bodies are very important to our identities throughout the life span and to our presentation of self—a topic to which we will return in chapter 3.

The social construction of old age is also apparent when we examine the depiction of the old cross-culturally and historically. The old have been revered or reviled in different times and places. For example, in classical Greece old age was seen as an "unmitigated misfortune" (Sokolvsky 1993, 51), while in Japanese culture, for many centuries elders enjoyed the greatest power in their society. In some places, such as Samoa, old age—especially when accompanied by good health—was considered to be the pinnacle of life; it brought with it the exclusive right to engage in important social realms (Sokolovsky 1993). Among the Abaluyia of western Kenya, respect for the old is a key cultural value: Children are expected to be quiet around adults and to obey them, and middle-aged people are similarly expected to be courteous and deferential toward their elders (Cattell 1997).

Despite the Western tendency to differentiate societies by preindustrial and industrial type, there is no simple correspondence between how old age gets constructed and societal type (Sokolovsky 1993). In fact, research on sixty mostly nonwestern societies reveals three different criteria for designating old age. The first and most common marker has to do with changes in social and economic roles, including such things as becoming a grandparent and shifts in productive activity. The second is based on chronological age. The third and least commonly used marker is a change in physical characteristics or capabilities (Sokolovsky 1997a). Further, industrialized nations are not sufficiently alike to assume similarity. For example, differences in self-concept among Dutch and Spanish old persons are attributable to the individualistic vs. collectivist orientations, respectively, that characterize the two cultures (Katzko et al. 1998). And although currently in flux due to women's increased labor force participation, the old receive greater reverence in Japan (Jenike 1997) than in the United States.

Historical changes occur in the construction of old age within countries. For instance, old age in the United States was not as exalted in the past as some might believe. Even in seventeenth-century New England, there existed some tension with regard to the old. Certainly, their control of land and other resources brought them power and respect, but not always affection. They often faced hostility from younger generations who desired these assets (Haber and Gratton 1994, 6–7). By the nineteenth century, people increasingly viewed the old as dependent and old age as a time of disease or "senility" (Haber 1983).

Current depictions of old age in the United States present it as something to be avoided. Scholars, policy makers and all manner of practitioners, and the general public have constructed growing old as a medical problem—a sickness that can be treated and cured. This "biomedicalization" of old age (Estes and Binney 1991) leads to a focus on diseases associated with old age. Thus, old age, equated with illness, is frequently seen as "pathological or abnormal," so that this condition, as well as those "afflicted" with it, are to be avoided (Estes 1991, 118).

Finally, social locations play a role in the construction of old age. In the United States, these locations include not only gender but also others, including race, ethnicity, class, and sexual orientation. Indeed, the respect accorded the old in the seventeenth century was by no means universal: Only landowning White men could command such honor. Similarly, the sorts of programs designed for the old in the nineteenth century reflected the inequality among them: "Private old-age homes were established primarily for native-born women and public almshouses for immigrant men;

in the large cities of the South, segregated, poorly maintained institutions housed the most unfortunate of elderly blacks" (Haber and Gratton 1994, 10). Of course, the likelihood of even reaching old age in the nineteenth century varied by class, race, ethnicity, and gender. For instance, because of the high mortality rate among women in childbirth, many women did not live beyond childbearing years. The industrial employment available to the poor and working class also curtailed life expectancy, as did the poverty and paucity of access to medical care for American Indians on reservations.

Thus, the contemporary biomedicalization of old age diverts attention from social arrangements that produce inequalities in old age, including differences in health and health care delivery. By making old age a medical problem, what should best be understood as a social issue is construed as a medical or personal problem that should be treated by medical intervention. Power relations based on class, race, ethnicity, gender, and sexual orientation are left untouched (Hendricks 1995).

Social constructions of old age have real consequences for those so defined. As a result, how scholars of aging define old age is critical at many levels—including policy formation, public perception, and self-concept. Scholars also recognize that old age has multiple dimensions. At the level of the individual, age identification is a complex process, involving much more than a simple reference to one's chronological age—the number of years since birth. Subjective age, which involves individuals' evaluations of their aging process in relation to their age peers (Uotinen 1998; Goldsmith and Heiens 1992), also plays a role in age identification. And of course, what individuals believe about others' perceptions of themselves matters in how one defines one's age (Goldsmith and Heiens 1992). Such perceptions could be based in part on notions of occupational age. That is, people may be considered "old" at different ages according to their employment. For example, a female model is typically old well before she turns thirty. A professional football player may be considered old in his early thirties. A baseball player may reach forty before that assessment is made, while a CEO is old in his early sixties. By contrast, a U.S. senator may be into his or her eighties before being seen as too old for the job. Finally, scholars also talk about functional age, which involves an assessment of an individual's physical and mental abilities in relation to an ideal type for his or her age group. For example, we sometimes hear of an individual who is chronologically sixty but who "has the body of a forty-year-old" and vice versa.

Scholarly arguments concerning how "old" is defined have cautioned against using chronological age exclusively and have centered on individual variations in the aging process. They point to the ways that physical or mental functioning do not allow lumping together everyone over a particular age. We would never, for example, allow generalizations to be made about a sample of persons aged fifteen to fifty-five based on their shared age. Yet, we accept results of studies of the "old," variously defined as beginning at age fifty-five, or including a forty-year span and several generations. Scholars also remind us not only of the great variability in aging but also of the effects of cohort or generational differences.

While the general public tends to see the old as homogenous and aging as homogenizing, aging scholars provide evidence to the contrary. Chronological age is a poor predictor of social, physical, and mental abilities (Arber and Ginn 1991a).

Indeed, there is vast heterogeneity in aging (Dannefer 1996). That is, aging experiences are shaped by individual variations in such things as genetic makeup, history, and personal biography. However, such individual differences are not the same as what we will later refer to as *diversity*—patterned differences that result from interaction among systems of inequality.

At the same time, scholars are not immune from stereotypes based on age. Schaei (1993) maintains that a "culturally based age bias" prevails in psychological research, a bias that makes negative or positive assumptions about the old on the basis of chronological age. He also challenges the way researchers operationalize "old," noting that the tendency to lump all those over a certain age, for example sixty-five, ignores the fact that "differences between those in their 60s and those in their 80s are greater than those between 20- and 60-year-olds" (Schaei 1993, 50). Furthermore, he notes a tendency to assume that the changes that come with age will be negative.

Implicit in the discussion of how we define old age is the reality that, regardless of what criteria or measures we use, the underlying construction of old age is negative. For instance, a recent survey conducted by the American Association of Retired Persons (AARP 1995a) discovered that younger people tended to define "old" in terms of years—if not chronologically, at least in terms of the number of years in a particular role such as worker or parent. By contrast, older people tended to define old in terms of social or psychological attributes (such as attitudes), or health and activities. Despite the different criteria used, however, both groups defined "old" in terms of decline or loss of roles (such as work or family/parenting) or of abilities.

It is not surprising, then, that a research finding first recorded over twenty-five years ago has changed very little today. A nationwide poll conducted in 1975 revealed that even the old resist the label; they don't see themselves as "old" (Harris and Associates 1975). A more recent survey on "Images of Aging in America" revealed similarly negative assumptions about "old" (AARP 1995a). Thus, the old themselves shun this label and reserve it for those in obvious physical or mental decline; they treat chronological age as irrelevant (Minichiello, Browne, and Kendig 2000). Not only has such rejection of the self as old long been prevalent in the United States, evidence suggests that it is accelerating. As advances in technology and medicine combine with the relative affluence and higher educational levels of many middle-aged people, preservation of youthfulness becomes even more desirable (Barak 1998). In fact, as people age they report increasingly discrepant age identities. Consequently, most old people see themselves as younger than their chronological age, leading to an inevitable tension between inner experience ("I feel young") and outward appearance ("I look old"). In a recent study as many as 80 percent of those in their sixties and seventies and 97 percent of those in their eighties reported subjective ages younger than their years lived (Goldsmith and Heiens 1992). There is little if any positive association with the term "old."

Ageism

The negativity that leads so many old people to scorn this label demonstrates the pervasiveness of ageism. Robert Butler first coined this term over thirty years ago to describe the "systematic stereotyping of and discrimination against people because they are old, just as racism and sexism accomplish this with skin color and gender" (Butler 1969, 243). Ageism allows people to see the old as different, as "other," as not "like them," thereby making it easier to see the old as "not humans." Pink triangles (for gays and lesbians) and Stars of David (for Jews) served that function in previous times by identifying those who were to be excluded but who might otherwise "pass" without visible means of differentiating. Constructions of old age and the visible markers of it matter in this way. Old people mask the bodily changes with good reason, as we discuss in chapter 3.

Similar to racism and sexism, ageism encourages viewing people not as individuals but as members of a social category (Quadagno 1999). Ageism is more than the attitudes and beliefs held by individuals in a particular society; it is also embedded in patterns of behavior and it serves as a social organizing principle (Dressel, Minkler, and Yen 1997). Further, ageism takes new forms over time. Images of the old as vulnerable have recently given way to images of the affluent "greedy geezer," whose selfish drain on society has left younger generations in poverty. Another new form of ageism, based on "the tendency to patronize the elderly and to be overly solicitous" (Quadagno 1999, 6), has also come to the fore.

We can see the influence of capitalism and culture on ageism when we look at our "moral economy," the rationale underlying particular notions of distributive justice. The "moral economy is the determination of what is a fair shake for any member of a category based on that person's presumed worth and contributions to social priorities" (Hendricks 1995, 59). Put simply, this is an evaluation of whether one "gets what one deserves," as well as which contributions people value in a society. Within capitalism, U.S. cultural values dictate that an individual's worth rests on his or her productivity and ability to maintain independence. This economic imperative devalues the old who cannot live up to its standards.

The institutionalization of retirement is a key illustration. The passage of the Social Security Act in 1935 did more than provide a minimum of financial support for (former) workers over the age of 65; it also created a new form of dependence based on age. The demarcation of age 65 as the time when one would be eligible to collect full Social Security benefits defined old age in terms of years since birth while also equating it with dependence. Prior to the institutionalization of retirement, there was no dependent group of adults based on age alone. Ironically, these new social policies also set the stage for the more recent claims that the old are an "economic burden" (Graebner 1980; Walker 1990). This process of first creating and then reviling an old "dependent" population has been conditioned by the needs of a capitalist political economy. During the Depression of the 1930s, business owners wanted to control workers, to push out more highly paid employees, to lower unemployment artificially and stimulate consumption. At the same time, labor unions wanted a way to insure job stability and seniority, and establish a forty-hour work week; they also sought a national system of retirement that would keep management from using pensions as a form of labor control (Graebner 1980). The result was the Social Security Act. Furthermore, while entitlement spending as a percentage of GNP has not varied much in the last twenty years (Quadagno 1996), the present hue and cry over welfare spending for the old (whether they are depicted as too dependent or too greedy), can also be viewed as having roots in class relations. Blaming the old for draining public coffers (a dubious argument at best) effectively turns public attention from the growing class inequality and blames the old for poverty among the young

(Minkler and Robertson 1991). Indeed, it ignores the great class inequity among the old themselves (Pampel 1998).

While Social Security's institutionalization of retirement has created dependence among the old, ageism does not equally influence all those over age sixty-five, nor does it equally influence persons of the same age. Many can avoid ageism by "passing" for younger ages through the use of cosmetic surgery, hair dyes, exercise, and the like; others use their wealth or position to escape stereotypes. Still others seem to avoid much of the stigma by virtue of group membership; for example, their families and communities may see them as offering wisdom (e.g., John 1999) in contrast with the larger social image. In other words, while the designation "old" often draws hostility, its application varies by other social locations.

Ageism and Inequality

In previous sections, we have demonstrated the prevalence of ageism in this society, and how it influences the general public and the old themselves. Now we turn more fully to the ways that ageism varies. That is, while those who are seen as "old" may experience ageism, when this designation occurs does not correspond neatly to the age of sixty-five; thus, if we are to understand when it occurs for some groups we need to examine some of the sources of ageism. Ageism interacts with other types of discrimination—sexism, racism, classism, and heterosexism—in ways that make the experience of ageism both similar and different across various groups. Below, then, we explore some of the ways that ageism interacts with other forms of privilege and oppression in ways that vary the timing, sources, and experience of ageism.

Dependence

One of the most negative attributes of being marked as "old" is dependency. We know that class, racial and ethnic, gender, and sexual preference inequities throughout the life course translate into a variety of factors that lead to dependence sooner for some people than for others (Estes 1991, 26). The most obvious is the way in which these relations exacerbate financial difficulties in old age, a topic we discuss more thoroughly in chapter 5. At present, we simply note that the main sources of income in old age—Social Security, pensions, assets, and earnings—vary accordingly. For example, the original Social Security legislation did not cover all occupations, and so certain groups of the elderly—particularly those of working class and racial or ethnic minorities, had to depend upon different, means-tested sources of social support in old age, such as Supplemental Security Income. This latter form of economic support for the poor marks those who receive it as less "deserving" (Estes 1983) than those who need not depend on welfare. Similarly, because later legislative revisions only allow "spouses" to collect benefits based on the earnings of a retired worker, those in same-sex partnerships cannot draw upon one another's benefits.

This is but one example of how class, race and ethnicity, sexual orientation, and gender can influence economic dependence in later life. Low lifetime earnings result in lower levels of Social Security; the inability to save or invest in a pension also reduces income in later life. Low lifetime earnings in turn are related to the intersections of these power relations. As a result, groups can see their disadvantages (or advantages) grow over their life courses (O'Rand 1996). For example, while a White, working-class man will often have lower lifetime earnings than a similarly situated middle-class man, a White working-class woman will not only have even lower benefits, due to lower earnings, but, if lesbian, will not be able to collect a pension or Social Security as spouse. Similarly, because of the types of jobs that Black men are more likely to occupy, they are likely to suffer both more spates of unemployment and higher rates of disability than White men (Gibson 1987; Hayward, Friedman, and Chen 1996). Thus, they are more likely to rely on unemployment or disability payments than are White men. As a result, they will also have lower Social Security benefits, and their economic dependence upon the state will be increased. In turn, lack of economic resources will exacerbate their physical disabilities.

Therefore, the structure of Social Security, welfare, and private pensions casts some groups of old in the role of "dependents." Other groups are privileged by ownership and income, and will be able to avoid economic dependence indefinitely or even altogether (Estes 1991). Here, we can see that the intersections of gender, race and ethnicity, class, and sexual orientation all play a role in dependence in old age through such things as property, which translates into greater power and better life chances. For example, we can see the class-based diversity of aging experiences in the tax reforms of the Reagan administration, which served to benefit the well-to-do elderly while disadvantaging those who were poor (Storey 1986). A more blatant example of class differences that divide the old came with the passage and subsequent repeal of the Medicare Catastrophic Act in 1988. This act would have benefited the old, particularly those without private health coverage, but was successfully fought by organizations such as

AARP that represent the old of higher class (Cox 1993; Day 1993). Those without coverage include members of racial and ethnic minority groups, women, and the working class—all likely to have been employed in occupations without such extended coverage, or who are not able to afford such premiums in retirement. In addition, partners in same-sex relationships will not be covered by their partners' benefits. Particularly disadvantaged would be those homosexuals already less likely to be covered due to their gender, race and ethnicity, or class. While this Act would not have changed the legal status of same-sex couples, it would have allowed anyone with Medicare to have extended coverage. Chances for economic dependence are also increased for homosexuals: Without legal rights and protections of legalized marriage, they cannot share Social Security or a pension with a partner, and such things as inheritance become questionable if other "family" intervene.

Lifelong inequities for women become exacerbated in old age, leaving them with less financial security in retirement due to labor market discrimination or episodic employment patterns. In addition, race and ethnic relations play a part in making minority women poor earlier in life, reinforcing their vulnerability to poverty in old age and to different forms of ageism as they turn to the welfare state for such benefits as Supplemental Security Income.

Here we see the relationship between economic dependence and the likelihood of physical dependence. For instance, we know that class relates to physical disability, both through the nature of working-class jobs (such as construction or other physically demanding labor) and through the lack of health benefits also more typical of working-class jobs. Poor physical health compounds with the inability to purchase needed health care, especially preventative measures. When people define aging in terms of physical disability, then, they will certainly see the disabled poor and working class as old much earlier in their lives than those with greater resources.

Although racial and ethnic minority groups are likely to fall among those described above by virtue of labor market discrimination and resultant employment patterns, racial and ethnic relations play an additional and distinct role. Beyond the fact that members of different racial and ethnic groups may vary in relation to the sorts of chronic conditions to which they are prone (Aranda and Knight 1997), research has demonstrated that non-White racial and ethnic groups do not receive the same quality of medical care as do Whites, regardless of income (Wallace 1991). These factors also make it more likely that non-White racial ethnic members of the working class will suffer physical disability and ultimately dependence.

We see the intersections of class and race in designating one as "old" in the results of a poll conducted by the Americans Discuss Social Security project. Findings from this poll reveal that, while people generally feel that old age occurs in one's early sixties, the higher one's wealth, the later the onset of perceived old age. Not surprisingly, African Americans and Hispanics see the onset of old age as occurring in the late fifties (Associated Press 1998). Obviously, class influences this, too: those minorities privileged by social class (who, for instance, have held the kinds of jobs free of hard physical labor and offering many years of adequate health benefits) will not grow old in the same ways as members of racial or ethnic groups who are disadvantaged.

Ageism and Old Bodies

The discussion above focuses on the way in which power relations result in some groups being more likely to become "dependent" than others. However, this is not the only source of ageism, of designating someone as "old" and "other." Another critical source of ageism is physical appearance, and this too varies by the intersection of social locations.

Bodies serve as markers of age. Gray hair, wrinkles, brown spots—each of these denotes "old." Yet if we think about it, these traits are not universally judged to signify someone is old. Not all gray-haired people are seen to be old, nor are all who exhibit wrinkles. Most of us have heard of the "double standard" of aging, by which we usually mean that women are seen to be old at an earlier age than men (Arber and Ginn 1991a). Recent attitude polls confirm that the gray hair and wrinkles a woman experiences mark her as old sooner (AARP 1995a). Why is this the case? How and why ageism based on physical appearance occurs is very much related to power relations. We begin with a focus on gender to make this clearer.

Why would people see an old woman wearing a miniskirt as deviant? Part of the reaction, and the rationale for regarding women as old earlier in their lives, arises from the fact that their value is based on their attractiveness to men and their reproductive abilities. Thus the old woman in the miniskirt is deviant for appearing sexual beyond her fertile years. By contrast, men's attractiveness stems from other sources not as quickly diminished. Indeed, sometimes age enhances men's attractiveness, especially if they are associated with public achievements, money, and power (Arber and Ginn 1991a, 42). Women even "age" more quickly than men in the workplace, where they do deal with money, power, and public achievement. This is particularly true if they are engaged in jobs where "attractiveness" matters—such as jobs dealing with the public or working for (predominantly White) male supervisors (Rodeheaver 1990). For instance, when airline attendants in this country were almost exclusively women, their unions fought the airlines on a number of occasions where women were removed from their jobs because they were seen as "too old" (in other words, no longer attractive). However, as we have noted, such issues are shaped differently in different societies. Thus, for example, we find that in Finland youthfulness and attractiveness are not as important for women as they are in the United States (Uotinen 1998).

Having said this, however, we must note that the preceding scenario is too simplistic. What women are we talking about? Do physical signs of aging result in ageism for all women in similar ways? If we accept the fact that people see employed women as old sooner than men, and that this hinges at least in some part on their attractiveness to White men, we must question what this means for the aging of Black women, for example, in the labor force. Are they sexualized in the same way as White women, earlier or later in life? How about women who live openly as lesbians? Or working-class women?

Class plays an important role in another way as well. As was apparent in our discussion of dependence, class—through economic resources—can play a critical role in denying or providing resources that allow the old to choose the ways in which they will manage growing old. To the extent that outward signs of aging can be forestalled by such physical transformations as face-lifts, the well-to-do enjoy an obvious advantage. "Remaking" aging bodies is expensive and time consuming and, hence, beyond the reach of the working-class or poor. At the same time, which women do the remaking, and how, tells us about racial and ethnic relations. Not all women feel the "need" to hide gray hair or diminish wrinkles.

Although early studies on gay men suggested that the influence of age on one's appearance is critical, and even more so or earlier than among heterosexual men (Berger 1982), more recent research has failed to corroborate this assertion (Gray and Dressel 1985; Adam 2000). Adam's (2000) recent study suggests that age preferences of homosexual men are as similar to and as complex as those among heterosexual men. Similarly, despite assertions that lesbians' changes in appearance with age appear to be more "acceptable," old lesbians still report feeling like outcasts (Copper 1986) and age still plays a role in the organization of gay and lesbian communities (Boxer 1997).

Finally, we return to our earlier theme that history and culture shape the ways in which social locations influence old age and ageism. For example, women who became adults in the 1950s lived in an era where motherhood and domestic life were "overvalued" for them. Partly as a result of this, these cohorts entered old age "economically and educationally disadvantaged by comparison to their male cohort-mates, and socially defined as sexual castoffs" (Rodeheaver and Datan 1985, 184). While women of later generations may not have achieved occupational parity with men, a topic to be further explored in chapters 4 and 5, the women's movement certainly brought them closer to that goal.

Similarly, the intersection between ageism and sexism is also shaped by culture. Women in some non-Western societies gain more power as they age, sometimes through their roles in life cycle rituals (Safilios-Rothschild 1977; Sokolovsky 1993). For example, in Muslim Hausa society in Nigeria, and despite the Western stereotypes concerning women's positions in such societies, old women have substantial power. Not only does this stem from realms traditionally associated with women, such as those of cultural conservators, but they also have independent sources of power, stemming from their power over younger women as well as their control over certain occupations (Coles 1991). Just as we found in the United States, however, we cannot understand the effects of gender on aging without reference to other social locations. For example, in both the United States and in Kenya, the shift to greater power appears to occur only among those women of higher status (Todd, Friedman, and Kariuki 1990). Cross-culturally, images of old women tend to be more diverse and dramatic than those attached to old men (Sokolovsky 1993).

Knowing the socially constructed and hence malleable nature of "old," we must still note that it remains negative across all groups. Whether the old appear in popular culture as vulnerable and potential victims or as affluent, the images are applied in a blanket fashion—that is, the old are seen to be homogenous—"all alike." This has led to additional problems for old women and members of racial and ethnic minority groups. For instance, the present ageist stereotype of the advantaged elder has obscured the class, racial, and gender stratification among the old. As a result, women, people of color, and working-class old remain disadvantaged, their problems ignored (Gonyea 1994).

Aging through a Gender Lens

Most research on aging[2] has paid little attention either to gender or to other hierarchies of privilege and oppression such as race, class, and sexual orientation. These interconnect to create differing aging experiences, but few scholars of aging have focused on age and gender as social relations— as interdependent dimensions of a complex set of historical relations between women and men, relations that are also shaped by other social inequalities. On the other hand, most feminists, while sensitive to gender and intersecting power relations, have virtually ignored old age in their theories and research—an issue to which we will return in greater depth in the final chapter.

A gender lens requires that we examine the power relations that underlie and result in multiple constructions of "old." There is not just *one* "old age" nor is there simply *one* ageism. In the remainder of this book, we explore old age through this gender lens, to uncover often hidden dimensions of social arrangements, those aspects that are taken for granted. We apply a critical eye to how one's position or location (gender, race/ethnicity, class, or sexual orientation, for example) shapes experiences of old age. While we focus on gender, in part because of research availability, we also attend to the many other locations that intersect with it. The old Latina woman's life and the old White man's life are shaped by more than their gender. Consequently, we should view their lives through a prism that allows us to explore the ways that their different social locations intertwine to create certain disadvantages as well as advantages.

While it may be tempting or easier to say, for instance, that all men are privileged over all women, this facile assertion ignores the fact that, for example, Black men receive lower Social Security benefits, on average, than do White women (Social Security Bulletin 1998). Although these men are privileged on one dimension—gender—their racial and, one could guess, related class disadvantages leave them in a worse financial situation than

---

[2]Sociological researchers on aging work in two disciplinary areas—social gerontology and the sociology of aging. Both fields have helped shape research on aging through their conceptual paradigms and methodologies—although aging research has sometimes been criticized for being theoretically underdeveloped and overly guided by positivist empiricism (Bengtson, Burgess, and Parrott 1997; Moody 1989; Cole 1995; Laws 1995). Moreover, despite the inroads made by feminist thinking in many disciplines, including sociology, the study of old age has remained relatively untouched by the perspective in general (Hooyman 1999).

White women—most of whom married White men. Furthermore, this example also points to another reality: Advantages that accrue to social location early in life allow individuals to gain further advantage so that, in old age, the gap between those who were disadvantaged and those who were privileged grows (O'Rand 1996). Think, for instance, of the contrast between the person born into poverty who spends his or her life working sporadically versus someone born into a comfortable, middle-class home who accrues a lifetime of advantages, such as health care and good education. The benefits of the latter provide lifelong advantages and underscore the point that the more resources one begins with, the more easily they will grow. For instance, while we know that our views about being old are gendered, with women seen as aging faster than men, we need also to recognize that some older women have less difficulty than others in dealing with the stigmas attached to old women in our society, as a recent study of retired professional African American women (Slevin and Wingrove 1998) demonstrates.

But even a picture of aging and old age that contains the many nuances shaped by multiple inequalities, by combinations of privilege and disadvantage, does not tell the whole story. A gender lens also requires that we pay attention to the importance of resistance—of human agency. Despite the disadvantages that shape the lives of many in our society, it is also the case that we actively shape our lives and in so doing may face various disadvantages with a spirit of resistance. Consequently, we must not only explore the problems diverse old people face, but also their strengths, how they overcome barriers, and how disadvantages can serve as advantages in certain contexts.

CHAPTER 2

Gender and the Study of Old Age

In this chapter we explore the ways in which traditional aging literature has conceptualized gender. In recent decades, particularly given the rise of feminist theory, we have come to recognize the extent to which mainstream theories in general, and theories of aging in particular, are based on the experiences of White, middle-class, heterosexual men. By looking at how our knowledge about aging and its underlying assumptions have been constructed, we illuminate how mainstream scholarship in social gerontology has influenced what we "know" about gender and aging. Ultimately, our exploration of the study of aging reveals the ways in which the discipline itself inadvertently perpetuates ageism. We argue that a gender lens is more comprehensive and inclusive and therefore enhances our understanding of old age.

Introduction

Those who study aging know the demographic reality that the vast majority of old people are women; life expectancy at birth and at age 65 differs by gender within all racial/ethnic groups. For instance, table 2.1 shows that life expectancy at birth has shown little narrowing of the gender gap: In 1998 it was 73.9 years for men and 79.4 years for women. Projections into the future yield a similar picture of greater life expectancy for women—in 2010 the projected life expectancy is 75.6 years and 81.4 years for men and women respectively (U.S. Bureau of the Census 2000). Thus, women will continue to predominate well into the twenty-first

Table 2.1

Life Expectancy at Birth, by Gender and Race

	Total			White			Black		
Year	**Total**	**Men**	**Women**	**Total**	**Men**	**Women**	**Total**	**Men**	**Women**
1970 at birth	70.8	67.1	74.7	71.7	68.0	75.6	64.1	60.0	68.3
1998 at birth	76.5	73.9	79.4	77.3	74.6	79.9	71.5	67.8	75.0
At age 65	X	16.0	19.1	X	16.1	19.2	X	14.4	17.5
2010 (projected) at birth	78.5	75.6	81.4	79.0	76.1	81.8	74.5	70.9	77.8

X= data not available
Source: U.S. Bureau of the Census, 2000. Statistical Abstract of the United States, Tables 116 and 117.

century. However, as table 2.2 demonstrates, the gender gap and gains are not uniform across all racial and ethnic groups; Asian and Pacific Islanders have the highest life expectancy at age 65.

Table 2.2 also suggests that a "quiet revolution" is emerging: We will witness a dramatic increase in the proportion and range of old who are members of racial and ethnic minority groups (Burton, Dilworth-Anderson, and Bengston 1992). For example, in 1995, non-Hispanic Whites accounted for 85 percent of all those over age 65. Demographic projections indicate that this percentage will diminish rapidly in the first half of the twenty-first century as Hispanics and non-Whites increase their percentages to 25 percent in 2030 and more than a third—34 percent—in 2050 (Siegel 1999, 2). The proportion of Hispanics among the old will quadruple, rising from 4 percent to 16 percent (U.S. Bureau of the Census 1996).

Given these demographic realities, one might assume scholars have turned their focus to diverse populations. Generally, however, they have not. We have little research on the wide variety of racial and ethnic old in the United States (Sokolovsky 1997b; Antonucci and Cantor 1994). For

Table 2.2

Additional Years of Life Expectancy at Age 65, by Race and Gender

Race	Men	Women
White	16.1	19.2
Black	14.4	17.5
Hispanic	18.5	21.8
Asian/Pacific Islanders	18.8	22.9
American Indian	14.9	18.3

Data for each group reflects different years as follows: American Indians 1993; Asian/Pacific Islanders and Hispanics 1997; Whites and Black 1998.
Sources: Hendley and Bilimoria 1999; John 1999; U.S. Bureau of the Census 2000.

instance, groups of "Hispanics" are frequently lumped together despite their vast cultural and class variations. The same is true for Asians, where we find groups as varied as Koreans, Japanese, Chinese, and East Indians all subsumed under one identity. Additionally, we know little about the wide range of American Indian cultures, and even less about urban Indians. This omission is especially problematic because American Indians are among those old who are poorest and who have the lowest life expectancy and quality of life (Antonucci and Cantor 1994; John 1994).

Similarly, the variability among African Americans—the racial ethnic minority group most extensively studied in general—has been ignored, for the most part. For example, middle-class African Americans have not been studied as extensively as their poorer counterparts (Antonucci and Cantor 1994). Further, the cultural diversity among "African Americans" (and the fact that this term is often inaccurately used) by region of origin has also been ignored, as has the diversity among Blacks who have more recently migrated voluntarily to the United States. Lastly, even studies of the aged that include racial and ethnic minorities often use theoretical models developed for White populations (Richardson and Kilty 1992).

While research on women has produced a burgeoning literature in the last decade or two, much of this newer work suffers from some of the problems identified above. Indeed, one of the most interesting aspects of this new research on aging women is that it virtually ignores the revolution in our knowledge about women and about gender provided by feminist scholars (Hooyman 1999). Major transformations have occurred in feminist scholarship in the past few decades. As a result, we have come to see gender as far from static or fixed and we have come to regard it as an embedded feature of social arrangements. We now understand that gender is constantly changing, that it is a process. These changes take many forms: change in meanings of what is involved in being a man or a woman, in being masculine or feminine; shifting relations between men and women (shaped by history, by culture, by situations) that lead to shifts in power and the (re)allocation of resources along gender lines. Thus, gender is much more than a one-time "identity" that one acquires through socialization; it is an organizing principle of social life (Glenn 1999).

Most feminist scholarship now also recognizes that gender is shaped by other forms of social inequality—whether race, ethnicity, class, age, or sexual orientation. For example, the life of an old, Latino, male migrant worker is quite different from that of a young, wealthy, White lesbian woman who lives in suburbia. While this may seem obvious, feminist theories give us a framework for exploring and explaining how and in what ways their lives might be different and similar, by focusing on the intersections of power relations. The former lives on the fringes of the economy and likely experiences all of the disadvantages of being poor and a minority, while still accruing some of the advantages of being male—especially in relation to women. The other's life is shaped by economic advantage and by membership in the majority group (White)—advantages tempered by the fact that this person is a woman and a lesbian. Thus, both will experience oppression but the nature of the oppression will differ given the social location of each. Finally, feminist scholars pay attention to the ways in which people shape their lives in positive ways within the constraints they experience. Oppressed people seldom are passive recipients; instead, they actively resist oppression and they do so in a variety of ways that may not always be apparent to those with privilege. Further, what might be seen as constraints or limitations from the standpoint of the majority also contain sources of opportunities or means to survive. For example, and as we discuss more extensively in the chapters on income, work, and retirement, the traditional domestic division of labor presents important barriers to employed women in terms of promotions, pay, pensions, Social Security, and other benefits. At the same time, it gives them daily survival skills that provide them greater protection against institutionalization than men upon the death of a spouse (Blieszner 1993). Similarly, the "kinkeeping" often associated with this division of labor also provides sources of support in old age often unavailable to men (eg., Barker, Morrow, and Mitteness 1998).

Several interlocking ideas form the basis of this chapter. First, we maintain that aging researchers have typically handled the issue of gender too narrowly in their analyses. Second, we argue that scholars of aging have not adequately used recent feminist scholarship to broaden and deepen the ways in which they conceptualize gender and issues of diversity. Finally, we argue that scholars of aging remain guilty of inadvertent ageism, and we illuminate the ways in which ageist biases shape their thinking about aging.

While theories of aging often remain implicit, their influence remains: "[I]nterpretive frameworks cannot help but be employed in gerontological research, whether or not one is an open advocate of conceptual models" (Bengtson, Burgess, and Parrott 1997, S72). Because underlying theories of aging influence how research is conceived and executed, we begin by asking how gender has been treated in traditional research on aging in recent decades, and we offer an alternative model, a gender lens, derived from feminist theories. We then show that this lens allows us—indeed requires us—to examine multiple social inequalities in an integrated manner. Through its focus on power relations, the gender lens approach that we advocate provides a framework for understanding diverse aging experiences as they relate to one another.

Gender in the Study of Old Age

Three approaches to gender underlie most of the work of scholars of aging and we briefly outline each below. To a great extent, these approaches reflect changes in how we have come to view gender in the social sciences in the last few decades. At the same time, they do not represent a linear progression as scholars themselves vary in their own understanding of gender relations, nor are they mutually exclusive. As a result, all three approaches can be found in present research.

Add Women

This first approach to gender analyses, the initial response to women's call for greater inclusion in scholarship, adds women into existing research models that use men as the implicit or explicit reference group. This conceptual strategy can guide research that focuses solely on women. Thus, for example, a study of women's experiences in retirement asks questions and makes assumptions based on what researchers know about men's experiences, instead of basing them on the complexities of women's lives. This research model treats women as adjuncts to men or examines them as part of an analysis of gender differences. For example, a comparison of men's and women's sexual activity that discovers that women attain orgasms less frequently than do men might ask, what is it about women that makes them different? What is the problem with their ability to have an orgasm? Because the questions derive from assumptions or models that are formed from men's experiences, they only illuminate how women do or do not "fit" this preconceived model. We still know little about women's experiences or about gender relations and, consequently, we really know even less than we should about the lives of women and men. Women's experiences have not been made central to the exploration and gender has not been explored as a social construction, embedded in social processes, that shapes the life experiences of both men and women.

In studies where women are "added" to the research model, we should question how gender differences are revealed and the uses to which they are put. If the questions and comparisons use men as an implicit norm, variations found can only tell us that women are "deviant" or even "inadequate" as they do not "measure up." As Diane Gibson (1996, 444) aptly notes,

> [W]e tend to refer to gender differences most often in terms of women's difference—women live longer, are higher users of prescription drugs, have higher rates of institutional care, and so on. We do not generally refer to men living shorter lives, being lower users of prescription drugs, having lower rates of institutional care, and so on.
>
> This in and of itself is not important. The comparisons are valid in either direction. It becomes an issue . . . when the orientation of the research—the questions asked and the research strategies employed—reflect the presumption of men as the dominant group.

Research conducted in this vein not only constructs women as "other," but also obscures the similarities between women and men. It also mystifies gender relations. For example, research on employed women often considers the impact of their family roles, but this is often neglected in research on employed men. Yet, family plays an important role in the careers of both—if for no other reason than women perform more reproductive labor, thereby freeing men to pursue paid job opportunities (Acker 1990;

Feldberg and Glenn 1978). Even though this "add women" approach focuses on differences between groups of unequal power, it ignores the power dynamics that underlie and produce these variations. This shortcoming undercuts our ability to fashion effective policy interventions.

Gender as a Variable

A second, more recent general strategy for including gender in traditional aging research treats it as a demographic or descriptive variable. While this strategy is by no means the exclusive purview of quantitative methods, one example of this would be research that includes sex in a regression equation, with an eye to possible differences that might arise. Such research presents whatever gender differences it found (in income, retirement, satisfaction, self-esteem, or occupation, for example) and leaves the discussion at that. Sometimes, gender is conceptualized as structural, but not with relational properties; that is, gender does not appear to be a characteristic of social organizations and identities that men and women constantly reshape (Glenn 1999). Instead, gender is a fixed variable that can be "accounted for" by the factors and processes that are of more central interest. Its influence can be controlled and "eliminated" relative to other variables such as levels of education, income, or occupations. This sort of research ignores the complicated impact of gendered structures, such as the ways in which women and men receive "different" educations or have varying experiences within the same occupation. In addition, such theoretical disinterest in gender leads to research conclusions that ignore relational similarities and differences between men and women. What appears to be "gender neutral," and hence "fair," assumes that there are no structural differences already reflected in the models employed.

Gender: For Women Only

A third approach, which often overlaps with the previous two, treats gender as being relevant only for women. Consequently, their analyses imply that only women "have" gender or have lives shaped by it. Earlier, we mentioned that gender relations are obscured when we ask only women, and not men, about family matters. This is one way in which researchers imply that only women are influenced by gender. For example, if we explore the influence of the division of domestic labor on retirement satisfaction only when looking at women, it is as though only women experience this component of gender relations—as if men's retirement satisfaction is not also related to the presence or absence of domestic labor in their lives.

Similarly, people often direct their concern with diversity into attention to the experiences of "special groups"—such as women, racial and ethnic minorities, or nonheterosexuals. They assume members of these groups to be the only ones whose lives are influenced by the inequality at issue. Ironically, when this approach considers the influence of such social locations, the majority group becomes the standard used by which to judge the minority group. For instance, an examination of gender uses men as the normative standard; one of race invariably uses Whites as the standard; one of homosexuality or bisexuality uses the lives of heterosexuals as the norm. The ways in which people use the findings of such research are also important. Too often researchers see them as relevant only to the minority or marginalized populations studied, with little or nothing to teach about the majority.[1]

A Gender Lens on Aging

A gender lens, which draws from more recent feminist critiques of conceptions of gender, offers a very different perspective from those discussed above. From this perspective, to understand gender we must examine how "women" *and* "men" are gendered, how each relates to the other. In addition, gender is embedded in social relationships at all levels, from individual interactions to structural or institutional processes. Thus, gender is an organizing societal principle—it shapes how we interact as individual men and women and it shapes, for example, how people conceive and implement government and other public policies. As we will show in chapter 7, care work policies, for instance, often assume that a family member, i.e., a woman, will be available and willing to provide it. Furthermore, a feminist exploration of gender implicates other social inequalities, such as race, ethnicity, class, and sexual orientation. Each of these represent power relations that again lead us to see that the privilege of one group is tied, intentionally or not, to the oppression of another. This insight allows us to see relationships among groups at many different levels. As Glenn puts it: "the lives of different groups are interconnected, even without

---

[1] For further discussion, see Calasanti 1999.

face-to-face relations. Thus, for example, a White person living in the United States enjoys privileges and a higher standard of living by virtue of the subordination and lower standard of living of people of color, even if she or he is not personally exploiting or taking advantage of any persons of color" (Glenn 1999, 11). Gender relations intersect with these other power relations such that we cannot simply say that an African American woman differs from a Hispanic woman because they are of a different race/ethnicity while they share their gender. Instead, each experiences a different sort of womanhood.

This understanding provides a very different angle from which to understand gender because, by definition, it concentrates on diversity. Incorporating diversity into gerontology through this perspective means something quite different than what we see in most studies of aging. It provides theoretical frameworks built upon the experiences of groups situated in a web of interlocking power relations (Calasanti 1996b). In contrast to the usual research design, it requires that we examine different groups from *their* perspective, privileging their knowledge. For example, because social institutions build upon and express the views of those with greater power, the taken-for-granted norms embedded therein can remain invisible to those with privilege, while those with less privilege are often far more aware of these relations. Thus, members of various minority groups are more keenly attuned to discrimination than are typical members of the majority. For instance, because hand-holding in public is denied them, same-sex couples recognize that this taken-for-granted activity is actually a privilege. Because heterosexuals can do it without rebuke, they don't even see this as an unearned advantage carefully regulated by a wide range of anti-homosexual denunciations. More insidious for well-being in old age are the rights denied them given the illegality of same-sex unions, a situation which doesn't allow for partners to assign survivorship benefits to the other. For the most part, heterosexual couples remain oblivious to these realities. Listening to the voices of the disadvantaged, and using the knowledge of oppressed groups that we obtain in this manner, provides the basis for comparison with more privileged groups. In this way, we can gain greater knowledge of both groups as we see their similarities and differences in relation to one another.

By focusing on and listening to the voices of marginalized groups through a gender lens, we take apart and rebuild taken-for-granted notions about gender. For instance, as we discuss in subsequent chapters, when we explore retirement and housework through this framework we can see domestic labor as part of the retirement experiences of both women and men, instead of women only. That is, White, middle-class, heterosexual men's ability to experience "leisure" time in retirement is tied to women's responsibility for domestic labor. The absence of this obligation in these men's lives provides them this opportunity to have "free time."

A Gender Lens and Diversity in Old Age: A New View on "Multiple Oppressions"

Viewing gender as a social relation renders a very different approach to examining diversity. It also solves a dilemma faced by some social gerontologists who recognize the diverse nature of aging experiences and seek to understand multiple oppressions in relation to aging. One approach to racial and ethnic as well as class differences over the life course suggests that old age serves to "level" these differences as groups become more alike, regardless of their starting point. For example, in terms of economic status, since racial and ethnic minority groups and the poor begin with lower incomes, they have relatively less to lose than do members of the dominant group. As a result, the logic suggests that the gap between them shrinks as all groups feel the effects of retirement on their finances (Pampel 1998; Dressel, Minkler, and Yen 1997). However, research has failed to demonstrate this leveling effect. For example, race and ethnicity continue to exert a strong influence in old age. The disadvantaged—and privileged—situations of old people are a direct result not of age but of their positions in hierarchies based on gender, race and ethnicity, and social class over their life course (Arendell and Estes 1991).

In part as a response to the leveling hypothesis, a "double jeopardy" approach gained prominence in recent decades. In its original formulation, it posited that old minority group members faced a double disadvantage in old age. Since then, others have talked about triple jeopardy and multiple jeopardy as a way of alluding to multiple disadvantages individuals might face in old age due to their social location. While a useful tool for advocacy, this approach ignores the strengths of different groups (Dressel et al. 1997). It also implicitly sets up an additive or even multiplicative approach to oppression. However, oppression and privilege do not simply add together: "An additive analysis treats the oppression of a Black woman in a society that is racist as well as sexist as if it were a further burden when, in fact, it is a different burden. . . . [T]o ignore the difference is to deny the particular reality of the Black women's experience" (Spelman 1988, 122). In the same way, we cannot view all men as privileged; they too are quite diverse (Benjamin 1999). The intersection of power relations leads to *qualitatively* different experiences.

A third general approach in the aging literature posits that people carry inequalities into old age at roughly the same rate and so *maintain* their status differences. In economic terms, this would mean that the gap in wealth among individuals earlier in life would be about the same when they are old. By contrast, what has come to be known as the *cumulative advantage/ disadvantage* approach (O'Rand 1996) has recently gained credibility. Focusing primarily on economic standing in old age, this framework argues that advantages from earlier in life allow one even greater possibilities to accumulate further advantages. On the other side, disadvantages are similarly compounded. As a result, inequality actually *increases* in old age.

How, then, does old age intersect with other systems of privilege and oppression? Clearly, one's position in later life results from both cumulative processes and factors relevant to this life stage, particularly policies targeted at the old alone, which serve to differentiate their experiences from those of younger people (Estes, Linkins, and Binney 1996). At the same time, these cumulative processes differ among the old because of their diversity. Our discussion of ageism in chapter 1 would suggest that, essentially, old age is overlaid on and intersects with other systems of privilege and oppression. Consequently, old age *does* matter, but *not* in the sense of "homogenizing" or making the old similar but instead, in the sense of creating multiple experiences of aging. As a form of oppression, ageism *does* touch on everyone, even those who are the most advantaged and privileged in our society. Ageism matters, then, as another form of oppression intersecting with previous ones. As a result, the content of each—ageism, sexism, racism, and homophobia—and the ways in which people experience each, are transformed by age relations as well.

Recognition of the diversity implied by the prior discussion can be daunting for some as "it leads to more than two worlds of aging—it implies dozens of worlds" (Pampel 1998, 76). How should social gerontologists deal with this? At one extreme stand those who ignore diversity and continue to focus on White, middle-class, heterosexual men, while at the other we might find detailed descriptions of a single group (Pampel 1998, 76). A gender lens offers an alternative, however, with its focus on the relational nature of aging experiences. It incorporates knowledge of diverse groups in a way that allows us to understand the aging experiences of everyone. It requires, first, that we understand the particular experiences of groups, by studying them on their own terms. Second, it leads us, through comparison of experiences of various groups, to explore the *bases* of different situations. For example, if we examine eldercare among Blacks, we find that "non-kin" are more likely to provide such care among this group than among Whites. If we begin our investigation with the lives of Blacks, we would not categorize this difference as a "deviation" as we would understand that, for many Blacks, such individuals are indeed considered part of their family. In addition, by then comparing eldercare among Blacks and Whites, on their own terms, we also come to see that strong informal support networks among Blacks have been developed as a survival strategy and in response to their disadvantages. By contrast, Whites have not developed such networks, given their more privileged status. Thus, we begin to understand the power relations that lead to particular situations: We comprehend the privileged position of some groups *in relation to* others. We understand not only the advantages enjoyed by one group, but also their roots in the disadvantages that plague another.

This perspective and relational understanding also uncovers biases in our theories, concepts, and research. For example, the notion that people center their lives around paid work, so that the main impact of retirement involves a loss of status and of co-worker relationships, reflects a male (and middle-aged) bias. This assumption hampers our ability to examine women's experiences and appreciate the family care or unpaid work traditionally more central to the lives of women than of men. Many women do not retire in the same way as men (Calasanti 1996a, 1993), and a gender lens surpasses the alternatives by treating both men's and women's experiences as equally important and then by theorizing the relation between them—for instance, the relative authority of employed men won at the expense of the low status of housewives.[2]

Finally, our approach to diversity offers us insights into alternatives and strategies for dealing with aspects of old age, including the effects of ageism. It helps us understand how people respond to oppression. It gives us directions for and clues to sources of empowerment, as well as insights that we might otherwise miss. Women's greater longevity is but one example. While from one perspective it might mean living longer in more chronically ill health, we rarely ask about the other side. For example, what

---

[2] Furthermore, to assume that paid work is or continues to be most central to the identities of men flies in the face of many recent studies that report a significant shift in which men in many post-industrial countries now rank fatherhood as more important to them than work (Coltrane 1999).

is it about women that makes them stronger and able to live longer (Gibson 1996)?

Similarly, examining aging from the standpoint of old women in Hausa society reveals hidden and important aspects of aging. Despite the fact that in this Muslim society women remain secluded, old women also enjoy considerable power, far more than previously assumed. Their power, which is enhanced by social class, rests on the fact of their seclusion into a woman-dominated world. They exert power through their control over younger women, "through activities that link gender-segregated sectors of society, in pivotal positions within the secluded world of women, through ritual and occupational activities which they monopolize, and as wealthy individuals influencing others through distribution of favors" (Coles 1991, 78). Attending to diversity in this context, then, teaches us about the informal channels through which power can be wielded, thereby expanding our notions of power, and sources of power, among the old. It also uncovers the ways in which gender relations underlie power—that the sources of women and men's power exist in relation to one another.

Attention to research on diverse populations forces us to question the very ways that traditional aging research views old age (Johnson 1994a). The amount of concern for "adaptation" to aging, the implicit belief that declines and losses lead to problems and the need to "cope," provides a case in point. Yet, despite the fact that old African American women report poorer health than do White women, they also report better mental health. Even among the oldest old, Black Americans report both worse economic and health situations in comparison to Whites, yet they also express higher morale. These findings suggest that, in general, African Americans may well use different criteria to assess their lives in old age. We know, for instance, that they have greater informal support, and that, specifically in the case of African American women, they are more accepting of aging as a natural part of life than are White women (Johnson 1994b; Gould 1989; Slevin and Wingrove 1998). Similarly, even though men and women share some of the same life events, such as care work or widowhood, the circumstances that present themselves as problems in advanced old age differ by gender (Barer 1994).

The attention to diversity and power relations we have outlined helps us not only to examine what we do with research on aging among different groups, but also to examine ageism itself. Now we turn this lens on the practice of gerontology.

Ageism in Social Gerontology

Like other forms of discrimination, ageism is institutionalized—not relegated only to idiosyncratic and overt actions but also prevalent in established and sanctioned behavior patterns. Ageism has thus been integrated in taken-for-granted aspects of our daily lives. Characteristics that we value in ourselves or in others, appropriate ways to behave in public, when or if we should have children—all of these and other areas of our lives include often-hidden ageist assumptions.

As members of a deeply ageist society, then, none of us can claim to be non-ageist. We can, however, strive to be anti-ageist, by which we mean that we can work to uncover ageism in order to fight it. This mode of action is itself critical and a key to recognizing our own ageism. As we discuss later, the usual tendency is to act as if age does not matter, to strive to be "age blind"—a position contradictory to unveiling and struggling against ageism. Rather than ignoring the role that age plays in our lives, anti-ageism asks us to become more aware of how age and age relations shape experiences.

As we discussed in chapter 1, the social construction of old age is critical to how it is experienced. Along these lines, social gerontologists are important as they help define old age and "problems" that accrue to this time of life: "the problems of the elderly are only those that experts, policymakers, and the public media define as true" (Estes 1991, 28). The often-inadvertent ageism of those who study old age is, therefore, critical.

How it is that gerontologists can end up being ageist, ultimately excluding the experiences of the old? In our discussion, we point to two interrelated ways in which this happens. First, they incorporate a middle-aged bias into theory and research—so that we define the old primarily in terms of their difference from the middle-aged. Second, gerontologists ignore the multiple experiences of old age, generally assuming that the old are White, male, heterosexual and middle class as well. Together, these erect an implicit standard against which the aging of all groups are compared, with the result that the latter will be found wanting and their experiences excluded.

At first blush, it might seem odd to find that a middle-aged referent would be embedded in gerontologists' theories, given their concern with the old. However, scholars draw upon intellectual histories in which middle age is central (Gibson 1996). That is, the sociological traditions underlying gerontological approaches themselves have tended to exclude old age; only in the last two decades or so have sociologists paid much attention to aging (Phillipson 1998; Arber and Ginn 1991b). As Arber and Ginn note, given the historical development of sociology in the nineteenth century, those over age 65 did not constitute a large segment of the population, nor was there such a thing as institutionalized retirement. In addition, the primary interests of sociology revolved around paid work and the related examination of modern industrial societies. As a result, implicit in sociology is a view that "people are valued primarily in economic terms, and . . . old age [is] a period of 'social redundancy' because most elderly people are not in paid employment" (Arber and Ginn 1991b, 260). While this contention may seem at odds with gerontology, we will show that this economic valuation has guided theory and research so that, ultimately, the conceptions of old age remain ageist.

The vast majority of theories of aging have posited ways in which individuals can age "successfully." For instance, early theories of aging viewed old age, at least implicitly, as an individual problem; old people needed to alter themselves to deal with this time of life, its concerns and anxieties. They focused on "adjustment" to growing old and the assumed "facts" of aging—role loss, such as retirement, or ill health and dependence. Never does this early scholarship either articulate the biases surrounding notions of how one should "adjust" to growing old, or challenge the inevitability of these "facts" of aging (Phillipson 1998; Lynott and Lynott 1996). The social creation of retirement, for example, received no scrutiny, and scholars did not question the social factors that might influence or construct health in systematic ways. Finally, regardless of whether the prescription for adaptation was to withdraw from roles and active social participation (disengagement theory) or strive to maintain activity levels in the face of losses (activity theory), the implicit standard was always middle age. Both approaches share a White, male, middle-class bias concerning the lifestyle and activities one would and would not be engaged in (particularly paid labor and a "career"). In effect, old age was assumed to be a "problem" with which people must cope: One was to "adjust" to a loss of the middle-age lifestyle.

Since the 1970s, political economists and, more recently, phenomenological and humanistic geronotologists have challenged some of the early approaches. In particular, they challenge the social construction of such issues as retirement and Alzheimer's disease, or the assumption of physical and mental decline and dependence (Phillipson 1998; Minkler 1996). As important as these critiques have been, these more critical approaches have not filtered into most theory and research on old age. A preoccupation with "problems" and "adjustment" remains in gerontological practice. In addition, and despite the attention often given to social inequality, the middle-aged bias has not been explicitly critiqued. Age relations themselves, and their relation to other social inequalities, remain unrecognized and under-theorized. As a result, the middle-aged bias, rooted in experiences of White, middle-class, heterosexual men, still permeates social gerontology, and this ageism continues to influence both knowledge and interventions: "[I]t is possible that research on old age, when conducted from one dominant (midlife) perspective, may not be age neutral in its consequences. The perceived disparity between objective circumstances and subjective well-being may be more a disparity from the perspective of the researchers than from that of the researched" (Gibson 1996, 438).

Below, we discuss "productive aging" as an example of this form of ageism at work. We illustrate how it takes middle-aged (men) as an ideal and urges the old to live up to it in order to demonstrate that they "deserve" social provisions or respect.

"Productive Aging"

Quite telling is the emphasis on "productive aging," a prescription that stems from attempts to convince politicians and the public that the old are, in fact, still "productive" even if not engaged in paid labor. Consequently, they are still "deserving" of entitlement.[3] Important to our discussion is not the political climate leading to this argument or the ramifications per se, but how productive—and, as we will discuss, "successful"—aging is defined. Even the terms of the debate—"productive" aging—reveal a class, race, and gender bias. Sensitivity to such biases has led some critical gerontologists to urge the majority to examine the meaning of productive and successful aging, to uncover the "socio-historical origins of such concepts, their roles and functions, and the degree to which they capture—or fail to

---

[3] Entitlements refer to federal program benefits "that were intentionally established to be outside the usual appropriations process [of Congress]. They are a protected type of spending, in part to ensure predictability for those who qualify for benefits" (Moon and Mulvey 1996). Benefits go to anyone who applies and satisfies legal qualifications. Examples of entitlement programs for the old would include Social Security and Medicare. In these cases, eligibility would include having achieved a certain age and having contributed to the programs through payroll taxes for a specified amount of time.

capture—the experiences of diverse groups of elders" (Dressel et al. 1997, 592).

The middle-age bias inherent in productive aging is more apparent when we dissect the term. It implies, for instance, that the value of the old is predicated upon their provision of goods and services for purchase. Shaped by the logic of capitalism, it validates only those old whose activities can be defined as relevant to a model of economic efficiency (Sicker 1994). Even tasks that are unpaid but productive, such as caregiving or volunteerism, are only considered valuable if they can be seen to have a monetary referent. The constraints imposed by this capitalist valuation disadvantage the oldest old, and particularly women and minorities, who live longer and under greater financial strain than do White men.

The attempt to show that the old don't fit the "unproductive" stereotype and that one couldn't deduce productivity from chronological age appears to be fighting ageism. However, the implicit message remains that as long as the old are *like* the middle-aged, then they are not "really" old—and therefore they do not fit the negative connotations of old. However, "[e]fforts to counter ageism by emphasizing the positive features of old age [within a traditional model of productivity] simply transfer old ageist stereotypes to those who have disabilities" (Holstein 1994, 21) or others who cannot conform. And of course, the positive aspects of old age are those most like the middle-aged.

The underlying ageism of productive aging, then, lies in efforts to demonstrate that the old are not different from others, again using middle-aged activity levels and values as the standard. In effect, being "old," in and of itself, is still *not* acceptable. Furthermore, gerontologists have implicitly reinforced these notions by their attempting to demonstrate that many of the old still fit the middle-aged referent.

Productive aging is but one example of how individuals might engage in "successful aging," a term that begs examination despite its taken-for-granted usage. Who, for example, would *not* want to age successfully? We return to discuss this in greater detail in chapter 8; here we simply note that the concept is imbued with cultural content that is, again, ageist. Indeed, the notion of "successful aging" in the United States is predicated on an ideology of individual responsibility and control, an ideology that is not shared in all cultures (e.g., Katzko et al. 1998). Affirmed in the literature on health and the literature on the body, this view reinforces ageism by suggesting that old age is something to be controlled. The plethora of articles and books on such topics in recent years confirms this preoccupation with "stopping the clock" thereby reinforcing the notion that aging can only be a negative phenomenon. Biomedicalization reinforces this trend as it tends to see aging as a disease and suggests that all problems of aging can be controlled by the proper intervention (Robertson 1991).

Social gerontologists walk a thin line in trying to combat ageism on the one hand without falling into it on the other. In part of his important discussion on ageism in psychological research, Schaei (1993, 49) argues that ageism involves "a cultural belief that age is a significant dimension by definition and that it defines a person's social position, psychological characteristic, or individual experience," and that we should not assume "that age is usually . . . a relevant dimension to variables under study." These assertions have some interesting implications. Among the most significant implicit messages is that, in fact, age does *not* matter, and that scholars ought to therefore be "age-neutral" or blind to age in their research. But age *is* a social position which carries with it particular consequences (McMullin 2000).

In the quest to show that "age does not matter," however, people make the implicit assertion that *old* age does not matter, just as Whites advocate "color-blindness." In the latter case, Whites maintain that race does not matter but, in so doing, use Whiteness as a standard. As long as other racial/ethnic groups "fit," they are acceptable, and thus race does not matter. But to be different—to be African American, for example—remains a problem. Similarly, gerontological theories and research gear toward demonstrating that the old are really not "old"—because scholars have adopted the same negative use for that term that permeates our culture.

"Age-blindness," wherein we adopt the stance that "age does not matter," reinforces systems of oppression in at least two ways. First, attempts to be age-blind or age-neutral push us to focus on individual perceptions and actions, thereby leaving intact taken-for-granted patterns of behaviors that underlie the more insidious, hidden forms of institutionalized discrimination. Second, and relatedly, such blindness implicitly uses the privileged as the norm, judging all others by that standard. For example, the age-blind expend much effort demonstrating that old people are acceptable because they are "much like young(er) people." The sort of ageism in which we try to turn a blind eye to the social realities of aging is akin to saying that women are actually OK because they are really like men, or that Black Americans are acceptable because they are really like Whites. In the words of Andrews (1999, 316), "this denial of difference, the erasure of the years lived . . . strips the old of their history and leaves them nothing to offer but a mimicry of their youth." A non-ageist position *would* maintain that the old *are* in important respects different from—as well as similar to—younger people, and that *such difference is OK*. One need not be young or middle-aged to be valued.

Arguments concerning the language we use reflect this struggle concerning ageism and age-blindness. For instance, in a recent editorial, a prominent gerontologist advocated that scholars no longer use the term "old" as it perpetuates ageism. Pejorative attributes given to "old" can reinforce the negative view of those over age sixty-five. He accuses gerontologists of using "old" as a euphemism for stigmatized statuses as "in decline" and he advocates that we be more direct in the terms we use (Palmore 2000).

Certainly, by "old" many people mean something akin to "in decline" or "senile." However, we propose a different solution to this problem. We should rather learn to use the word "old" in a positive or neutral way—much in the same way that we use terms for other age groups. Despite the negative characteristics often attributed to the "young," for instance, no one suggests that we use a different term in order to avoid scorning them. Were we to develop a new term for the old that distinguished them from other age groups—to whom we also refer in terms of their age (young, teenaged, middle-aged)—then we would inadvertently suggest that the old were deviant. There is nothing wrong with being old, and though popular common sense disagrees with us on this point, what we would teach we shall first do by example. We use "old" with respect and invite others to join us in this practice.

Thus in this book we use the term old, and not older, in all contexts. We hope to naturalize its use so that someday soon we will no longer describe this time of life with euphemisms or by allusion to other age groups.

Where Do We Go from Here?

The movement to a non-ageist position is made all the more difficult—and necessary—by the reality of diverse experiences of old age. We tend to view aging as a discrete and uniform phenomenon, and talk about the "realities" of aging in terms of statistical norms. However, as we discussed above, those who do not fit the numeric profiles cannot be treated, implicitly or explicitly, as "deviant." In chapter 1, we discussed the Images of Aging poll, which found people to be fairly knowledgeable in relation to selected "facts on aging." Still, fears about old age remain and these fears related primarily to respondents' own past experiences. So women, members of racial and ethnic minority groups, and the working class were more likely to have experienced financial problems. They were thus also more likely to express moderate to strong levels of anxiety about financial issues in aging. A similar situation existed in relation to health. One way of dealing with the prevalence of fears, despite overall levels of knowledge, is to say that we need even greater education. But this in fact assumes that such fears are "wrong" because they did not coincide with the "facts on aging." But *are* they wrong? For everyone?

If our old age is inextricably linked with our entire lifetimes, and these are in turn shaped by the confluence of relations of privilege/disadvantage, then it makes more sense to talk about aging in terms of different modalities—or, to put it differently, there are many realities to aging. So those who demonstrated a lack of congruence, "incorrectly" viewing their own aging more negatively than statistics warrant, but who do so based on their own experiences, may in fact be revealing a "correct" notion of aging, one in which their anxiety appropriately matches their past and probable future. The fact that men who were college educated and had experienced no financial or employment difficulties also did not predict financial difficulties in old age makes sense—they are far less likely to experience them. By the same token, those who showed more pessimistic beliefs and greater anxiety about the future—women, those who were employed in nontechnical and lower-waged jobs, and those who experienced financial and health difficulties—likely are projecting a realistic appraisal as well. They may represent a minority experience of aging, but their experience remains important to the study of aging. A gender lens approach to aging, with its focus on diversity, takes this into account. It includes diverse experiences not as statistical deviations but as norms for those groups and attempts to explore how these experiences of aging for all groups are intimately connected through systems of power.

The rest of this book explores, through this gender lens, aspects of life in old age. We cannot cover all relevant issues, but we will examine some that seem to be central to researchers and to public fears about growing old, such as finances, work, and retirement. People also fear bodily changes, and we will discuss these in relation to ageism, power relations, sexuality, and the care work that bodily changes can require. Areas neglected in this sample include health, other family relationship issues, friendships, widowhood, bereavement, and dying. Even for the topics that we raise, we focus on just a few dimensions as we demonstrate the ways in which a gender lens refocuses theory and research practice. This book will demonstrate the gender lens rather than provide comprehensive review of the experiences of the old.

Likewise, we focus on gender as a relation, rather than on women per se. Gender relations define women and men in relation to each other, and distribute resources unequally between them. Neither women nor men matter more to this process; and so, whenever the research available allows it, we discuss old men as well. Finally, in the last chapter, we turn the gender lens back on itself, so to speak, to examine ageism in feminism. Despite its emphasis on power relations and its incorporation of diversity, considerations of age have been largely ignored in the feminist literature—perhaps because of the relative youth of those working in the second and third wave of feminism (Arber and Ginn 1991b). This exclusion is both ageist and important; and we end the book by speculating on ways that feminist theories could benefit from an age lens that examines both old age, on its own terms, and age relations.

CHAPTER 3

Bodies in Old Age

Common sense tells us that bodies are important for understanding old age, particularly since so many people equate old age with physical decline. However, our focus on old bodies is not on physical abilities per se but is instead on the ways that old bodies, in their plurality, are shaped and experienced. We use a gender lens to explore the ways that ageism intersects with sexism and other social inequalities to frame how the body is constructed in contemporary society. In particular, we highlight issues of physical appearance   of body image—based on individuals' experiences with their looks as well as others' responses. Although very limited, research on old bodies also offers us some suggestions about how old men and women inhabit their bodies, and we conclude the chapter by suggesting how a gender lens might enhance our understanding of how aging is experienced in the gendered body.

The Social Significance of the Body

Introduction

Attention to the body as an important topic for understanding aging has been largely absent in social gerontology (Oberg 1996). This omission is especially noticeable when we consider that the body is a critical marker of age. In addition, to understand ageism we need to recognize that the body is a principal—albeit mostly silent—point of reference in identifying the old: "our most immediate sense that somebody is young or old usually comes from encounters with their corporeal appearances" (Laws 1995, 4). In observing the body we draw conclusions about people's age, as well as their sex, race, social class, ability, and health. In addition, the body is an important part of our identities over the life course and, as such, deserves attention. To the extent that the body has been the topic of research among scholars of aging at all, it has largely been confined to the area of geriatrics. Here the focus typically has been on assessing the functional body and the ways in which the old are physically independent or may need help to carry out various tasks.

Outside of social gerontology, there has been a tremendous growth in scholarship on the body in recent decades. Certainly Foucault's work stands out as an early and influential examination of the growing importance of the body in contemporary societies. In *Discipline and Punish* he demonstrates the emergence of a societal discipline aimed at producing "docile bodies" whether in the army, schools, hospitals, or other institutions (Foucault 1979). Similarly, through his analysis of the civilization of the body, Elias (1978) documents how modern institutions produce many forms of bodily discipline through such things as table manners, etiquette, and decorum. The modernization that gave us military drills, waiting in line, and table manners also gave us precise instructions for the performance of female beauty—application of cosmetics, careful training in poise, sitting, walking, speaking, and acting in a demure or "lady-like" fashion (Bartky 1990). More recently sociologists and feminists from a variety of disciplines also have explored the body (e.g., Oberg and Tornstam 1999; Brumberg 1998; Weitz 1998; Connell 1995; Butler 1993; Turner 1992; Featherstone, Hepworth, and Turner 1991). Finally, psychologists have not ignored the body's importance, either. They have examined physical attractiveness and societal responses to it as well as self-perceptions of body image and resulting levels of self-esteem (e.g., Cash 2000; Grogan 1999; Cash and Pruzinsky 1990).

Given the patriarchal nature of societies where the importance of appearance for women is paramount, it is not surprising that much of the discourse on the body so far has concerned women's bodies. Ageism and other prejudices have shaped researchers' approaches, leading to a general focus on younger women's bodies and on White affluent women's bodies in particular. Thus, much has been written about dissatisfied body images and eating disorders (particularly *anorexia nervosa* and *bulimia* which are primarily the domain of young, affluent White women) and the increasing medicalization of women's bodies (e.g., PMS). By contrast, literature that explores the male body has been scarce until very recently (Connell

1995; Grogan 1999). Substantive literature on aging and the old body continues to be very sparse. Indeed, it is not an exaggeration to say that the old body has largely been invisible in contrast to the overexposure of young bodies.

The Aging Body in Contemporary Society

Self-identity and the body's importance to our sense of self—particularly as we age—are increasingly significant in contemporary societies. That is, our bodies have become evaluative markers, culturally judged in ways that define our worth. Self-identities are increasingly bound to how we look and how our bodies perform. Postmodernists remind us that we live in a time when uncertainty and rapid change are the norm. As a result, things that were more fixed or given in the past are now subject to fragmentation and change. Consumer cultures today provide options and choices that were unimaginable until recently. As a consequence, we can now "actively determine *how to be old*: what to wear, what to own, where to live, how to look and so on" (Oberg and Tornstam 1999, 631). For a price, we can avail ourselves of pharmacological interventions like anabolic steroids, Viagra, and hormone replacement therapies; we can merge bodies and machines to prolong life; we can surgically make the body look younger or restore erections; we can replace hips and other joints; we can allow postmenopausal women to give birth; and we can avail of the miracles of genetic engineering. As a result of such options, available to those who can afford them, the meanings that not so long ago accompanied notions of chronological aging or being old are not so fixed anymore (Biggs 1999). What marketing experts refer to as "generational blur" has grown over the last twenty years. Indeed, some postmodern notions, at their most optimistic, imply that "the promise, as far as aging and identity are concerned, is that one might somehow choose *not* to become old" (Biggs 1999, 47; emphasis added).

In recent decades, the attempt to avoid old age—at least in the visual bodily sense—is increasing across Western societies. We also see a greater fluidity of social images and expectations with regard to aging and to aging bodies specifically (Biggs 1997). Not only do those who are growing old in our society consume youthful lifestyles, they also have increased opportunities to remake and reshape their bodies (Featherstone and Wernick 1995). The growing popularity of body building and cosmetic surgery for women and men illustrates this point. The body is viewed as increasingly malleable, allowing aging members of society greater lifestyle choices and identity choices through physical discipline that include the increased ability to masquerade as younger than their chronological years.

The various ways that the media create and sustain our body-beautiful and youth-dominated culture are widely debated. Certain trends are apparent, however. First, ageism is pervasive in the messages that are promulgated about the aging body and about being old. The media convey in a variety of ways that to be young and beautiful (which almost always means to also be White, affluent, and Western) translates into being "good" and possessing desirable social resources, including culturally valued tastes and knowledge. By contrast, to be old is to be ugly, to be "bad," to be avoided, and to possess fewer of these resources.

Second, ageism interfaces with sexism to put pressure on women to be a particular shape and size, to portray a youthful image even if old. While the prevalence and effects of these pressures on women vary by social location, they are more pronounced than those experienced by men. For instance, the most recent national survey of women's body images in the United States reveals substantial body dissatisfaction among women from 18 to 70 years old (Cash and Henry 1995). Evidence is compelling, for example, that media images of attractiveness in women have changed over the past several decades from a more voluptuous body ideal to one that is more lean and angular (Fallon 1990; Heinberg 1996). That the norm of thinness for women dominates the popular media (Lavine, Sweeney, and Wagner 1999) is reflected in the changing shapes of both Playboy models and contestants in the Miss America Beauty Pageant (Wolf 1991). As a consequence, there is an increasing gap between the media-hyped bodies of models and those of typical women. Consider, for instance, that the average North American woman is five feet four inches in height and weighs 140 pounds, while the average model is five feet eleven inches and weighs 117 pounds (Underwood 2000). The print and television media also have increased their focus on weight-loss and dieting issues and their target audience is overwhelmingly women (Wiseman, Gunning, and Gray 1993; Wiseman et al. 1992). In studies that compare women's and men's magazines, researchers find that women's popular magazines are significantly more likely to focus on body shape and on diet articles and advertisements than is the case with men's magazines (Malkin, Wornian, and Chrisler 1999; Anderson and DiDomenico 1992). Interestingly, studies also show that women are even harsher on themselves than men are on them, with women exaggerating men's preference for thinness (Rozin and Fallon 1988).

A third aspect of the media's increasing attention to the body is seen in the fact that the body has become a critical vehicle for marketing multiple products, particularly "anti-aging" products, whether one of the 1,700 available creams (such as Ponds, which advises "Don't deny it; defy it"), machines, or lifestyles. Notions of self-preservation and self-maintenance go beyond what we might consider reasonable concerns for healthy lifestyles and take on a new and confrontational urgency in contemporary societies. The aging process is increasingly presented as one of conflict between our aging bodies and our forever youthful spirits (Andrews 1999). Thus, the dominant language of the cosmetic industry, for instance, is one that promotes the imagery of war with the body—one is exhorted to do battle with growing old, to "fight," to "defy" signs of aging with multiple creams, therapies, and surgical interventions. But even beyond the cosmetic industry there is increasingly a general societal attitude that we can transcend age, become "ageless" (Andrews 1999).

As well as its fundamentally ageist character, this attention to fighting bodily signs of old age is labor intensive. Within this context the body can be viewed as a site to be managed, an object of discipline. For example, the growing politicization of the body has led to governments' increasing involvement in regulating the body in new ways—whether through policies on abortion, AIDS, surrogate parenting, suicide and death—with women's bodies being especially targeted for such regulation. Furthermore, physical fitness, general "wellness," and cessation of "vices" such as smoking, overeating, and indulgence in casual sex have become a growing focus of the State, the medical establishment, and employers who connect certain behaviors to risk and to medical and health insurance benefits.

Further evidence that the body is a site to be regulated and managed is seen when we consider how the body serves as a "message board" that, with appropriate discipline, conveys age and gender-appropriate messages. The current craze in our culture for body piercing and tattoos among the young and the pressure to dye gray hair among the middle-aged and old (for women and, increasingly, men too) underscore the way age norms get translated into body messages. In the latter case hair dyeing represents an attempt on the part of those who do it "'to pass' as members of a groups with greater power, privilege, and prestige than the group to which they in truth belong" (Gerike 1996, 156). The rise in recent decades of *anorexia nervosa* in young women as well as the growing concern among young men about being muscular highlight how gender influences responses to the body and the various cultural messages about "ideal" bodies (McCaughey 1999). Finally, the influence of age and gender is apparent when we consider that movies rarely show the bodies of old men or women unless in a setting such as in a hospital or nursing home where their bodies might be expected to be exposed. Furthermore, in the few instances where we see flattering portrayals of the old in movies or on TV shows, they are much more likely to be men than women. Indeed, when they are included, old men are much more likely to be presented as attractive and sexual and as having sexual relationships with younger partners (Grogan 1999).

Body Image and Body Dissatisfaction

Tied to the increasing emphasis on the self and hedonistic self-expression, we have witnessed a phenomenal growth in consumerism centered upon personal leisure and pleasure. This shift has further amplified the body's significance to a point where it is increasingly seen as a "central paradigm" for the self—perhaps even a proxy for the self (Brumberg 1998, 197). Indeed, one of the consequences of this shift is that the body in modern societies has become a focal point for self-image (Oberg and Tornstam 1999). Moreover, cultural images of "ideal" bodies, hence "ideal" selves, are intimately coupled with notions of youthfulness.

Studies that explore the complexities of body image are fraught with a variety of methodological problems that influence what we know currently, and deserve brief mention. First, the data are overwhelmingly cross-sectional and few studies exist that examine body image assessments over the life course. Consequently, we have no way of knowing, for instance, whether a middle-aged person's reported discontent is new and is truly related to aging concerns or whether that person was dissatisfied with his or her body as a younger person. Furthermore, interpretations often ignore the critical role played by historical time periods in shaping people's attitudes toward their bodies. Another concern is the absence of studies that explore body image issues among people over thirty-five years of age. As a consequence, while we know that "people are increasingly overwhelmed with messages of youthful ideals," we know virtually nothing about how these images affect people's experiences as they grow old (Oberg and Tornstam 1999, 629). This omission in the literature underscores a point we make throughout this book—researchers themselves are frequently ageist in their choice of topics and populations to study. Thus, while we are necessarily forced to concentrate on existing data in this section, we must also exercise caution in the ways that we extrapolate from these data as we try to understand the old as well as other understudied groups. A last methodological limitation of body image research concerns the instruments used to measure body image attitudes. They vary greatly from study to study, making comparisons across studies difficult, and their reliability and validity are sometimes questionable.

Bearing these caveats in mind, we explore a number of interesting points about research findings on body image. First, studies of body image illustrate that negative body image is not only commonplace but increasingly prevalent in the United States (Cash 2000). Furthermore, men and women consistently differ in the extent to which they rely on their physical appearance to define their sense of self. This is not to imply that looks are not of concern to men; more than half of both genders feel their appearance is important (Oberg and Tornstam 1999). However, women of all ages are more invested in their looks than men, although evidence sometimes suggests that the differences are greatest in adolescence and early adulthood (Feingold and Mazzella 1998; Pliner, Chaiken, and Flett 1990). Not only are women more attentive to and concerned about their appearance than men, it appears to be the case that they are also increasingly more unhappy with their appearance—especially with body weight and shape (Cash 2000). Feingold and Mazzella's (1998) meta-analysis of 222 body-image studies from the past fifty years finds a widening gender gap in body image, with women becoming increasingly more dissatisfied with their bodies. This gender gap in body concern is not restricted to the United States. While the size of the gender differences may vary, studies in England, Australia, and Sweden find women expressing greater discontent with their appearance than men (Oberg and Tornstam 1999; Thompson et al. 1999). A similar gender difference is noted among the Chinese in Hong Kong (Davis and Katzman 1997) and among Iranians (Akiba 1998).

Explanations for women's greater body dissatisfaction generally center on the sexual objectification of women and the consequent enormous pressures placed on them to be physically attractive to men. It is hardly surprising, then, that heterosexual men, who are consistently less concerned than women about their own appearance, place great importance on the physical appearance of their female partners (Siever 1994). Attractiveness, especially sexual attractiveness and desirability, are important factors that influence how we view our bodies. This is especially the case for women because their sexual candidacy depends more on physical appearance than is the case for men (Sontag 1979). Moreover, on these issues, age relations intertwine with gender. Underscoring these interconnections, feminists argue, for instance, that women's sexual value—intimately connected to their appearance—decreases with age in ways that highlight how stigma can be both gendered and ageist. A woman's appearance as she grows old is likely to be viewed less kindly than that of a man at similar ages; indeed, getting older tends to work in men's favor—at least for several decades longer than is true for women (Sontag 1979). This argument is, of course, oversimplified; we know that not all women are equally stigmatized, nor all men equally advantaged. As we illustrate shortly, class, sexual orientation, and race/ethnicity combine with gender and age to create considerable diversity in these regards.

The Cult of Thinness

To what extent our societal obsession with thinness persists into old age is mostly unexplored. We know, however, that concern about bodily weight is the central factor that contributes to an individual's overall body image and it is this issue that produces the greatest gender difference (Cash and Hicks 1990). Despite varying methodologies and measures, women almost universally are reported to be most concerned with their lower body—particularly with the stomach, thighs, buttocks, and hips; men generally are most concerned with muscularity and tone, especially in the upper body—chest, shoulders and biceps (Grogan 1999). Uniformly, women want to weigh less than they do. For women it is preferable to weigh too little than too much—something that is the opposite for men. Consistent with this idea, studies show that generally men are more satisfied than women with their weight in every weight group, except among those men who are underweight—where perhaps fear of "the 98-pound weakling" phenomenon surfaces. By contrast, when women are underweight they are most satisfied with their bodies (Rothblum 1990). This might explain why women report feeling happiest with their bodies first thing in the morning before eating, when they feel lightest and slimmest (Grogan 1999).

Garner's (1997) *Psychology Today* national survey sheds additional light on body dissatisfaction among women and men. His data indicate that 56 percent of the women and 43 percent of the men evaluated their overall appearance negatively. The extreme power of the current cultural norm of thinness is illustrated in a rather startling finding for the responding population: 24 percent of the women and 17 percent of the men claimed that they would give up more than three years of their lives in order to be their ideal weight. *wow, that so extreme*

Two particularly interesting recent examples highlight both the importance of weight for females and how Western conceptions of the ideal female body are being successfully transported to non-Western cultures. The first example comes from a study conducted in two parts of Peru—one region that had little exposure to Western cultures and the other less remote and more exposed to Western notions. Men were shown images of women that depicted a range of body shapes from fat to thin. Researchers found that in the less remote villages, those influenced by Western ideals of thin women, men picked thin female ideals, in contrast to the remote villages where men selected heavier and more "tubular" shaped women as the most attractive and healthy looking (Underwood 2000). A second example of the spreading Western obsession with thinness concerns the recent coverage given to the arrival of Hollywood television shows in Fiji, where only one television channel is available. A group of Harvard Medical School researchers studied young Fiji women's body images in light of a sudden infusion of Western cultural images of thin women in such shows as *Beverly Hills 90210*, *Melrose Place* and *Xena, Warrior Princess*. While there have been very few studies of body-image in non-Western cultures, in most, thinness is seen as a sign of malnutrition; by contrast, plumpness indicates prosperity, health, and wealth (Grogan 1999). In a culture such as Fiji where women and men have historically preferred robust body shapes and placed great importance on generous feeding and voracious eating, it is telling that researchers found a sharp rise in eating disorders among Fiji girls in the years since the introduction of Western television. In fact, five times as many teenage girls reported vomiting to control weight in the time period studied (1999 news release, Harvard Medical School Office of Public Affairs).

The above discussion highlights how the current devotion to disciplining the body—to dieting, sports, and fitness—has taken on new meaning in today's secular world. Indeed, some scholars argue that this illustrates a transference from older religious conceptions of the body (Turner 1992) and that in contemporary society the body has replaced the soul to "become an object of salvation" (Oberg and Tornstam 1999, 631). Past religious conceptions depicted the body as God's temple, requiring its owners to take good care of it in order to respect its sacredness. Thus, where people in previous centuries dieted to manage the spirit and the life of the soul, they now diet for "the purpose of longevity and sexuality" (Turner 1992, 47). Thinness has become synonymous—at least indirectly—with good character. Being overweight, by contrast, is seen as an indication of laziness, as a lack of will power or self-control. Being overweight or obese and stigma are closely connected, especially in the United States. A comparison of U.S. and Mexican attitudes toward being overweight confirms the greater likelihood that those from the United States stigmatize people who are heavy and blame them for lack of personal control (Crandall and Martinez 1996). Indeed, even physicians harbor similarly negative attitudes toward their overweight patients (Fallon 1990). The extent to which women carry the desire to be thin into old age is unclear. However, as others pressure the old to appear more like the young and middle-aged, aging women will probably try harder to discipline their bodies.

Intersections of Gender and Age with Other Social Inequalities

While women of all ages historically have been the ones most concerned about appearance and body image, men also are joining them in this concern. Boys and men are paying more attention to their bodies and to body image, especially in Western societies where advertising has increasingly capitalized on young, shapely male bodies to sell various products. Evidence is mounting that the pressure to look good has intensified for males in recent decades. Men are now bombarded with pictures of unattainably perfect bodies in various media—whether magazines, newspapers or television. Such relatively new and intensified pressure may, at least in part, explain the recent 9 percent increase in appearance dissatisfaction among men—reported to be up from 34 percent dissatisfied in 1986 to 43 percent dissatisfied in 1997 (Cash 2000). As might be expected, however, the growth in male attention to the body highlights a critical gender difference. Men emphasize their body's physical fitness and its physique. Men are more likely to view their bodies in terms of their physical strength and athletic prowess in competition with other men (Siever 1994). Women are generally more likely to view their bodies as objects for aesthetic evaluation.

As well as the existence of a clear gender gap in body image, race is also relevant when we examine how culture shapes responses to one's body and to issues of body image. For example, evidence suggests that African American perceptions of beauty are flexible and that they include, and go beyond, physical characteristics (Parker et al. 1995). Thus, Black Americans, especially women, are more likely to assess body image in themselves and others in terms that are much less rigid, more multi-dimensional than typically appears to be the case for Whites. As a consequence, for African Americans in general and African American women in particular, having a sense of style and "looking good" are important aspects of how one presents oneself, and these entail much more than body shape. Personality, grooming, "attitude," how one moves, and, simply, "making what you've got work for you" are all aspects that point to a certain fluidity in how African Americans assess themselves and each other in terms of body image (Parker et al. 1995).

The above characterization of a racially distinct approach to appearance or body image on the part of Black Americans helps us understand the complexity of approaches to the body in general and body image especially. Evidence with regard to racial differences in weight suggests that African American women tend to weigh more than White women—even when education, social class, and number of live births are held constant (Klem et al. 1990). At the extreme, obesity and its related mortality complications are a serious health issue for African American women when compared to White women (Flynn and Fitzgibbon 1996). Yet, despite their overall greater weight, Black women (as well as Black men who show little weight differences when compared to White men), are less likely to consider themselves overweight and have more positive body images than White women, and are more accepting of diverse body types and physical differences (Parker et al. 1995; Huffine 1991). This greater tolerance among Blacks for different and heavier body types is highlighted in a recent national survey that shows that African American women are both more satisfied with their looks and less preoccupied with weight and dieting that are White and Hispanic women (Cash and Henry 1995). Other studies suggest that Afro-Caribbean, Hispanic, and Asian women are more accepting of larger and heavier body shapes and have overall less weight concerns than White women (Abrams, Allen, and Gray 1993; Harris 1994).

How various racial/ethnic women view their bodies and especially assess ideal body weights is not simple or straightforward, however, as other factors intertwine with ethnicity and race to create differences even within the same racial or ethnic group. Thus, despite evidence that Black women are less concerned than Whites about their weight, this generalization may not apply to *all* Black women. For instance, social class may intertwine with other identities to create diversity among Black women— a possibility that has been generally ignored. For instance, Slevin and Wingrove (1998) found in their sample of old, middle- and upper-middle-class African American women that, although they were more positive about being old women than a similar sample of White women, some of these privileged Black women also fretted about their weight gain in old age. In addition, the findings of a recent study of Latina and non-Latina women (Lopez, Blix, and Blix 1995) underscore the importance of paying attention, especially in the case of immigrant women, to the extent of their immersion into U.S. culture. Thus, despite similar social class backgrounds, Latinas who immigrated to the United States after age sixteen picked a larger silhouette for their ideal body image when compared with Latinas who immigrated to the United States prior to age seventeen. The latter women were more likely to match the ideal body choices of White American women, leading the researchers to speculate that "early socialization to the dominant cultural values has an important impact" (Lopez et al. 1995, 9).

It is also suggestive that Black men who, in a national survey, were found to be more invested in body image than White men and as invested as Black women in appearance, were also found to be the most positive of all groups about their body image (Huffine 1991). The racialized importance of "styling" may be a factor here, especially for African American men. In this regard, styling—which involves a high level of attention to one's physical appearance, to looking "cool"—may provide an avenue for empowerment for Black men who might otherwise go unnoticed (Parker et al. 1995). Huffine (1991) also speculates that the difference in available role models by race may be a factor. First, Black male role models are overwhelmingly sports and entertainment figures for whom physical attractiveness and physical fitness are important. Thus, Black men may invest greater energy in their appearance than White men who have available a wider variety of male role models from a wider variety of occupations. The persistence of these attitudes and behaviors into old age remains unknown, however.

Sexual orientation may also influence body images and emphases on certain body types. To date, research findings are clearer for men than for women (Cash 2000). When compared to heterosexual men, several studies find that physical appearance among gays is highly valued. Thus, gay men are much more invested in being physically attractive and physically fit than are heterosexual men (Beren et al. 1996; Finch 1991; Siever 1994; Wagenbach 1997). Siever posits that gay men and heterosexual women are the most likely groups to share body dissatisfaction because "the gay male subculture imposes similarly strong pressures on gay men to be physically attractive. Gay men, like women, experience extreme pressure to be eternally slim and youthful looking" (Siever 1994, 252). Possibly because, like heterosexual women, gay men are also subject to the male gaze, there is within the gay subculture a heavy emphasis on body shape and especially on the importance of the male athletic body (Gough 1989). In fact, Siever, who studied both homosexual and heterosexual men and women, concludes that gay men appear to be the most unhappy with their bodies. He suggests two dimensions that may help explain this finding. First, like heterosexual men, gay men are concerned about having bodies that are strong and athletic; second, like heterosexual women, they may doubt their physical attractiveness (Siever 1994). Ageism is also likely to be a factor within the gay subculture. A heightened concern for youthful bodies among gay men is likely to create problems for old gay men and, in fact, pressures to remain youthful and especially to look young may serve to marginalize old gays within their own subculture. However, evidence on the impact of old age is still mixed (e.g., Gray and Dressel 1985).

For lesbians the empirical evidence is also mixed. Some scholars (e.g., Wolf 1991) predict that lesbians may downplay the importance of physical attractiveness and have higher levels of body satisfaction than heterosexual women. Other researchers, who find no such differences, argue that gender is a better predictor of body dissatisfaction than sexual orientation (Brand, Rothblum, and Soloman 1992). Although the issues are complex and under-researched, current research suggests some provocative avenues for inquiry. For instance, Bergeron and Senn (1998) discover substantial overlap in body attitudes among heterosexual women and lesbians but also find that lesbians appear less dissatisfied with their bodies and particularly with the size of their thighs and buttocks. While both heterosexual women and lesbians appear to be similarly exposed to and aware of cultural messages about ideal feminine bodies, lesbians are buffered from certain views—at least to some extent. Perhaps because of their heightened awareness of societal oppression, lesbians, while not immune from the pressures to be thin and youthful, are better at resisting the full force of ideal body images. Some researchers speculate that their ideology may encourage lesbians to nurture themselves and other women and to promote greater acceptance of one's body (Altabe and Thompson 1992).

At the same time, examining race, class, and cohort differences may indicate that lesbian culture is not as homogeneous or generally accepting of diverse body sizes as frequently assumed. For instance, current research suggests that older lesbians differ from young lesbians on body image issues. Young lesbians who have experienced less marginalization and who are influenced by the 1990s decade of "lesbian chic" and "lipstick lesbians" may be more mainstream in their values regarding beauty ideals than are older lesbians (Beren et al. 1997). Indeed, the beauty ideal among college-age lesbians is "thin but fit—and not too 'fem' [*sic*]" (Beren et al. 1997, 435).

Exploring how class shapes responses to the body or how it intersects with other locations such as sexual orientation, race, or ethnicity is difficult because researchers generally focus on body images among middle class or the affluent. What little data there are tend to support the notion that, especially in the case of women, those who are the most affluent or *class?*

privileged are also the most concerned about their body images and are most likely to be dissatisfied with their bodies (Grogan 1999). Others have suggested that modern mass communications have created a democratization of body shape ideals that cross class divides (Featherstone 1991). However equal the pressure to conform, class certainly influences one's ability to acquire or keep the ideal bodies that come at a cost of time, money, and effort. Consequently, the affluent will have more ready access to these resources than will those of lower classes. Indeed, the body itself has become a vehicle for conspicuously demonstrating social class differences (Fallon 1990). In this regard, Bourdieu (1984) argues that social class creates an important distinction in how one relates to the body: Those from the dominant social classes treat the body as an aesthetic and ongoing project for improvement. They choose specific activities (golf or aerobic exercise, for instance) with an aim to improving health or appearance. By contrast, he argues, those from the lower classes treat the body as a functioning instrument and, unlike the affluent, are more likely to choose sports that represent a means to an end, such as weight-lifting for strength or soccer for fun.

Growing Old in Gendered Bodies

We begin our discussion of old bodies by summarizing and extending our previous arguments to directly address old age. Bodies are not merely symbolic, nor are they only cultural sites. As Connell (1995, 51) aptly puts it, "The surface on which cultural meanings are inscribed is not featureless, and it does not stay still." Bodies also have materiality; they do matter, as bodies: "They age, get sick, enjoy, engender, give birth. There is an irreducible bodily dimension in experience and practice" (Connell 1995, 51). To the extent that this is the case, old age and old bodies are not *only* social constructions. To be sure, what we take old age to be, when we believe it occurs, and the meaning and evaluation we place on it are social. However, the material reality of bodies changing cannot be denied.

Our interest, then, is in how both changes in appearance and decrements in certain physical abilities are experienced and lead to being seen—by self or others—as "old." Bodies do age and, in so doing, lose some abilities and perhaps gain other capacities. And these changes differ for men and for women. Questions about the interaction between aging bodies and gender lead us into a consideration of the ways in which masculinities and femininities are intertwined with bodies. The plural reflects the fact that, as the previous section showed, social locations such as race and ethnicity also shape masculinity and femininity. At the same time, some of these visions of manhood and womanhood attain an importance as ideals for all people. The ideal form of manhood dictated by "hegemonic masculinity" (Connell 1995) is predominantly about "doing," whereas a hegemonic femininity is primarily about appearance. Of course, women and men may cross these boundaries—looks do matter for men, and actions for women—but always in gender-defined ways. Thus, muscularity in men may be important (but this is also related to the implied connection to "doing"); women's abilities to bear children certainly is about "doing" but it is also tied to their femininity. The point of hegemonic masculinity or femininity is that people are held to these standards, just as old people are held to the standards of youth and especially middle age. These two body dictates interact such that old women and old men have similar but different body ideals.

For women, the emphasis on appearance is central to how much of the age-based bodily changes will be felt and dealt with. Old women must struggle to be seen as still feminine *and* as not "old." Men face related but different issues which center on how their bodily changes may interfere with "doing." In this regard, old men will face two problems. For all men trying to enact hegemonic masculinity, having a body that is unable to "perform" in appropriate ways is problematic. Further, they have to fight against being labeled as not only "nonmasculine" but "old" as well. Thus, old men and women are dealing with issues of body image based on the intersection of gender and ageism. But in addition, both are faced with increasingly recalcitrant bodies. Biological aging does limit "the degree to which the body can be reconstructed" (Oberg and Tornstam 1999, 632).

Focusing on the interconnections between ageism and sexism reveals, for instance, that even though women have certainly gained new freedoms in our society, new forms of oppression also have arisen. Although women's culturally required preoccupation with youth and beauty is not new, "its deployment throughout the life-cycle," and the increasing power of the visual media to reinforce it, are (Bartky 1990, 80). Still, we know little about the consequences of such body images on the old. Researchers and social observers certainly have tended to assume, especially in the case of women, that older people share the same body ideals as the young, leading to growing discrepancies between current and ideal body images and to feelings of inadequacy. On the surface, this assumption has a plausible ring to it. Especially among women, growing old means moving further and further away from the beauty ideal that is most valued for them—being young, having smooth and unwrinkled skin, having a thin and firm body, and so on (Wilcox 1997; Brownmiller 1984). Supporting the notion of a double standard of aging, men are judged less harshly as they grow old and, indeed, signs of aging may be seen as enhancing their attractiveness. It comes as little surprise, then, that currently older women are much more prone than are older men to use age-concealment techniques and also to report that they will do so in the future (Harris 1994).

Thus, nowadays we might find that a grandmother is obligated in ways similar to her teenage granddaughter to police and discipline her body and to maintain certain standards of "femininity" that are heavily vested in notions of youthfulness. Women of all ages are encouraged to compare themselves to models who are very young, very thin, and very beautiful. The gap between this image and reality becomes ever more apparent as women get old and it results in a growing sense of shame and guilt about aging and the inevitable bodily changes that accompany old age (Grogan 1999; Tunaley, Walsh, and Nicolson 1999). Thus, it is hardly surprising that women over 60 are as concerned as adolescents and young adult women are about their appearance (Pliner et al. 1990). Importantly, however, this concern may not translate into the same level of body dissatisfaction that younger women record (Oberg and Tornstam 1999). At the same time, we should note that we are still quite ignorant about what such "dissatisfaction" actually *means* to those being assessed, whatever their age (Tunaley et al. 1999).

There is general agreement, nevertheless, that the social dictate to be young and slim intensifies the pressure to manage bodies in order to avoid looking old. Until the mid-twentieth century, older women in most Western societies were expected to have "mature" figures and to dress accordingly (Dinnerstein and Weitz 1994). Starting in the 1950s and accelerating at a rapid pace each decade thereafter, we have witnessed a breakdown of the demarcation between "mature" and youthful bodies for women. With growing consumerism and globalization, we have seen the rise of a fitness craze and a powerful fashion-beauty industry that seeks to persuade women to spend ever-growing amounts of money on products touted to perpetuate youthfulness and deny the biological realities of growing old.

But the relationship between women and the beauty industry, with its clothes, makeup, and cosmetic surgery, remains complex and often paradoxical. Women who adhere to norms of youthful beauty are not "cultural dopes" (Davis 1995; Grogan 1999). Indeed, "a woman's pursuit of beauty through transformation is often associated with . . . self-creation, self-fulfillment, self-transcendence, and being cared for" (Morgan 1998, 154). Furthermore, women (especially the affluent and well-educated) can be "highly critical consumers" of beauty products. Thus, Davis (1995) argues that women confront an ideological dilemma when choosing, say, cosmetic surgery. They can see through the conditions of oppression even as they comply with them.

Whatever the debates about the role of choice in transforming the body, the commercial and social pressure to remain youthful is growing such that it is increasingly impossible for us to imagine bodies becoming old "naturally." Former First Lady Barbara Bush, who commanded considerable media attention for her insistence on aging naturally and resisting cultural dictates to dye her hair or to alter her face and body in order to appear less "matronly," illuminated the limits of resistance when she explained that she wore her famous three strands of pearls to hide her sagging neck (Dinnerstein and Weitz 1998). In this context, it is worth emphasizing that internalizing the cultural norm of youthful appearance discourages solidarity from forming between young and old women. Young women learn to dread growing and looking old. In learning to be ageist toward women older than they are, they also learn to turn against their future selves as old women (Woodward 1999). There is some evidence also that lesbians are no more inclusive of old women in their subculture than is the case within the mainstream heterosexual culture (Copper 1986).

Men, we have argued, are increasingly affected by this intensified attention to the body as well, albeit in a different way. Because men are more likely to be judged for what they do rather than how they look, they may be allowed to grow old more gracefully and with less pressure to live up to unrealistic standards. However, the notion that men's status and wealth have more enduring value than their looks (Oberg and Tornstam 1999) is based on critical assumptions concerning class and race at the very least. Masculinity can be demonstrated in many different ways; physical appearance is only one, important insofar as it is a manifestation of physical abilities. Thus, middle-class men are more likely to be defined by skill than by strength in their jobs (Connell 1995), one reason perhaps that such things as graying hair are not perceived negatively. By contrast, bodies themselves tend to be economic assets for working-class men; through their active use these men make their livings (Connell 1995). This reality, however, also presents some different challenges for aging. Manual laborers may experience becoming physically "old" sooner than men of other classes. Further, such bodily changes as a loss of strength may be all the more threatening to masculinity for these men.

Thus, we might guess that the decreases in physical capabilities that accompany aging, rather than appearance per se, might be more problematic for old men than for old women. However, scholars have yet to examine men's experiences with such losses in relation to ideals of manhood. Research on disabled men of many ages finds a wide range of responses to their physical challenges in relation to masculinity. One reaction, reliance, involves continued adherence to standards of masculinity—continued frustration averted by working hard to show strength. Others redefine masculinity in terms of their present abilities—for example, substituting financial independence for physical autonomy. Finally, others reject such masculinity altogether, perhaps focusing on "personhood" rather than "manhood" (Gershick and Miller 1994). As their physical capacities diminish, old men certainly may fall anywhere along this range. Indeed, the fabled "midlife crisis" in which men seek younger partners to prove their sexuality may well be a reaction to signs of aging and the specter of diminished masculinity. Cosmetic surgery in the form of facelifts and similar interventions may amount to women's resistance while penile implants may constitute men's response. Nevertheless, these middle-class responses represent only a small fraction of the ways in which old men and women may assert and reshape their gender identities.

We have argued that ageism interfaces with gender in ways that make the body problematic in different ways for old women and old men. Among the more interesting ironies that emanate from this intersection of ageism with sexism, however, is the fact that as technology increasingly allows us to postpone outward signs of old age, we are called to start at younger and younger ages to labor against appearing "old." Indeed, the more accessible cosmetic surgery and other body modification technologies become, the more that "looking old may . . . become even more culturally unforgivable" (Oberg and Tornstam 1999, 633).

Negotiating Old Bodies

The arguments presented above risk exaggerating the extent to which the old accept without question the equation of beauty with youth. In fact, many people can reject or challenge such ideals; and many of the old grew up before the relentless bombardment by our unrealistic standards began. Even if we accept that the old are now influenced by ideals of thinness and youth, we must still allow that they may reject or reshape what they see as unrealistic standards.

For instance, a recent study of old, White, working-class women in England illustrates that their constructions of growing older involve a sense of greater freedom and earned enjoyment—even in the context of realizing that slimness is the beauty ideal (Tunaley et al. 1999). Interestingly, the old women in this study were at a stage of their lives where they were less worried about being sexually attractive than was true when they were younger, or at least in the same ways. Indeed, they were "more concerned with meeting their own needs and desires than they were with meeting the needs of others" (Tunaley et al. 1999, 755). The words of a seventy-year-old interviewee, Ruth, illustrate this point:

> Sometimes I know it is wrong to be greedy and then I think "Oh well, what the heck! Now you're 70 why not enjoy what you've got while you've got it?" I mean I don't eat many sweet things, but there are certain things that really appeal to me like— you know—such as I went out and we had a raspberry tart, and I love raspberries and of course I had to have two pieces with cream on it, didn't I, where one would have been quite sufficient. But it was so enjoyable I had to have another piece. (Tunaley et al. 1999, 755)

Social gerontologists should also explore the matter of political ideology. Survey findings suggest that feminists, while certainly not immune to unrealistic cultural body standards, appear to be somewhat less caught up in meeting the standards than are women with more traditional gender ideologies (Garner 1997). It is at least possible, then, that some among the baby boomers will resist the full strength of body image messages as they grow old.

A third issue that may shape how the old consider their bodies can be gleaned from the social comparison literature. Explaining how older people can maintain self-esteem and life satisfaction despite the losses that can accompany old age, Heidrich and Ryff (1993) hypothesize that old adults compare themselves with other old adults who are having more difficulty along a particular dimension. Thus, a seventy-year-old woman may feel that she is attractive compared to other seventy-year-old women, and her goal may be to look sixty years old, not thirty (Wilcox 1997).

Sorting out the complexities of how the old respond to their bodies is not an easy task, and the influences of age, cohort, and social inequalities will no doubt result in a diverse range of experiences. Any combination of influences already mentioned will likely frame how the old respond to their bodies. Such thinking makes sense when we consider the findings of a sizable study that included a representative number of the old in Sweden. In this instance, older women were found to be *more* content with their bodies than were younger women. Furthermore, gender differences in satisfaction with bodies decreased with age. Among those aged 75 to 85, 80 percent of both men and women said they were satisfied with their bodies (Oberg and Tornstam 1999). Gender differences in body satisfaction may well be less pronounced among the old (Franzoi and Koehler 1998) but how and why this is the case needs further exploration.

Conclusions

The growing cultural emphasis on transforming the body to maintain youthfulness and to defer the visual evidence of aging illuminates contradictions and problems that bear scrutiny. First, a society that emphasizes notions of agelessness, of masking one's chronological age, is a society in which growing old is seen as problematic and even unacceptable. Such a society is ageist. Second, attempts to thwart biological aging, to "stop the clock," may create consequences where increasingly aging can become a "nightmare" or trauma in which the psyche is at war with the body, leading to "an end-game in which older people are at war with themselves" (Biggs 1999, 63). Third, dealing with the growing choices that prevail as we age requires that "the body needs to be progressively managed" (Biggs 1997, 558)—significant time, effort, and money must be spent on masking aging.

Bodies are shaped (literally) and influenced by such things as the values and norms of a particular culture at a particular time. At the same time, we must bear in mind the fact that the body is more than a social construction (Butler 1993). It is more than a site of response to culture. Bodies are biological and physical entities with their own imperatives. So, old age and its relationship to the body are especially critical. Even if we have opportunities to replace and resurface their various parts, our bodies nevertheless progressively age—and therein lies the tension between an old body and the possibility that its owner desires it to remain young or, at least, youthful and spry. Old men have more prostate problems than young men do, and they have penises that are more likely to lose erections or have less hard ones than young men do; old women have droopier breasts and are more likely to have osteoporosis than young women. Furthermore, outward changes in physical appearance accompany old age. Change to the skin is one of the most apparent—with loss of elasticity, dryness, and the presence of "age" spots. The subcutaneous fatty layers thin and leave one with increased boniness and more hollows. Furthermore, bodies change shape as they age. These are physical realities that we must understand and consider in conjunction with the power of social construction if we are to begin to understand the body and its relationship to growing old and being old.

But what if, as women and men, we claim to willingly comply with normative notions of youthfulness? Some may say, as Jane Fonda did when discussing her cosmetic surgeries and intense exercise regime, "'What the hell is the big deal about trying to buy yourself a few more years?'" (Dinnerstein and Weitz 1998, 96). Surely, looking good, feeling good about one's self, and having a fit body are all good things. However, the cultural shift toward agelessness, denial of the aging body, and increasing pressure to discipline the body to maintain a youthful appearance contain certain contradictions. If our culture tells us that growing old makes us unattractive, that being old is undesirable, how much choice are we exercising when we elect to try to postpone the visible signs of being old? Perhaps it is the case that "what appear at first glance to be instances of choice turn out to be instances of conformity" (Morgan 1998, 155). Women's lifelong conformity to the norms of youth amounts to adherence to norms of heterosexuality. As feminists have argued, one cannot underestimate the power of ideals of femininity in sustaining patriarchy and overcoming resistance to it (Bartky 1998; Morgan 1998). In a world that puts so much pressure on women to be attractive, which of these "choices" is "free"?

Further, attempts to "stop the clock" typically cost money as well as other resources. Therein lies the root of another form of inequality—one that restricts access to sophisticated body management techniques to society's most affluent members. Our gender lens requires that we bear such class inequality in mind.

CHAPTER 4

Sex, Sexuality, and Old Age

We shift the focus in this chapter from exploring the social significance of the body to our understanding of old age, to examining sex and sexuality within the context of aging. As might be expected, the topics of sex and sexuality in later life are fraught with misconceptions and prejudices. We begin by examining the ways in which various social constructions and cultural stereotypes shape our notions of and attitudes toward sex and sexuality, especially for the old. Next we provide a very broad overview of what researchers tell us about sex and the old. We continue by exploring how gender shapes sex and sexuality, particularly in later life. Included in this discussion is a brief look at the physical changes related to sex that women and men experience as they age. We then examine the problems with the available data: the types of studies available, their implicit and explicit assumptions, and sampling issues. Finally, we turn our attention to sex and sexuality among the old by applying a gender lens that critiques existing knowledge and prompts us to rethink how we conceptualize and study these topics in old age.

Introduction

Recent scholarship in the area of sex and sexuality has been particularly useful in challenging the view that sex is nothing more than a "natural instinct," an overpowering natural force (especially centered in the male genitalia) that requires expression. In prior eras, assumptions of sexual essentialism were persistent and pervasive in Western cultures. Embedded within the folk wisdom of Western societies was the notion that sex is "eternally unchanging, asocial and transhistorical" (Rubin 1993, 11). Both feminist and gay and lesbian scholarship have been especially effective in highlighting the importance of both social construction and power relationships in shaping our approaches to sex and sexuality. Past certainties have been challenged and have largely been replaced with the argument that what we know of sex and sexuality is socially shaped. Increasingly, scholars' attention focuses on the fact that while the biological body is the site for what happens sexually, issues of sex and sexuality are more about beliefs, ideologies, and imaginations than about the physical body (Weeks 1996).

The Social Construction of Sex and Sexuality

Modern Western societies appraise sex acts according to a hierarchical system of sexual value. Marital, reproductive heterosexuals are alone at the top of the erotic pyramid. Clamoring below are unmarried monogamous heterosexuals in couples, followed by other heterosexuals. Solitary sex floats ambiguously. The powerful nineteenth-century stigma on masturbation lingers in less potent, modified forms, such as the idea that masturbation is an inferior substitute for partnered encounters. Stable, long-term lesbian and gay male couples are verging on respectability, but bar dykes and promiscuous gay men are hovering just above the groups at the very bottom of the pyramid. The most despised sexual casts currently include transsexuals, transvestites, fetishists, sadomasochists, sex workers such as prostitutes and porn models, and the lowliest of all, those whose eroticism transgresses generational boundaries. (Rubin 1993, 14–15)

To explore how sexuality is shaped by society and history, we can examine various norms, values, and attitudes and thus illuminate the variety of ways in which our notions about sex are socially constructed. We can also begin to understand that the social organization of sexuality is neither fixed nor stable. For instance, religious beliefs, as well as notions about morality, are especially powerful influences in this regard, even if not always obvious or explicit. Western cultures are steeped in negative notions about the sinfulness of sex and sexuality. Sex is considered to be "a dangerous, destructive and negative force" (Rubin 1993, 13). Consider the predominant nineteenth-century and early Victorian Western views in which sexual activity unconnected to reproduction—in other words, sex for the sake of pleasure—was claimed to cause serious physical harm. Masturbation was said to cause blindness, insanity, and heart disease, and oral sex was said to cause cancer (Giddens and Duneier 2000). But, within these contexts, sex could be redeemed if performed within marriage for procreation rather than pleasurable purposes.

As the opening quotation suggested, our notions about sex in modern Western societies also are infused with a pervasive sense of hierarchy—one that is socially constructed, rooted in Western religions, and shaped by modern medicine and psychiatry (Rubin 1993). These forces, often intricately interwoven, shape what forms of sex get labeled as "normal" or "pathological" at any given time. It is hardly surprising, then, that the most privileged sexual behavior—heterosexual intercourse between those who are married—is the only adult sexual behavior that is legal in every state in the United States.

However, we suggest that an additional but essentially invisible hierarchy exists within the one Rubin articulates. In our society, dominant notions of age-appropriate sexuality, as well as ageism, shape this invisible hierarchy. Thus, in addition to the more visible ways that sexuality is shaped by, for instance, gender or sexual orientation, it is also structured by age considerations. As a consequence, whatever the point in the pyramid, whatever the sexual behavior we consider, the level of disapproval or stigma is highest when an old person engages in it. This line of reasoning might lead us to conclude that while people may accept or abhor sexual acts that they label as appropriate or deviant when they are carried out by the young, our greatest level of censure is bestowed upon the old who engage in these acts. What may be considered virility among the young is labeled perverse when the actor is old. Thus, from the top to the bottom of the hierarchy, the "dirty old man" gets "dirtier" and "more perverse" as we envisage him in the various sex acts. At the same time, male sexuality—even among the old—is at least subject to speculation—in contrast to the sexuality of old women, which is virtually ignored.

What we mean today by the term "sex" also illustrates that what constitutes sex means different things to different people and that social location is a key to understanding how one approaches sex. Accordingly, various social constructions shape our ideas. The variety of activities, which include fantasies, are as great as the human imagination. For some, sex may mean phone sex or cybersex in which the participants talk/write/fantasize about various sexual acts. For others it may mean oral sex or vaginal or anal intercourse. A similar variety of notions accrue to sexuality, which is also best viewed as a social construction, a historical invention. Thus, in addition to actual behavior, sexuality includes desired and actual sexual attraction, emotions, and fantasies (Lorber 1999). It is best understood as describing a "series of historically shaped and socially constructed beliefs, behaviors, relationships and identities" that relate to the body and its pleasures (Weeks 1996, 368).

Cultural blueprints provide the members of a society at any particular time with maps, accompanied by legends, which guide how individuals think about what is desirable, appropriate, "normal," or "perverted" about sex and sexuality at different ages. The previous discussion of the sexual hierarchy illuminates the current content. In general, at all stages of the life cycle, society's dominant groups associate "normal" with heterosexuality and with penetration, intercourse, and orgasm. Other sexual identities and practices are marginalized. In addition, romance and love are associated with society's young. Only firm, youthful bodies are seen as attractive, and thus sexual interest and activity are considered the rightful domain only of the young. The idea that old people with wrinkled and sagging bodies might be sexually interested or, even worse, sexually active, strikes most as perverse, as "sick" or "disgusting" (Hodson and Skeen 1994). Time will tell how the baby boomers will reshape these ageist notions as they enter old age.

The Importance of Social Locations

Our social construction of gender plays a key role in shaping sexuality (Connell 1999). "[P]atterns of female sexuality are inescapably a product of the historically rooted power of men to define what is necessary and desirable" (Weeks 1996, 377). Thus, for instance, we must acknowledge that the language of sexuality is overwhelmingly male (and heterosexual); the various metaphors used to describe it (e.g., penetration, insertion) are almost exclusively derived from men's sexual experiences (Weeks 1996). One result of the encoded dominance of one sex over the other is a gendered imbalance of power that, in turn, shapes sexual attitudes and behaviors. Thus, for instance, women's sexuality is most often viewed as an adjunct to men's sexual desires because men are defined as the active sexual agents. Despite women's progress in many Western societies, many still believe that women are to be passive sexually, and thus they should learn about themselves sexually from the perspective of men (Tolman 1994).

Sexuality has been viewed differently at various time periods. For instance, people have viewed women as everything from dangerous, to sources of disease, to guardians of moral purity (Weeks 1996). Consider also the gendered ways we construe sexual desire. What are the stereotypes we have learned about men and women and their desire for sex? Among them we certainly can cite the idea that men can "never get enough" and that "nice" women (or "good girls") need to be persuaded to "do it" (Schwartz and Rutter 1998).

Of course, when we examine in more depth the notion that women are not as interested in sex as men, we find that other identities and locations intersect with gender in powerful ways to shape this notion. For example, the notion of girls' and women's comparative frigidity is largely restricted to Whites, especially those in the upper classes. Hence, consideration of race/ethnicity, class, and sexual orientation illuminates how membership in different groups forms our notions about sexuality—underscoring that when we talk of sexuality we need to recognize that there is not just *one* sexuality. In fact, there are many different sexualities to consider (Weeks 1996). For example, men and women of color have been the victims of sexual stereotyping by Whites for centuries. Black men and women have been labeled as "lustful and hot-blooded" (Bartky 1990). Similarly, the stereotypes of the Latin "Casanova," the mysterious Asian seductress, and the insatiable gay man also highlight the importance of exploring how social location shapes sexual notions.

Add consideration of age to these pictures and we uncover an even more complicated set of issues. For example, media images of an old body (naked or close to it) presented in a flattering sexual manner are very rare. Contrast this invisibility of old bodies with the overwhelming presence of young ("hard") bodies. In this way we come to see how ageism explicitly and implicitly plays an important part in our conceptions of sexuality. We can also see how sexism interfaces with ageism when we consider our notions about appropriate cross-generational sex and gender—it is acceptable for older men to have considerably younger women as partners but it is not similarly acceptable for old women to have young lovers.

The many jokes and stories in our culture that ridicule sexuality among those who are no longer considered young point to an ageist hostility toward both sex and old age (Hooyman and Kiyak 1999). Several themes permeate the myths of sexuality concerning the old: First, the old are not sexually desirable; second, they are not sexually desirous; and, lastly, they are not sexually capable. Images of the sexless old or "dirty old men," "old biddies," and "old hags" abound (Minichiello, Plummer, and Seal 1996). The recent spate of Viagra jokes makes clear that the drug is wasted on old men. But such ageist humor focusing on old men's sexual dysfunction at least makes visible *their* sexuality, in contrast to the wall of silence about old women's sexuality and sexual needs. Sexuality in later life remains, for the most part, little researched, very private, and invisible despite biomedical and behavioral studies that demonstrate that older people both continue to desire and have the capacity for sexual intimacy (Weg 1996).

Clearly, ageist notions about sexuality in later life are deeply embedded in our society, despite the fact that we are increasingly tolerant about sexual self-determination for most other segments of our population (Hooyman and Kiyak 1999). We have grown, for example, increasingly tolerant toward sexual self-determination for teens, single adults, unmarried couples, and homosexuals in our society (Hodson and Skeen 1994). Yet, we continue to hold firmly to the view that sexual interaction among the old in our society is absent or unacceptable. For instance, college students expect that aging leads to a fairly steep decline in sexual activity from age thirty onward (Zeiss 1997). Even physicians vary in their understanding and acceptance of sexuality among the old, as do other health care providers (Wallace 1992; Butler and Lewis 1988). Furthermore, for the old who are institutionalized, policies about sexual activities reflect a variety of taboos about sexuality among the old (Weg 1996). Family members also demonstrate prejudices and ignorance when it comes to the issue of sexuality and their elderly relatives. Finally, the old as a group also have internalized, albeit perhaps in different ways and to a lesser degree, ageist ideas about their own sexuality. And, however much this is true for elderly men, no doubt older women have been subjected to (and have internalized) even stronger prejudices against themselves as healthy sexual beings (Woodward 1999). It may be especially difficult for old women to challenge family expectations of celibacy (Read 1999). Our silence about sexuality among the old in general is magnified in our lack of attention to the needs of old women. Sexism combines with ageism to produce particularly negative consequences for old women, as they tend to outlive men.

Despite increased research on sexual orientation in general, studies on old gay men and lesbians are sorely lacking, and this is even more noteworthy for those who belong to racial and ethnic minorities (Boxer 1997). This lack of attention is all the more regrettable because what little we do know about old gays and lesbians suggests that they may have important lessons to teach both old heterosexual men and women concerning healthy adjustment to multiple stigma (Quam and Whitford 1992) and more egalitarian and reciprocal sexual relationships (Connell and Dowsett 1992).

Sexuality and Old Age: What Researchers Tell Us

The minimal investigation of sexuality among the elderly reflects ageist assumptions about what is important in scholarly investigation, our general "cultural illiteracy" about aging, and long-established cultural biases about the sexless old (Matthias et al. 1997; Weg 1996; Cole 1992). In addition, when scholars have chosen to focus on sex and sexuality in later life, the results have been fraught with sampling and other biases that have reduced the generalizability of results (Schiavi 1996).

The 1948 report on male sexuality and the 1953 report on female sexuality by Alfred Kinsey and colleagues are viewed as the beginning of modern scientific research on human sexuality in the United States (Walker 1997). As an indication of the importance that sexuality among the old garnered from these researchers, note that in his first report, Kinsey and colleagues devoted a total of three pages in a 735-page report to the subject of sex and aging (Schiavi 1996). Despite studies with overall large sample sizes of several thousand, the sample of those over 60 years of age totaled 126 men and 56 women. In fact, Kinsey's suggestion that three-quarters of men over age 80 were impotent was based on a sample of four (Kellett 1991). Nevertheless, these were the earliest studies to consider the relationship between age and sexuality and they represented the most comprehensive look (18,000 individual histories) at sexual activity in the United States. Kinsey's report demonstrated that, contrary to popular beliefs, sexual practice persisted among the elderly, albeit at a reduced level, and that women *were* interested in sex. In addition, they found that 37 percent of all males reported at least one homosexual encounter leading to orgasm (Kinsey et al. 1948).

Masters and Johnson (1966, 1970) continued the exploration of sexual behavior in the United States through clinical studies that examined the physiology of sexual responses. Among the most relevant of their findings for sexuality in later life, two are particularly worth highlighting. First, the aging process may slow human sexual response but it certainly does not terminate it (Masters and Johnson 1966). Second, the best predictor of level of sexual activity in later life is the level of sexual activity in earlier years (Masters and Johnson 1970). However, the findings on sexuality among the old were based again on the inclusion of very small samples—in the case of the first Masters and Johnson study (1966), twenty males formed the basis of their conclusions about sexuality in later life.

Key conclusions from predominantly White samples in more recent research suggest that while sex continues to play an important role in the lives of elderly men and women, sexual activity declines over time. Sexual interest also declines, but more slowly. A number of factors influence the extent of sexual interest and activity in men, including past experience, age, health factors, and social class. For women, the factors that shape activity and interest in sex are marital status, age, and past enjoyment of sex. Availability of a partner is also critical for (heterosexual) women (Minichiello et al. 1996).

Other national studies of sexuality in recent decades that have garnered attention are the Hite Report on female sexuality (Hite 1976), The Janus Report on Sexual Behavior (Janus and Janus 1993), and the most recent and highly publicized national study of adult sexual activity, the National Health and Social Life Survey (NHSLS) conducted by a team of University of Chicago researchers (Laumann et al. 1994). All three ignore the old entirely or nearly so. In the case of the Hite Report (N=1,844), only 19 women in the study were 60 or older. The Janus Report did not focus on the sexual behaviors of the elderly but did have a sample in which 34 percent were aged 51 and above. Their findings support those of earlier studies that document a wide range of sexual interest and activity among aging populations. The most recent national survey headed by Laumann and colleagues excluded those over 60 years of age.

Studies of sexuality in later life reveal a number of consistent themes (Quadagno 1999). First, assuming a reasonable level of health and an available and functioning partner, sexual activity continues, although at varying levels, even in the lives of the very old. Second, a decline in sexual activity and, to a lesser extent, in sexual interest, ensues with increasing age, usually beginning around the age of 50. For instance, a national survey of *Parade Magazine* readers over age 65 reports that the old continue in sexual activity. By the same token, the percentage declines with age, ranging from a high of 55 percent among those aged 65 to 69 to a low of 13 percent among those over age 85. Many more would like to be sexually active, but cannot due to lack of a suitable partner (26 percent), impotence (18 percent), and health problems (16 percent). Further, the frequency declines, with those over 65 reporting sex an average of 2.5 times a month, compared to 7.1 times a month for those aged 18 to 65 (Clements 1996).

That said, sexual activity or interest does not cease at a specific chronological age; considerable individual variation exists. Being sexual, which is shaped in important ways by earlier interest and activity, continues to occupy an important place in the lives of most of the elderly. For instance, a study that explored the sex lives of white men and women who were 80 and above found that 38 percent of the women and 66 percent of the men reported that sex was currently important to them. The majority of both women and men most frequently engaged in touching and caressing (Bretschneider and McCoy 1988). The old need intimacy just as much as the young; several studies document the insignificance of age differences in sexual satisfaction and enjoyment (Schiavi et al. 1994; Levy 1994; McKinlay and Feldman 1994). In fact, a recent AARP study reveals that the majority of midlife and older adults sampled consider a satisfying sexual relationship important to their quality of life (AARP/*Modern Maturity* 1999). At the same time, men of all ages are more likely than women to say sex is important (Clements 1996).

To a very great degree, the studies reported above assume that their respondents are heterosexual, and it is thus impossible to glean from them what similarities and differences might be found based on sexual preference. Tentative suggestions stem from the few studies that do focus on old gay men and lesbians. Importantly, however, samples are not only small, but researchers often include those whom we might consider to be middle-aged—those aged forty to fifty—in their study. Nevertheless, these few studies find that, similar to heterosexuals, most gay men and lesbian women report that sexual activity continues into old age, though perhaps less frequently, and sexual interest does not wane (Kimmel 1995; Pope and Shultz 1996; Berger and Kelly 1996). Further, and also similar to heterosexuals, some older gay men report greater satisfaction with sex as "it is less focused on the genitals and more on the whole person" (Kimmel 1995, 294). The speculation that old gays and lesbians may be less interested in maintaining traditional notions of masculinity and femininity (Berger and Kelly 1996) may also have a bearing on their sexual behavior in old age, for example, making typical notions of virility in men less important, perhaps even forestalling psychological barriers to impotence. Such speculations await research on the influence of notions of masculinity and femininity on sexual behavior in old age.

Age and Physical Changes

The term "climacteric" is used to describe the physical and behavioral changes that occur during middle age for both men and women (Byer and Shainberg 1994). Generally, men experience the climacteric some eight to ten years later than women. For women, menopause, which occurs usually around age fifty, signals a host of physical changes in the female body.

Menopause

The menstrual cycle ends, the ovaries stop functioning, and the body produces lower levels of the female hormones estrogen and progesterone. A range of physical symptoms accompanies menopause—some are experienced by most menopausal women, others are highly variable. Whatever the changes, *no* loss of women's established multi-orgasmic capacity occurs and the clitoris continues to be the center of female orgasmic response—although orgasms are noticeably shorter between the fifth and seventh decades and longer periods of stimulation are needed to achieve orgasm (Weg 1996). All women experience a decline of estrogen, which causes vaginal changes that may trigger physical and emotional consequences for older women (Weg 1996). Estrogen deficiency causes the walls of the vagina to thin, the body produces less vaginal lubrication, and it takes longer to produce lubrication. As a result, sexual intercourse may become less comfortable. In addition, hormonal changes contribute to urogenital atrophy, altered body shape, diminished muscle tone, and skin elasticity (Weg 1996). One of the body changes that occurs is that breasts become less firm due to a diminution of skin elasticity, muscle tone, and glandular tissue.

Numerous treatments are available to alleviate the various menopausal symptoms and this stage of women's lives is increasingly medicalized in Western cultures (Defey et al. 1996). Treatments include creams and jellies to lubricate, psychotropic drugs, and hormone replacement therapy (HRT)—a controversial medical intervention that re-introduces higher levels of estrogen and progesterone to the female body, thus alleviating some of the symptoms associated with menopause, such as hot flashes (which are experienced by most but not all women at this stage). Changes associated with menopause for some women include mood swings, fatigue, irritability, and reduction in sexual interest and desire. However, most postmenopausal women report little or no change in their levels of sexual arousal and no impairment in their level of orgasmic response (Leiblum 1990). Yet, as suggested above, it is also the case that gynecologists, especially in the United States, categorize menopause as a crisis associated with loss and anger: They "tend to emphasize the 'dark' side of menopause (depression, anxiety, etc.)" and, as a result, their approach centers on pathology and medical treatment (Defey et al. 1996, 1454).

While menopause heralds for women a very clear cessation of reproductive capability, middle-aged men also experience physiological changes, albeit less dramatic than women's. Clearly, men can father children into their eighth decade, although they do experience declining testosterone in their fifties and sixties. Other changes, most notably in the ability of the penis to obtain and sustain erections, occur. Typically older men take longer to achieve erection than do younger men and, in addition, erections are likely to be less rigid than in earlier years. These changes are likely to gradually alter the nature of intercourse in heterosexual older men. Frequency may drop and intensity may be diminished. Nevertheless, older heterosexual couples may benefit from slower erections for men and the need for greater stimulation for women to the extent that both may now have more time to experience arousal (Weg 1996).

In extreme cases, men can experience erectile dysfunction or impotence. By age 65, approximately 25 percent of all men are impotent (Walsh and Worthington 1995). Because men typically equate masculinity with the ability to have an erection, "performance anxiety" –a psychological phenomenon that triggers impotence—occurs more frequently as men age. Indeed, an important reason elderly men do not have intercourse is fear of being impotent and the resulting sense of self-devaluation.

Finally, health status is a critical factor in sexual behavior and sexual satisfaction among the old. Declining health affects both performance and satisfaction as people age, and this may be compounded by the side effects of medication (Kellett 1991; Clements 1996). That said, the most recent AARP study on sexuality among those 45 and older confirms earlier claims that reasonably good health and an available partner assure sexual activity into middle and ultimately old age: More than half of those surveyed who report no major diseases or depression claim to engage in sexual intercourse at least once a week (AARP *Modern Maturity Sexuality* Survey 1999). Interestingly, findings from this survey also illustrate that despite the most commonly reported health problems of high blood pressure (37 percent of both men and women) and arthritis and rheumatism (32 percent of women and 19 percent of men), substantial minorities are not seeking treatment for some of these ailments that may affect their sex lives (AARP 1999). Perhaps reflecting a cohort effect that could diminish as the baby boomers grow older, this study also finds that only a small minority of those with self-described sexual problems are currently making use of treatments to enhance sexual performance (AARP 1999). For those who avail of drugs or treatments (for example, Viagra for men or hormone treatments for women), a majority claim that their sex lives are improved (AARP 1999).

Conceptual and Methodological Concerns

The study of sexuality and old age is fraught with many difficulties. First, the frank and open discussion of sexual activity is frequently considered taboo in *any* age group, and thus respondents may not be entirely honest (Schwartz and Rutter 1998). Indeed, they may overestimate or underrepresent their sexual activities. For instance, we know that there is frequently a gendered phenomenon at play in sex surveys—men exaggerate their level of sexual activity and women underestimate it (Reiss 1995). This raises important conceptual as well as methodological questions. As important as the concern about the validity of data due to distortion is a much subtler issue: how societal norms, shaped by patriarchal values, influence what both old men and women consider "normal" or desirable in terms of levels and types of sexual activity. Of particular interest, for example, is the exploration of how old women regulate their sexual desires and activities in order to reflect normative cultural stereotypes of their presumed asexuality. It is difficult for old women to express their sexuality when the community that surrounds them does not see them as sexual beings.

These issues highlight the challenges of sex research, particularly when we study sex and sexuality in later life. A cohort influence may also be at work. Today's old people, especially women who were expected to be modest and guarded about sex, may be less open than future cohorts such as baby-boomers who came of age in a more sexually permissive era. Specifically, we might expect women who have been raised in a climate of greater sexual permissiveness to be more aware of their sexual needs and desires. Thus, one might predict that more female-centered sex practices could lead to different results than recently indicated in a national survey that showed that heterosexual women are less than half as likely as men to report having an orgasm (Laumann et al. 1994).

Moreover, researchers are themselves frequently uncomfortable exploring this sensitive topic. They are likely, even if unwittingly, to share the biased notions about old age and sexuality that permeate our culture—where a myth of "nothingness" still pervades much thinking on the topic (Hodson and Skeen 1994). Yet, in those rare studies where researchers have been especially open to issues of sexuality among the old, results debunk popular myths of asexuality (Minichiello et al. 1996). For instance, Wiley and Bortz report that, although a majority of their elderly participants generally were satisfied with their sex lives, "a large percentage of men and women desired more frequent sex" (Wiley and Bortz 1996, 144). Indeed, their finding that 48 percent of men and 55 percent of women over 70 years of age "desired to have sex two or more times a week" (1996, 145) underscores two important points. First, current levels of sexual activity are not necessarily considered ideal by the old; and second, notions of old women's sexual desire appear to be mistaken in terms of levels of interest both in general and relative to old men's. The assumptions of absence of sexual activity among the old lead not only to an obvious inaccuracy but also to an increasingly deadly consequence—the frequently unrecognized and untreated phenomenon of geriatric HIV/AIDS (Crisologo, Campbell, and Forte 1996).

Sex research is also difficult because sexual activities almost always occur in private, without witnesses. Consequently, researchers must rely on self-reports rather than on direct observation—a fact that introduces the possibility of all sorts of distortion. In addition to the difficulty of relying on self-reported behavior to study sexual behavior and sexuality, there is the equally important issue of researcher influence. Researchers' prejudices, whether toward the old, or toward people of other races or sexual orientations, shape research projects. Their definitions of what constitutes the repertoire of sexual behavior and activities determine the issues investigated and the questions asked. Consequently, sex studies give us more than a particular set of findings, they also tell us about researchers and their world views (Eriksen and Steffen 1999). Thus, when most researchers were White heterosexual men, we learned little about issues such as nonconsensual sex or AIDS. Those researchers privileged heterosexuality and maintained "an obsessive interest in female sexuality and the problems it caused for men" (Eriksen and Steffen 1999). Not until feminist researchers devoted attention to sex and sexuality from female perspectives did we begin to see studies that placed women at the center of inquiry. We still await, however, substantive feminist attention to old age and sexuality beyond menopause.

Current research also rarely considers the fact that the old can define and express their sexuality in more diffuse and varied terms, or that they may feel less pressure to be as goal-oriented in their sexual expressions (Walker 1997). Certain types of sexual practices and activities, such as frequency of intercourse leading to orgasm, have been scholars' focus, to the detriment of other important practices, such as oral sex, touching, and caressing. For instance, in their study of self-reported sexual practices of elderly men and women, Wiley and Bortz (1996) report that when asked to rank preferred forms of sexual activity currently and ten years ago, the importance of intercourse and orgasm declined significantly for men and preferences for loving, caring, and oral sex rose. For women, regardless of age, loving and kissing were highly rated (Wiley and Bortz 1996).

Finally, research has concentrated on narrowly defined and executed samples. In relation to the old, attention has been greatest to married, heterosexual male sexuality. By contrast, sparse attention has been given to women (Segraves and Segraves 1995), to nonheterosexuals (Boxer 1997), and to those who are unmarried. Even in studies where older women have been included, their numbers have often been very low; that social class or racial/ethic variations might also exist has also been frequently ignored (Schwartz and Rutter 1998).

As a consequence of the issues discussed above, the data are not only distorted but gendered as well. For instance, many studies define sexual activity and interest as the same thing. Clearly, this assumption is problematic in general, as the earlier cited Wiley and Bortz (1996) study that reports a difference between current and desired levels of sexual activity among their elderly participants demonstrates. However, the conflation of sexual interest and activity is especially troublesome in the case of old women. Elderly heterosexual women confront a demographic reality that constricts and constructs their sex lives. Given the dearth of old men and the taboo against younger partners, their interest in coupled sexual activity may remain unexpressed because they lack available or functioning partners. Family members' taboos may also contribute to sexual inactivity among elderly women (Read 1999).

A Gender Lens on Sexuality and Old Age

We have considered how our notions of sexuality are socially constructed and how patriarchal values underpin our approaches to sex and sexuality throughout life. Here, we discuss the ways in which gender relations, embedded in various patriarchal conceptions and assumptions, influence the way researchers study sex in later life, and we explore how a gender lens would influence studies of sexuality among the old.

Gender Relations and the Social Construction of Sex and Sexuality

Gender relations shape our most personal definitions of ourselves as sexual beings as well as our most intimate and private sexual activities.

Although we are increasingly familiar with the idea that gender is a factor in the U.S. workplace, for example, the notion that male dominance shapes the most intimate sexual relations of average, everyday humans is perhaps less evident.

We can begin to see how gender relations shape our sex lives (at whatever age) by exploring the ways in which our notions of sex and sexuality are shaped by male heterosexual perspectives. As we have noted, our ideas of real or normal sex are based on "male-oriented frameworks" (Minichiello et al. 1996, 187) and thus center on penetration, intercourse, and male orgasm; other sexual activities are defined as "foreplay." Language also reflects the male experience such that in discussions of sex we use the verbs "to penetrate," "to take," "to insert." Consequently, both heterosexual men and women have learned a construction of sexuality that on its face is genderless but in reality is predicated on an unacknowledged male dominance. Perhaps this helps shed some light on why it is that women are five times more likely than men to report having been forced to do something sexual that they did not want to do (Laumann et al. 1994). In addition, attention to the fact that men's sexual desires dominate leads us to recognize that, especially with older women, the obsession with penetration may be counterproductive—yielding a less satisfying sexual experience than manual manipulation or other sexual expressions. Privileging men's sexuality over women's also helps us to understand the resounding silence about old women's sexuality, their pleasures and desires. Finally, implicit or explicit notions of appropriate heterosexual sexual practices centering on penetration, intercourse, and orgasm render lesbian sex invisible.

As the above discussion implies, issues about sexuality ultimately concern power—male domination and female subordination (Millett 1972). Indeed, men's domination has been eroticized (Pringle 1992) and this is most obvious in the gender scripts that control sexual relations between men and women. Indeed, images of male conquest and female submission are so pervasive that women and men internalize the message that male-dominated heterosexuality is the only "normal" form of sex. Underpinning our social constructions of sexuality, then, are unequal gender relations, including women's obligation to please men.

In this regard, women's duty can be seen in the ways in which, as men and women, we learn to see our bodies throughout the life cycle. In the previous chapter we noted that girls learn quite early to discipline their bodies in order to meet patriarchal notions of bodily acceptability, and women more than men are constrained by an increasing cultural preoccupation with beauty and youth throughout their lives (Bartky 1990). In a way that is less pronounced for men, appearance for women is intimately connected to their sense of self as sexually attractive and desirable. But as women age they are no longer subject to the male "gaze," and they become increasingly invisible. Indeed, the calendar is a greater arbiter of women's sexual candidacy than is true for men: "Women become sexually ineligible much earlier than men do" (Sontag 1979). Indeed, men, middle aged and older, can have gray hair, be paunchy, and yet be considered vital and attractive (Weg 1996). By contrast, the Tina Turners and Jane Fondas of the world aside, we generally do not see the typical sixtyish woman as sexually attractive. This gendered (and racialized) double standard in our notions of old men and women and their sexual attractiveness is reflected in the fact that old women's sexuality and self-image tends to be influenced more by sociocultural expectations than by physiological changes (Hooyman and Kiyak 1999). As *Vogue* magazine reminds us, "a woman's self-worth *still* resides in her body" (Radner 1995). Thus, it is hardly surprising that those who base their self-esteem on such factors as youthful attractiveness are likely to find aging more troublesome, even traumatic (Greenwood 1992).

Gender relations and ageism also influence whether or not we consider it at all appropriate for people to be sexually active beyond a certain point in life. For example, there is still a strong cultural link between sex and procreation, especially for women. If menopause heralds the end of a woman's reproductive capabilities, then it also opens up the question of how we consider her sexuality as a postmenopausal woman. While menopause is a physical event in a woman's life cycle it has enormous social and political ramifications that determine how it is experienced and perceived (Zita 1997).

The notion that older lesbians might escape some of the double standard that old heterosexual women face is challenged by evidence that indicates that older lesbians are invisible both within and outside the lesbian community (Fullmer, Shenk, and Eastland 1999; Copper 1986). Furthermore, gender and ageism shape the lives of older gay men in some of the same ways they shape those of heterosexual men insofar as both share a preference for younger partners (Lee 1987). But this latter preference is also centered in the body: If you look fit and youthful—i.e., "not your age"—then you are considered a more acceptable partner (Adam 2000).

Toward a Gender Lens Approach

Much of what we have written in this chapter illustrates that our current knowledge about sex and sexuality in later life is inadequate. That is not to say that early studies, however problematic, did not serve very useful purposes in bringing sexuality in later life to the public arena. However narrow their focus, they helped dispel some of the myths about asexuality among the old. They also helped establish that the physical capacity to be sexually expressive is lifelong (Weg 1996). But how might a gender lens approach the topics differently? We have alluded to much of this throughout this chapter; here we summarize and extend some of our thoughts.

First, a gender lens asks that we be aware of how patriarchal assumptions shape our research efforts. To date, this awareness has been scant. Because gender has largely been ignored as a major constituent of sexuality (Pringle 1992), scholars of aging have failed to place gender at the center of their thinking about sexual behavior. Paying attention to the rich interdisciplinary feminist literature on relevant topics is a necessary first step toward ensuring that we move beyond defining women's experiences through a male prism.

When researcher assumptions are predicated (implicitly or explicitly) upon notions of "normal" sex as heterosexual, male-dominated, and focused upon penetration and orgasms, researchers have de facto relegated women and sexual identities and practices outside the heterosexual model as marginal, as deviant (Connell and Dowsett 1992). Consequently, lesbians and gay men are automatically excluded from the picture. Furthermore, when researchers concentrate exclusively on the quantitative aspects of sex, they miss the opportunity to explore different ideas about sex such as more nuanced and intangible aspects of sensuality. Consequently, little attention has been given to issues like the need for affection and intimacy in various forms, sexuality within the context of lesbian or homosexual relationships in later life, and so forth. Female-centered notions of eroticism, especially in old age, are also missing; "women's eroticism is defined as either nonexistent, pathological, or peripheral when it is not directed to phallic goals" (Morgan 1998, 151). By concentrating on the penis and men's performance, researchers not only ignore women's perspectives on sex and sexuality, they may also reinforce sexist and ageist notions about male prowess and male dominance. As a result, they may even contribute to men's performance anxieties.

When we assume that "real" sex by definition involves penile/vaginal intercourse, the natural biological changes that accompany aging for both women and men become, in themselves, "problems." Thus the decline in sexual activity that accompanies old age, along with the natural changes that lead to slower and less firm erections in men and vaginal dryness in women, may create self-fulfilling prophesies of decline, performance anxieties in men, and avoidance in women. From this perspective we can see that the gender inequalities that result in sex and sexuality being defined in terms of young men not only hurt women throughout their lives but also hurt old men. Finally, even when we acknowledge a wider range of sexual activity such as touching and caressing, we still hold the young or even the middle-aged as the implicit standard. We recognize, for instance, that old people gain satisfaction and pleasure in these activities as their bodies and sex drives change, but we ignore the ways in which the young themselves might enjoy touching and caressing. Implicit in this omission is that this "deviation" between young and old is, perhaps, acceptable in the old, but it is somehow compensatory and not as valued as the activities of the young or middle-aged.

As we have indicated, feminists often ignore aging issues and are guilty of ageism, too. Thus, new approaches to understanding sex and sexuality in old age require that feminists also be sensitive to the images about the old that we have absorbed, that is, to their own ageism. This new or heightened awareness of the intersections of ageism with other social inequalities would mean that we would no longer ignore issues such as HIV/AIDS in elderly populations. We might presume that this oversight has been fueled, at least in part, by assumptions that the elderly are not sexually active and have no sexual past; therefore they do not contract sexually transmitted diseases.

Overcoming the ageism in research on sex and sexuality becomes possible when we begin with the experiences of the old. This would seem obvious, given the lack of research, but a gender lens requires that we do more than simply include old people in our samples. Instead, understanding sex and sexuality among the old in an anti-ageist manner dictates that we begin our exploration with them and their experiences, without the mantle of young or middle-aged sexuality draped around us. Giving voice to old women and men, instead of merely treating them as the research objects, would lead us to reconceptualize our notions of sex and sexuality based on their lives, without assumptions concerning such issues as more or less penile/vaginal intercourse. We would begin with their thoughts and actions regarding sexual expression, for instance, rather than assuming, say, young, male, and heterosexual notions—ideas against which any group *not* young, male, and heterosexual would fall short.

By implication, a gender lens would urge us to move to a more relational (and perhaps more qualitative) exploration of sex among diverse elderly populations. The White, sixty-five-year-old professional woman who has had access to years of information and expertise about menopause, sexuality, and aging will likely approach these topics in a very different manner from her working-class counterpart. A lesbian of similar age who may have resisted traditional gender socialization and who may fight negative stereotypes about old women as asexual beings may share this more positive orientation to her body and her sexuality with old, middle-class, African American heterosexual women (Slevin and Wingrove 1998). Still, each may have varying interests in, and find different possibilities for, sexual expression. And an old working-class man who is experiencing sexual difficulties and is too embarrassed to seek help would share some similarities with and yet diverge from a similarly aged middle-class man who has the educational and financial wherewithal to avail himself of treatment and even normalize its use.

The bottom line is that understanding sexuality requires that we recognize the wealth of diversity in how old people, whatever their social location, experience it. Topics that deserve attention include power dynamics in sexual relationships, varieties of sexual needs and expressions, the influence of demographic imbalance among the old and especially the very old, and the issues of sexuality among heterosexual women, who survive an average of eight years longer than men. We know little, beyond the observation of gradual decline, about the specifics of how we change as sexual beings in later life. Furthermore, limited but provocative studies of elderly lesbians and homosexual men suggest productive avenues of exploration. Berger and Kelly suggest, for instance, that older gay men and lesbians "are likely to have less personal investment in following traditional notions of virility and masculinity or sexiness and femininity, respectively. The physical changes that accompany old age, then, may not seem like insurmountable hurdles" (1996, 309). Thus research into marginalized populations can also teach us about how social inequalities can foster important adaptation skills that bear attention from more privileged elders. A gender lens on sex and sexuality offers fertile ground to begin more diverse and comprehensive investigations that can do much more than simply alleviate fears about sexual declines in old age; it can also uncover new possibilities.

CHAPTER 5

Gender, Social Inequalities, and Retirement Income

Most people believe that retirement equals freedom: freedom from a forty-hour work week, from the same routine, from supervision or, conversely, from feeling the weight of too much responsibility. This attitude comes across in questions asked of retirees such as, "So what do you do with all your free time now?" Or by fears expressed by some contemplating labor force withdrawal, "What will I do with my time?" Similarly, investigations of the retirement transition presume such freedom and measure satisfaction in terms of personal responses to this new freedom, the "lack of structure."

We built this mythology by seeing labor force withdrawal as a male experience, concentrating research almost exclusively on men and assuming that men maintain continuous labor force participation, regardless of marital status or family type. But after years of being overlooked, the retirement experiences of women have also received attention. Drawing on the feminist insight that work involves more than paid labor, we have begun to see how both work—paid and unpaid labor—and retirement are shaped by the intersections of gender with race and class. Once we begin to examine the gendered nature of work and retirement, we see that the ability to experience retirement as "freedom" is closely related to privileges conferred by race and class as well. We also see that, for the most part, a woman's work really is never done.

In the next two chapters, we examine the gendered nature of work and retirement in old age from different vantages: the activities of productive and reproductive labor over the life course; their impact on income; and the similar and different meaning of work and retirement to men and

93

women. In this chapter, our primary focus is on retirement income. We chose this emphasis partly because finances can have an enormous impact on later life. Monetary difficulties can lead to a situation where "retirement does not mean freedom but restriction, and, in the extreme, imprisonment" (Braithwaite and Gibson 1987, 11). In addition, the obvious relationship between paid and unpaid work on one hand and retirement income on the other makes the latter an ideal choice for examining the gendered nature of retirement. In this way we show that, for instance, women's greater likelihood of poverty in old age than men's is not, strictly speaking, either a natural result of demographic trends, such as greater life expectancy (itself partly influenced by social factors) nor is it random: It is a result of patterned social processes, such as the ways in which old people get access to income, among other things. Further, these social processes are racialized such that White women may in fact have higher retirement incomes than men of color due, in part, to their marriages to White men. It is women of color who are particularly disadvantaged.

To clarify the arguments we put forward in this chapter and the next, we need to lay out the broad context undergirding our analyses. Putting women's lives at the center of analysis reveals the wide range of productive activities which men and women perform that have economic value, including paid labor, unpaid labor, and services provided to others (Calasanti and Bonanno 1992; Herzog et al. 1989). When we define work this way, we see that, at all ages, women perform more productive activities than do men (Herzog et al. 1989) and that retirement does not mean leisure or freedom from labor. This latter point is the focus of the next chapter; but we discuss productive activities here as well, as they have a direct impact on paid work and retirement income. Gender relations structure the productive activities in which men and women engage: which ones they do, the rewards for these, and so on. Gender relations play out over the life course and through retirement such that men's and women's experiences of this time differ in critical ways: in terms of income and the meaning of retirement. When combined with sensitivity to race and class, we find that the "golden years" await only a select group of predominantly White and privileged men. Many women, men of color, and members of the working class must continue a range of productive activities in retirement, in both the formal and informal economy, unless poor health precludes this. In addition, women continue their unpaid domestic labor. By contrast, more privileged men have choices in this regard: They can choose to engage in paid work, and they can choose to be involved in domestic labor. The voluntary nature of these activities underscores the power differences based on gender, as well as race and class. Who has the freedom to choose to perform labor, and what types, in their retirement years?

Women's continued work in retirement is not "freely" chosen when it is predicated on financial need or power relations within the family. Instead, it is built into workplace and state policies, and also results from "normal" behavior within families—the expectation (and mandate) that women will have primary responsibility for domestic labor. Simply put, family obligations of employed women constitute a "second job" which men generally do not undertake. Women continue this domestic labor (typically regardless of class or race) over the course of their lives while men retire relatively free of it. Although most men perform some domestic labor, they generally do not take primary responsibility nor do as much as most women. At the same time, class and race play a role. On one hand, women of higher class, most of whom are White, may maintain responsibility for domestic labor while paying other women, working-class and often women of color, to perform it (Glenn 1992). On the other hand, many men are also not living this "dream": White, middle-class retired men's unearned advantage in the labor market, and their resultant ability to secure stable, "career" jobs, is based on the disadvantages experienced by women, working-class White men, and people of color.

Gender, the State, and Retirement Income: Social Security

One of the most important sources of income in retirement in the United States is the public pension, Social Security (Atchley 1997). However, gender inequities in both paid work and family have been embedded in this program since its inception in 1935. Social policies that assume the existence of a traditional nuclear family tend to reinforce the gender inequities embedded in that family form (Estes 1991). Social Security is but one example of this process, with critical consequences for men's and women's retirement benefits.

Social Security originally covered only those who contributed to the program—specifically, retired workers. In so doing, it also assumed a particular form of unequal gender relations: that women always depend upon men in heterosexual (marital) relationships, and that women would be homemakers and men would be breadwinners. Just as the "family wage" assumed a patriarchal family head (May 1987) who would provide for other members, Social Security assumed the same in retirement. Thus, men's presumed labor force history—a long-term, stable career with ever-increasing rewards—formed the basis of benefit eligibility and calculations. Never mind that some minority and working-class men were virtually excluded by this formulation as they were shut out of family wages and "careers."

At the same time that reproductive labor was seen to be a woman's "job" and her implicit basis for economic support, it was not valued as highly as men's paid labor. As Harrington Meyer (1996) notes, when wives and widows were added as beneficiaries in 1939, their eligibility was non-contributory. That is, their benefits were not based on their own contributions as workers but instead by virtue of their marital status alone—solely as (former) wives of eligible workers. Further, a spouse "dependent"—originally referred to as "the 'wife allowance'" (Harrington Meyer 1996, 458)—is entitled to only half of the main benefit amount. Importantly, while domestic labor may have been assumed by virtue of marital status, this was not the basis for the benefit; actual performance of such tasks was never a condition of benefit receipt (Harrington Meyer 1996). Social Security further reinforced women's subordination by distinguishing between deserving and undeserving women. Widows could collect Social Security based on their spouse's work histories, but divorced women could not (Rodeheaver 1987). Regardless of the reasons for the divorce, women were felt to be at fault for somehow calling upon themselves their abuse or abandonment. Despite changes in Social Security over time, such as the ability of divorced women to collect benefits if they were married for at least ten years, the reduced spousal benefit remains in effect.

In addition, Social Security ignored the reality of female breadwinners—despite the fact, for instance, that in 1940, 40 percent of Black women held jobs (compared to 15 percent of White women) (Amott and Matthaei 1996). Indeed, by assuming only one breadwinner and tying benefit levels to earnings, Social Security pays some dual-earner couples lower benefits than it pays to a traditional couple in which the man earns that amount alone (Harrington Meyer 1996). Thus, Social Security legislation concerned itself neither with women's lower wages nor with family obligations that might interfere with continuous labor force participation. Again, it devalued women's reproductive labor by not counting years engaged in reproductive labor in their benefit levels.

We can see the cumulative impact of gender relations within the family when we look at how Social Security benefits are calculated. First, benefit levels are tied to earnings: The more one earns, the greater the likelihood that one will receive the maximum benefit, which was $1,373.10 per month in 1999 (Social Security Administration 1999). Women tend to be clustered in a relatively small array of low-paid jobs, a factor which in itself deflates

Social Security benefits. But in addition, benefits are also based on the earnings of the best 35 years of work. Due to family obligations, women are far more likely than men to have worked fewer than 35 years, and thus have years of zero earnings included in the calculation. Thus, women who leave the labor market usually receive less pay upon their return and lower Social Security benefits later on. Men's ability to have, on average, only one zero year out of 35, compared to women's average of 12 zero years (Harrington Meyer 1996) is firmly rooted in the gender division of family labor.

Thus, gender relations in family and work influence the retirement experiences of both men and women through the formation of pensions. Public pensions, such as Social Security, and private pension schemes are fashioned on the basis of men's experiences of work and production, as well as traditional, heterosexist notions about the domestic sphere. The emphasis on traditional couples excludes those who are never married, including for reasons of sexual preference. Further, while both paid and unpaid activities make important economic contributions (Calasanti and Bonanno 1992; Herzog et al. 1989), most pensions are based on White, middle-class men's work history, and therefore ignore reproductive labor (Quadagno and Harrington Meyer 1990; Scott 1991). As a result, pension plans treat men's labor as more valuable, and reward it more highly than women's in retirement, despite the fact that men's ability to engage in more highly paid labor likely relied upon women's reproductive work—that is, the primarily domestic work involved in maintaining people. Conversely, the assumption that individuals spend their lives as members of traditional nuclear families translates into policies that reinforce women's dependence on men for financial security in old age (Harrington Meyer 1996; Rodeheaver 1987), such as Social Security's spousal benefit.

To illustrate, in their study of a national sample of men and women, DeViney and Solomon (1995) found that, even after controlling for type of industry and occupation, gender was still a significant predictor of retirement income for two reasons. First, in terms of age, the older a man is, the higher his retirement income. The same is not true for women. Second, being continuously married to the same person is much more important for a woman's retirement income than for a man's. Only for women, even among those presently married, does discontinuous marital history matter; having been divorced or widowed earlier in their lives has an important impact on their retirement income. Women who had been continuously married to the same person had a monthly average retirement income of only $83.52 less than similar men. By contrast, women whose marital history was interrupted received an average of $356.35 less than men with interrupted marital histories. Thus, it appears that women still accrue a substantial penalty for "[d]eviation from 'traditional' marital careers" (DeViney and Solomon 1995, 98). Similarly, research in Great Britain uncovered a link between marital status and pension receipt for women but not for men (Ginn and Arber 1999).

A racial bias embedded in the original Social Security legislation excluded occupations typically held by people of color, particularly agricultural labor and domestic labor. These exclusions interest us because they reveal the intersections of gender with race and class. As we have noted, domestic labor is devalued as it is seen to be part of the private sphere and remains unpaid. When such devalued labor is in fact paid—that is, when others are hired to perform such tasks as housecleaning and caregiving for the old or young—it is relegated to those groups with the least amount of power: women, but especially women of color (Glenn 2000). The exclusion of domestic labor, then, particularly disadvantaged working-class women of color, who find both their paid and unpaid labor devalued. Figures from the 1940s, important years in the earnings history of present retirees, reveal that retired women of color were often employed as domestic laborers. Depending upon the group one is examining, between one-fifth and one-half of women of color were employed as domestic laborers, compared to only 12 percent of European American women (Amott and Matthaei 1996; King 1992). Despite legislative changes that have broadened coverage to almost all workers, still only 83 percent of Blacks aged 65+ (men, 81 percent and women, 84 percent) and 74 percent of non-White Hispanics (men, 77 percent and women, 72 percent) received Social Security in 1996, compared to over 90 percent of White men and women (Social Security Administration 1998a, table 1.9). Lack of Social Security coverage also jeopardizes health in later life. In addition to the loss of pension benefits, Medicare benefits automatically accrue only to those who receive Social Security. If one is ineligible for Social Security, one also does not receive Medicare.

The intersection of race, class, and gender is also evident when we examine other ways in which marital status is rewarded. Social Security recipients are considered "dually entitled" if they qualify for benefits both as retired workers and as a present/former spouse, but receive the larger, spouse's benefit. Again, the larger benefit is based on marital status—having been married continuously for at least 10 years. However, not only is the proportion of ever-married women decreasing, but Black women are far less likely to have been married at least ten years. As a result, they are less likely to qualify as dually entitled than are White women (Harrington Meyer 1996). At the same time, Black men as a group receive much lower wages than do White men. As a result, those Black women who would be able to opt for a spouse's benefit are also less likely to find that it is appreciably higher than their own retired worker benefit. Thus, their class position also prevents them from having equal access to a higher, spousal benefit.

Finally, as implied above, Social Security benefits also maintain class privilege. First, working-class members enjoy less job stability than do middle-class workers. As a result, they receive lower benefits due to the impact of number of years of continuous work on payment levels. Second, benefit levels are tied to past earnings through a progressive formula, which means that while people with low lifetime earnings receive a higher replacement rate (their benefits represent a larger percentage of their previous earnings), people with high lifetime earnings receive higher absolute benefit amounts. Overall, then, tying benefits to past earnings advantages high-income workers.

We now turn briefly to some of the ways in which gender relations within the family and workplace also influence retirement income.

Gender Relations in the Family and the Workplace

Though most women work for pay, they still bear primary responsibility for household tasks (Twiggs, McQuillan, and Ferree 1999; Press and Townsley 1998; Coverman and Sheley 1986). Decades of research have shown that women take on the vast majority of housework, in part because no one else will do it and in part because everyone, including women, expects them to do so, as if to prove that they're real women. Men, on the other hand, tend to avoid such labor as "women's work" (Szinovacz 2000, 78). The power relations and advantages that accrue to men in this domestic division of labor have long appeared in household research. As Hartmann (1981) noted decades ago, the addition of a husband to the household increased a wife's domestic burden. Examining men and women over several years, Gupta (1999) finds that, while men decrease their domestic labor when they take on female partners, and increase it only when single, women do the opposite. They put in a lot more housework to take care of male partners than they do when they're alone. Women consistently do more across a wide array of living arrangements and marital statuses, including cohabitation. But the biggest gender discrepancy is among those who are married (South and Spitze 1994). Men add work to women's lives, whereas women toil to make men's lives easier.

This domestic division of labor influences retirement in terms of both the jobs that people take and their upward mobility. Among today's retirees, women often entered the labor force later than men, had to work particular shifts, turn down promotions or enter particular types of jobs in order to maintain their domestic labor roles. Domestic labor time also has an impact on other labor market outcomes, such as earnings (Coverman 1983). Importantly, this does not imply that women expend less energy at work; in fact, evidence indicates that they work harder than men (Bielby and Bielby 1988).

Men are privileged by this division of labor in ways that go beyond pay levels. White middle-class men are able to take jobs, promotions, and geographic moves to maximize their economic security. Indeed, their ability to even have "careers" or engage in paid work is based upon their not having to be concerned with household work (Acker 1990). They can take advantage of particular job opportunities, for example, a move into a more time-consuming position or to a different city, well supported by their wives' unpaid work at home. Race and class shape this situation as well. For instance, the opportunity to even consider mobility for a promotion is not equally available to different minority or class groups.

In addition to household tasks, women predominate in a number of care work activities throughout their lives. Although care work may bring with it a number of benefits, it may also have a negative impact on such things as retirement income. Many women appear to partake in what has been called serial caregiving. That is, they do not commonly care for children and elder adults at the same time, but instead tend to follow one with another: spouses, grandchildren, or others (AARP 1995b). While we return to the topic of caring for others later, at this point we emphasize the impact of this activity for women's retirement incomes. Among older employed women, it is important to note that acting as unpaid caregivers for frail elderly can impede their labor force activity (Stoller 1993; Harrington Meyer 1996). Although women, particularly African American women (Hatch and Thompson 1992), typically do not drop out of the labor force when involved in caring for adults (Moen, Robeson, and Fields 1994), they may reduce hours or productivity levels, or change jobs to accommodate their care work demands. These factors typically translate into lower retirement incomes.

The cumulative impact of gender relations within the family on retirement income is evident in many ways. The assumption of a male breadwinner has served to justify women's lower wages and mobility, which in turn further justifies women's predominance in care work and other domestic obligations. From this vantage point, we can see that both women's and men's retirement income is firmly rooted in the gender division of family labor.

The highest incidence of poverty among old women occurs among the never married. In part, this is because they lack spousal benefits—benefits denied to those who do not form traditional couples—from Social Security as well as possible private pensions. At the same time, never-married old men—who do have lower retirement incomes than married men (Mitchell, Levine, and Phillips 1999)—are not as likely to be poor as a result. Thus, gender relations in the family tell only part of the story. Women receive low wages over the life course, whether working continuously, as is likely to be the case among never-married women, or intermittently.

Gender relations in the workplace result in occupational segregation: Women and men tend to work in different jobs. In itself, this might not be a problem; but compared to men's jobs, women's jobs—primarily in the service sector—pay substantially less (Mitchell et al. 1999). These jobs also offer less mobility and fewer benefits, including pensions (Farkas and O'Rand 1998). Even women who work in traditionally male occupations earn less than their male counterparts. Before the 1970s, women retirees earned, on average, 50 to 60 percent of men's wages; today, women still only make 73 cents to the male dollar (U.S. Bureau of the Census 1999a). This labor force discrimination has a cumulative effect; women are less able to save for the future while employed, and they receive less Social Security income later.

Pensions

Private pensions are a potentially important source of retirement income. Contrary to public beliefs concerning the importance of individual choices, receipt of private pensions depends first and foremost on the job—whether or not it includes pension coverage. The kinds of jobs women, and many minorities and lower-status workers, tend to hold, such as service sector and non-unionized jobs, are among those with the lowest rates of pension coverage (Stoller and Gibson, 2000; Farkas and O'Rand 1998). Indeed, the approximately 56 percent of full-time workers covered by pensions are disproportionately White, well-educated, and work for large firms (Johnson, Sambamoorthi, and Crystal 1999, 320). As a result, older cohorts of women have generally not been covered by pensions (Farkas and O'Rand 1998). Further, working in jobs with coverage does not insure that one receives an adequate pension or any at all, as we discuss below.

Defined Benefit versus Defined Contribution Plans

Defined benefit plans rely on employer contributions; the benefit to be received is predetermined, based on a formula that takes into account such things as employees' years of service and earnings in order to calculate payment levels. Historically, women and minorities have been excluded from such programs, as plans tended to be located in noncompetitive manufacturing and unionized industries (Farkas and O'Rand 1998). In addition, pension rules have tended to disadvantage women in the same way Social Security does: They also assume continuity of work and so penalize women with intermittent work histories (Quadagno 1988).

Defined contribution plans, on the other hand, contain variable benefits that depend on the contributions made to the plan by both employee and employers, as well as any relevant investment and interest earnings (Graham 1994). Defined contribution plans place much greater risk and responsibility on workers to plan for their retirement than do defined benefit plans (Chen 1999; Kennickell and Sunden 1997). They are analogous to savings plans in that they are not age-related and thus do not require one be a particular age or retired to withdraw the money, though withdrawal prior to age 59^1/$_2$ can incur a 10-percent penalty as well as income tax on the amount (Fronstin 1999). As a result, one can borrow money from the plans or even withdraw it all together; significantly, women, minorities, and workers with lower incomes (below $25,000) are most likely to do so (Korczyk 1996) in order to meet pressing needs. Estimates are that the vast majority of such pensions are never reactivated (Farkas and O'Rand 1998). Even if one begins investing in these pensions again, the losses incurred have a cumulative effect and the worker is permanently penalized in terms of retirement income.

Importantly, these plans do not necessarily require an employer contribution at all. They may not even require that the employee contribute either (Fronstin 1999). That is, they may simply offer the opportunity—but not the mandate—to put money aside for retirement. Further, employers often do not match employee contributions to defined contribution plans for three to five years (if they match them at all); as a result, such plans "tend to be substantially underfunded and are not likely to perform as well as traditional defined benefit programs that involved compulsory deferral of wages in the form of pension entitlements" (Atchley 1997, 11).

In recent decades, pension coverage has changed, with important gender, race, and class implications. As of 1993, those employees covered by pensions were about as likely to be participating in defined contributions programs as defined benefit programs. This is quite a change from 1975, when 87 percent of employees were covered by the latter (Atchley 1997; Kennickell and Sunden 1997). The move to defined contribution plans has, on one level, helped women. They have been beneficial by virtue of the fact that they offer coverage to employees in smaller firms and non-unionized industries with higher concentrations of women (Farkas and O'Rand 1998). Thus, they offer an opportunity for retirement savings previously denied many women. In addition, pension rules of defined benefit plans made it difficult for women to be vested—have enough years of service to qualify—and to be able to take their pension with them when they moved to new jobs. However, defined contribution plans are no panacea. Since women earn less, they have less to contribute to such plans. Lower payments are cumulative over time, increasing the gap between lower and higher contributors. Initial evidence suggests that the present cohort of middle-aged women have found pensions more accessible to them due to the shift to defined contribution plans. However, they still face a significant risk of saving too little (Farkas and O'Rand 1998). Participation in such plans also varies significantly by race and ethnicity as Whites both have more plans available to them and are far more likely to avail themselves of them when accessible (Chen 1999). In 1993, 36 percent of Whites had access to such plans versus 26 percent of Blacks and only half as many Hispanics (18 percent) (Chen and Leavitt 1997).

In addition, working-class members are likely to be conservative investors. Evidence suggests that those with lower educational attainment (less than a high school degree) and low household incomes are more likely to invest in interest-earning assets than in stocks or diversified portfolios. While this could owe to financial inexpertise, these workers also hold low-paying jobs with higher risks of unemployment. This economic uncertainty may make it more prudent for these workers to engage in low-risk investments (Kennickell and Sunden 1997). Women are also more conservative investors than are men. As a result, they are less likely to lose a lot of money through risky investments and also not likely to increase their savings very much (Shaw, Zuckerman, and Hartmann 1998). Overall, then, the median amounts accumulated in defined contribution plans are fairly low, despite the fact that the overall contribution rate has increased (Kennickell and

Sunden 1997); this will have an important impact on financial security in retirement.

Pension Receipt and Amounts

Pension coverage rates, low as they are, do not tell us the whole story, however. They provide the upper boundaries—the limits of how many people might receive a retirement pension. But they do not tell us how many of those potentially eligible actually receive pensions. In 1996, less than half (45 percent) of those 65 and older received a pension, and between one-quarter and one-third of women did (Chen 1994; Estes and Michel 1999). One-third of Whites but only one in five Blacks and one in seven Hispanics receive pensions (Chen 1999; Chen and Leavitt 1997). The intersection of race and gender is apparent when we look at marital status. Women are far more likely to have pensions as a result of marriage to a man with a pension than to have one on their own (Shaw, Zuckerman, and Hartmann 1998), and White men are far more likely to have been employed in jobs that offer such coverage. In addition, such pensions are substantially higher. Unmarried women can expect pensions of about half the amount of similar men, while married women's pensions are almost as high as those of married men (Mitchell, Levine, and Phillips 1999, 27). Finally, pension receipt varies with class; those in the higher income brackets also receive the bulk of pensions (Woods 1996).

As should be clear, pensions expand inequities in old age. Less than one-fourth of all elderly households receives almost 70 percent of all pension and annuity income (Woods 1996, 22); almost one-third of this income goes to those in the top 10 percent of income (Woods 1996, 24, table 11). Women's mean pension benefit is only about one-half that of men (Johnson, Sambamoorthi, and Crystal 1999). So, men are twice as likely to receive a pension, and their benefits are twice that of women. This gender gap will continue, as men's median pension wealth is currently 76 percent greater than women's (Johnson, Sambamoorthi, and Crystal 1999). And if we take marital status into account, unmarried women have only 59 percent of the pension wealth of their male counterparts (Mitchell, Levine, and Phillips 1999, 26).

We can also see the impact of racial discrimination and its influences on gender relations within families. Recall that public and private pensions are based on a White, middle-class, and heterosexual model of "family" wherein a man is a breadwinner and a woman is a housewife. This notion of family implicitly assumes that men have the opportunities to be bread-winners, with high enough earnings to support stay-at-home wives. Findings on expected retirement wealth reveal the race and gender biases in this depiction. Using data collected as part of a national, longitudinal study of men and women approaching retirement, Mitchell, Levine, and Phillips (1999) examined expected pension incomes and retirement wealth by race and ethnicity, gender, and marital status. Table 5.1 recasts some of their data.

All the men and women benefit from marriage, but do all benefit in the same way? When we compare the expected incomes of each group with that of similarly situated White men, it is apparent that White men fare best in all cases. But when we look within racial and ethnic groups as well, we can see that the gender and race dynamics are quite complex. To be sure, being married benefits all racial/ethnic and gender groupings, both rela-tive to White men (with the exception of Hispanic men) and, absolutely, in terms of overall income. But if we look *within* racial/ethnic groups, we find that White and Hispanic women's incomes increase relative to their male counterparts. By contrast, Black women's income decreases relative to Black men's. It is evident, then, that while being part of a traditional couple in-creases the income of all groups, Black men benefit from marriage more than Black women do. This reality no doubt reflects Black men's greater likelihood to experience unemployment than Black women and to find employment in occupations without benefits.

Turning to retirement wealth, Mitchell et al. (1999) found the gender gap is much greater among Whites and smaller within racial/ethnic mi-nority groups because minorities have relatively little wealth upon which to draw. Importantly, marriage nearly triples White women's expected re-tirement wealth, while it only doubles that of Black and Hispanic women. Taken together, these findings demonstrate that the benefits of marriage are not felt equally across race and gender groups.

It should also be clear that retirement income inequities result, not from individual choice, but from the structure of employment. The national study noted above discovered that most of the gender-based gap in retirement income results from occupational segregation and the gender gap in pay. That is, when researchers took into account such individual factors as num-ber of years employed and educational level, they found that two-thirds of the retirement income gap was still due to these gender-based features of the jobs: the number of women employed in the occupation and gender

Table 5.1

Projected Pension Incomes by Marital Status, Gender, and Race and Ethnicity

	Amount of projected pension income	Percentage of similar White men's income	Percentage in relation to same racial/ethnic men
Married White men	$12,638	100%	100%
Married White women	$11,321	90%	90%
Married Black men	$10,119	80%	100%
Married Black women	$10,268	81%	104%
Married Hispanic men	$4,415	35%	100%
Married Hispanic women	$5,204	41%	118%
Unmarried White men	$8,670	100%	100%
Unmarried White women	$3,825	44%	44%
Unmarried Black men	$3,341	39%	100%
Unmarried Black women	$4,228	49%	127%
Unmarried Hispanic men	$3,314	38%	100%

Source: Social Security Administration 2000a, 10.

differences in pay (Mitchell et al. 1999). Thus, women make less than men not because they "choose" domestic burdens but because they work in women's jobs, which pay less. Of course, many employers justify low pay for women because women are supposed to depend upon the wages and pensions of their husbands.

Race as well as gender governs these unequal pay scales. For example, in contrast to the work histories of White women, Black women's labor force participation in the twentieth century has been relatively continuous (Belgrave 1988). Still, Black women receive relatively low wages and so have among the lowest retirement incomes. Importantly, instances of relative comfort in retirement don't negate Black women's disadvantage. For example, the Black professional women, whose dogged success and preparation leave them relatively secure financially in retirement, would have prospered even more had they had the advantages of being White men (Slevin and Wingrove 1998). Taken together, the accumulation of disadvantage over their life courses leaves racial and ethnic minority women, particularly Black women, with the highest poverty levels in old age (Social Security Administration 1998b).

Further, the likelihood of "careers" is not merely gendered but is shaped also by the intersection of gender with race and class. In the case of working-class Black retired men, for instance, racial discrimination and their placement in secondary labor market jobs result in their movement into and out of the marketplace throughout the life course. As a result, they do not experience the clear transition into "retirement" that more closely typifies middle-class White men's labor force withdrawal (Gibson 1987). The same is also true for many Hispanics—particularly Mexican Americans and Puerto Ricans—who spend their lives working in similar jobs and with similar results: a blurring of boundaries between work and retirement. In addition, working in low-paid, unstable employment with few if any benefits translates into a need to continue working, whether in the formal or informal labor market (Calasanti and Bonanno 1992). In fact, both Blacks and Hispanics over age sixty-five receive a larger percentage of their income from earnings than do Whites, signaling their greater need to continue paid employment in old age (Quadagno 1999).

Economic (In)security in Retirement

Data on the sources and levels of retirement income give us critical insights into retirees' lives because they demonstrate the financial foundations that shape the lives of different groups in old age. Although economic resources are just one of many social resources important to old people's lives, retirement income has obvious and immediate effects on whether or not one feels a need to continue to work for pay after retirement, as well as more distant effects on where one lives, the medical care one can seek, and how one spends one's leisure time, all of which have an important impact on how one ages.

Given the unequal gender relations in work and family, a 200-dollar gender differential in Social Security benefits comes as no surprise. As we show in table 5.2, at the end of 1999, retired men's average monthly benefit was $904; women received $697 (Social Security Administration 2000a, 159-60). Closer inspection of these data reveals the importance of race. The gender gap within races is smaller among minority racial/ethnic groups than among Whites, but this is because both men and women were so much more disadvantaged relative to White men. In fact, White women average only slightly less than the amounts racial/ethnic minority men receive.

Table 5.2

Average Monthly Social Security Benefit by Race and Sex, Dec. 1999

	Total	White	% of similar racial/ ethnic man	Black	% of similar racial/ ethnic man	% of White man	Other	% of similar racial/ ethnic man	% of White man
Men	904.80	922.80	100	756.00	100	82	716.00	100	78
Women	697.00	706.30	76	626.80	82	68	597.60	83	65

Source: Social Security Administration 2000a, 159–60 (Table 5.A.1).

The policy bias toward traditional families appears when we examine subgroups of elderly poor. For instance, women make up three-fourths of the elderly poor, and poverty rates are highest among unmarried women (Glasse, Estes, and Smeeding 1999). Importantly, the vast majority of old women, and particularly women of color, are unmarried. Just over one-fourth of Black women, one-third of Hispanic and American Indian women, and 42 percent of White women are married (Conway-Turner 1999; John 1999; U.S. Bureau of the Census 1996, table 6-2). Finally, a woman's likelihood of experiencing financial difficulties in old age increases over time. Given that the average 60-year-old can expect to live an additional 21 years, nearly one-third may experience poverty at some point (Rank and Hirschl 1999). Single Black women with less than a high school degree are especially vulnerable; almost 9 of 10 will be poor prior to age 85 (Rank and Hirschl 1999).

People often blame the gender gap in retirement income on women's "choices": to move in and out of jobs, to choose jobs that mesh well with family obligations, to take part-time work, to take days off in favor of sick children and other household duties. This common view, which blames women for their poverty, contains two serious problems. First, it may not make a lot of sense to speak of "choice" when it comes to the childcare, husbandcare, and eldercare that women do. Such work is expected of them without complaint and for love and, in turn, they have come to expect to do it. Second, even women who devote themselves more to career than to domestic duty risk being called bad mothers, and must deal with employers who assume both less commitment to work and a greater likelihood of intermittent work patterns. Such women, who maintain a male pattern of employment, may find it difficult to obtain high-status jobs and promotions because bosses assume that all women will be distracted by the call of home duties and responsibilities. As a result, women who work continuously still do not do better in old age. Full-time employed women do not earn comparable wages to men and thus enter retirement at a disadvantage. For example, never-married women—4 percent of old women— are the group one would expect to have the greatest continuous labor force participation rates. Yet their poverty rate, 23 percent, exceeds the poverty rate of widows, which stands at 18 percent. Indeed, the only group with a higher poverty rate, 27 percent, is divorced women (7 percent of all old women are presently divorced). The number of never-married old women will probably increase to 5 percent by 2020, and it is expected that their poverty rate will jump to more than a third (35 percent) (Smeeding 1999, 9–10). Indeed, the recognition that never-married old women will be poorer than ever-married women underlies the call to consider marital histories when examining the impact of future Social Security benefits and possible program reforms, a topic to which we shall return (Butrica, Iams, and Sandell 1999).

At the same time, the Social Security program has not adjusted to the marital status changes that have occurred over the last several decades (Rix 1993). Between 1970 and 1997, the marital status of women ages 45 to 49 changed dramatically, suggesting future problems in old age. The percentage divorced has more than tripled, standing at 17.7 percent. Divorced women tend to fare the worst in old age. Regardless of reasons for not being married, the percentage of women who are part of a couple decreased from 81.4 percent to just over two-thirds (Estes and Michel 1999).

The capacity to accumulate wealth and economic security is not randomly distributed across the population; glaring disparities in old age point to lifetimes of differences. For example, women's poverty in old age results from life course factors that make them vulnerable to poverty throughout their lives. Thus, whether widowhood leads some women to be poor "depends on their economic resources just prior to the event. But the financial resources available in old age, in turn, depend very much on their long-term economic status throughout much of their adult lives" (Choudhury and Leonesio 1997, 17). Thus it is critical to uncover the life course factors that increase some women's vulnerability to poverty (Choudhury and Leonisio 1997).

Huge disparities in wealth in old age exist by race as well. The median net wealth of Whites aged 70 and over is $103,000. This figure is more than five times higher than that of Blacks ($19,000) and six times as high as that of Hispanics (Chen 1999). These differences are not based on behavioral variations—such as a propensity to save—but instead result from cumulative, structural disadvantages. For example, in addition to workplace and income inequities, from the 1930s onward both banks and the federal government engaged in racialized lending patterns that negatively influence minority wealth in old age. While many such practices are now illegal, institutional discrimination remains. As a result, home ownership rates for Whites (84 percent) exceeds those of Blacks (67 percent), and the home equity of older Blacks is presently less than half that of older Whites (Chen 1999; Quadagno 1999). Such wealth disparities have even longer-term consequences as they influence generations: minorities have less wealth to pass on to children, so the race gap continues to grow (Oliver and Shapiro 1995).

Tables 5.1 and 5.2 suggest that a focus on gender differences alone misleads. The biggest gaps appear when we look at intersections of race and gender. For example, in examining Social Security recipient data from 1997, we can see that 9.9 percent of White women recipients are poor, twice the rate of White men (4.4 percent). However, one in five (19.6 percent) Black men are below the poverty line, as are 17.3 percent of Hispanic men. Racial and ethnic minority women are especially marginalized, reflected in the fact that among Social Security recipients, more than one in five Hispanic women (21.8 percent) and more than one in four Black women (26.2 percent) are poor (Hendley and Bilimoria 1999, 61).

As tables 5.3 and 5.4 show, Social Security is the largest source of income for those over age 65. At the same time, it is far more critical to the economic security of some groups than others. Who relies on Social Security?

Table 5.3

Sources of Income for Those Aged 65+, 1999

Table 5.4

Percentage of Income from Social Security for Those Aged 65+, 1999

Sources of income	Percentage from income source	Percentage of income from Social Security	Percentage of persons
Social Security	90	100	18
Assets	62	90–99	11
Retirement benefits (pensions, annuities, etc.)	43	50–89	35
		<50	36
Earnings	22		
Public assistance	5		
Veteran's benefits	5		

Sources: Social Security Administration, 2000a, 10, Charts 1 and 2.

Turning first to gender, we know that, despite their lower average benefit levels, women rely on Social Security far more than do men. Present and future cohorts of retired women will receive just under half their income from Social Security (Butrica and Iams 1999). Similarly, if we examine the importance of Social Security to racial and ethnic minority groups, we find that among Social Security recipients, about three-fourths of racial and ethnic group members rely on these benefits for more than half of their income, compared to only two-thirds of Whites. Further, for almost half of these minority group members Social Security makes up 90 percent of their income; for a full one-third, it comprises all of their income in old age. Comparable proportions for Whites are less than one-third (29 percent) and 16 percent, respectively (Hendley and Bilimoria 1999, 60). Obviously, Whites have additional sources of income in old age. Thirty-one percent of Whites received pension income, compared to only 21 percent of Blacks and 15 percent of Hispanics. In terms of the importance of this source for overall income, pensions comprised one in ten dollars received by old Whites, but only one in fourteen dollars among Blacks and Hispanics. More significantly, two-thirds of Whites have asset income, compared to one-third (33 percent) and just over one-fourth (27 percent) of Blacks and Hispanics, respectively (Chen and Leavitt 1997). It is no surprise, then, to find that only one in twenty old Whites receive public assistance, but more than one-fifth (22 percent) of both Blacks and Hispanics do (Chen 1994).

Looking at this from another angle, table 5.5 shows that old Blacks and other racial/ethnic minority group members are disproportionately likely to receive Supplemental Security Income (SSI) benefits, a means-tested (one must prove one is below poverty level) federal program for the old and disabled. Nearly one in four and one in six SSI beneficiaries are Black or other racial/ethnic minority group members, respectively (Scott 1999), a percentage far above their representation in the general population. Given the widening disparities in pension coverage between White and minority workers, the latter's reliance on Social Security will likely grow (Chen and Leavitt 1997).

Table 5.5

SSI: Average Monthly Payments and Recipient Characteristics, December, 1999

	Women				Men			
% of SSI recipients	72%				28%			
	White	Black	Other	Unknown	White	Black	Other	Unknown
% by race	58.7	25.7	13.8	1.9	58.8	19.1	19.7	2.4

Average SSI benefit: $293.00

Percentage of SSI beneficiaries who also receive Social Security: 59%

Average Social Security benefit: $381.66

Source: Social Security Administration, 2000a, 276–77; 2000b, 24–29.

Finally, Social Security makes up the largest share of total income for low-income retirees. Table 5.4 reveals that in 1999, almost one in three old people relied on Social Security for 90 percent or more of their income. In

1998, among the poorest fifth, Social Security comprised 82 percent of their income, and pensions made up only 3 percent (Social Security Administration 1999, 22). Overall, the median income of the poor was only $5,579, with the bulk (80 percent) coming from Social Security, 11 percent from Supplemental Security Income (a needs-based program for poor elderly), and only 3 percent from either pensions or dividends and the like. By contrast, the median income of the non-poor was $15,284, of which Social Security made up 41 percent of income; dividends, interest, and rent comprised 23 percent; and pensions, annuities, and the like were 19 percent (Social Security Administration 1999, 152, table 3.E3).

The importance of Social Security for minorities and especially minority women appears in the way in which it lifts certain groups out of poverty. For example, drawing on 1997 data on Social Security recipients only, Hendley and Bilimoria (1999, 61) note that without Social Security, 41.7 percent of White men and 53.2 percent of White women would fall below the poverty line, compared to the present rates of 4.4 percent and 9.9 percent, respectively. But the numbers are far worse for Blacks and for men and women of Hispanic origin, whose rates would range from 55.7 percent to a full 65 percent among Black women. Similar rates might be expected for American Indian elders, as 52 percent depend on Social Security for more than half their total income (John 1999). Further, in 1999, poverty rates among Whites would jump from 7 percent to 47 percent; among Blacks, six of ten would be poor without Social Security (Social Security Administration 2000a, 11).

We know little about the impact of sexual preference on economic resources and standing in retirement; but suggestive data and knowledge of the income policies laid out above allow us to speculate. Data on this population are hard to collect, and the samples used—such as subscribers to upscale magazines—are often biased toward more well-to-do individuals. A recent review of studies suggests that if we look across samples and attend to national surveys, the economic status of lesbian and gay households appears similar to that of heterosexual households, though it might also be that gay men reap somewhat lower monetary rewards (Badgett 1998). This research compares gay men to men within heterosexual households and lesbians to married women working full-time. Lesbian couples face the same gender discrimination in the workforce and lower wages as do heterosexual women and are, as a result, similarly disadvantaged in old age in terms of private pensions and Social Security benefits.

Also, retired gay and lesbian adults cannot be legally married. Though heterosexuals usually take it for granted, marriage as a legal and social institution provides a wide range of protections for couples throughout the life course. In relation to finances and retirement and old age, privileges denied gay and lesbian couples include the ability to provide health insurance for partners, various tax exemptions, and rights of inheritance (Badgett 1998). In terms of our focus here, recall that most pensions have assumed a traditional family form. As a result, gays and lesbians cannot receive benefits specifically for spouses in retirement, including survivor's pensions, and Social Security spousal and survivor benefits. In addition, the gender gap in pay means that lesbians are doubly disadvantaged as a group. While it is certainly possible that some were married previously and might qualify for spousal or widow benefits from Social Security, it is likely that some of them can be found among the never-married poor women discussed above.

Economic status influences quality of life in many ways; among the old, one of the most important avenues is through its impact on health. Aside from the influence of gender, race/ethnicity, class, and sexuality on health over the life course, finances in old age have additional effects through access to care, ability to purchase needed prescriptions and other health aids, and the like. While the provision of Medicare helps, many of the old spend large portions of their income on health care.

For instance, even with Medicare, the old spend, on average, more than one-fifth of their income on medical treatment, about $3,142 in 2000. This proportion, projected to increase to nearly one-third by 2025, is not evenly distributed, however (Maxwell, Moon, and Segal 2000). In fact, the lower the income, the larger the percentage spent on out-of-pocket health care expenses. The poor already spend about one-third of their income on medical costs. Further, as many as one-half of poor Medicare beneficiaries do not receive Medicaid (Gross and Brangan 1999; Crystal et al. 2000).

Gender differences in out-of-pocket health care costs also reflect women's lower incomes in retirement. Although the amount each group spends is about the same, it represents a larger proportion of old women's income. Thus, on average, old women spend one in four dollars of their income on such costs while men's expenses represent 19 percent of their income. Old women of color are especially disadvantaged in this regard as they spend a higher proportion than either White men or women. Further, old women in poor health spend more than half their income on health care—a burden expected to rise to 71.8 percent by 2025 (Maxwell et al. 2000). The 1997 legislation that will cause monthly premiums that the old must pay for Medicare Part B coverage to more than double to $105 a month in

2007 means that a woman with an annual income of $10,000 will also pay 10 percent of her income for this program alone (Estes and Michel 1999b).

While supplemental health insurance might alleviate some out-of-pocket costs, employer-sponsored plans tend to be available only to retirees from the largest firms. As a result, women and people of color are less likely to have this option available to them. Of course, among those whose employers do give them this chance, those with lower incomes and no pensions are least likely to avail themselves of it (Loprest 1998). This trend is reflected among those who face the prospect of purchasing supplemental insurance on their own; Blacks and female heads of household are least likely to purchase supplemental insurance (Lillard, Rogowski, and Kington 1997). Thus, the relationship between retirement income and health is heavily shaped by gender, race/ethnicity, class, and sexuality.

Below, we look to the future of retirement income. We draw from the understandings gained in our previous discussions of the gender, class, and race relations embedded in present income sources to examine Social Security "reform" proposals. Rather than increasing income adequacy or equalizing the present state of affairs, these proposals would likely create an even greater divide among groups of retirees. As a result, the unequal gender, race, and class experiences of later life might well increase in the near future.

Social Security "Reforms"

As we have tried to show, some groups are poorer in old age because of the way in which gender, race, and class relations are embedded in social institutions. This means that they must rely on Social Security more than those elderly persons with greater privilege, while their disadvantages are simultaneously reinforced by Social Security. This understanding provides a context through which we can examine proposed Social Security reforms. Although the specifics of particular plans continue to change, the general ideas—changing the benefit formula or age at which one can collect full benefits, or privatization—have not. Below we briefly examine these general proposals to demonstrate that, as presently formulated, none of them challenge the gender, class, and race logic of Social Security but instead build upon it.

Policy makers have suggested changing the number of years of paid employment that are used to calculate benefits from 35 to 38 or even 40 years. National economic simulation models suggest that any change in the averaging period upon which lifetime earnings are calculated will have a larger impact on lower earners. For those with average monthly incomes of $477 or less in 1998, benefits would decrease by 90 cents for each dollar decrease in their average monthly earnings (Sandell, Iams, and Fanaras 1999).

Women would be much more adversely affected than men as they tend to work fewer years and earn less over the course of their work lives than men do. Despite women's increased labor force participation, in 2030 only 40 percent of women would have the full 35 years of Social Security contributions presently required (Quadagno 1999, 350). Indeed, in 1999, only 15 percent of female and 57 percent of male retirees could meet the 38-year requirement (Fierst 1997, 137 in Rix and Williamson 1998, 16).

To offset the potentially negative impact of this proposal, some have suggested that a minimum benefit level be implemented. This minimum benefit, which would guarantee poverty level income, would not offset the gender, race, and class impact of the increased years for averaging, however. While such a provision would give women with low lifetime earnings a 4.7-percent increase in their benefit levels, this minimum is only guaranteed if one can demonstrate 40 years of paid work. Thus only 8 percent of women would qualify; and only 63 percent would qualify for a partial benefit (Sandell et al. 1999, 12). The gender gap in impact would remain as the minimum benefit applies only to the lowest earners (Sandell et al. 1999). In addition, women with lower earnings tend to be married to men with lower earnings, and vice-versa (Butrica, Iams, and Sandell 1999). This would of course have an impact on such women's retirement benefits as dual entitlements (98 percent of all recipients of dual entitlements are women) as well, as their combined benefits would still lag behind women from higher classes.

Finally, increasing the averaging period to thirty-eight years would also disproportionately affect members of racial and ethnic minority groups. Black men would be the most adversely affected among all groups of men, while (White) Hispanic women would suffer the largest cuts among women. Whites of either gender would receive the smallest cuts. The minimum benefit provision would decrease but not erase the negative effect (Sandell et al. 1999). Many would still receive benefits below the poverty level as, again, the minimum benefit level guarantee requires that one demonstrate forty years of taxable earnings.

In addition, increasing the age at which one retires could hurt single women, as women in general tend to have more chronic conditions that might cause them to need to retire sooner than men; yet they would be required to continue to work or face even lower benefits for early retirement. While it is not clear if this would be the case for women, it does appear that members of racial/ethnic minority groups would in fact be adversely affected (Quadagno 1999). Thus, minority women might suffer the most. In addition, those who might need to continue paid labor must face the gender, race, class, and age discrimination in the labor market. For instance, low-wage workers in physically demanding jobs or jobs with high rates of skill obsolescence would be disproportionately affected (Rix and Williamson 1998) by proposals to increase the number of years required for Social Security benefits. Such workers tend to be disproportionately women, people of color, and working class.

Perhaps the most controversial changes would convert varying amounts of Social Security benefits into more of a defined contribution pension plan. Several gender inequities are built into this change and vary according to different plans. In general, the problems already noted with the shift to defined contribution plans for private pensions would be incorporated.

One suggestion is that workers (but not employers) be required to pay an additional 1.6 percent tax that would go into an individual account. This account, which would provide a specified number of investment options, would presumably offset some additional changes that would result in reduced benefits. If it did, which is not certain, it would still not increase benefit adequacy, a problem many women face already (Rix and Williamson 1998). Of perhaps greatest significance to women are two other changes. The first is a proposal to alter widow's benefits: A widow could opt to receive her own benefit, her husband's benefit, or three-fourths of their combined benefit. For the small number of high-earning women, this would be a positive change, but this would not be true for the majority of women. In addition, the dependent benefit would be reduced to one-third, rather than one-half, of spouse's benefit (Shaw et al. 1998). This last change particularly disadvantages divorced and separated women and reinforces the assumption of permanent heterosexual relationships, despite reality.

One last proposal calls for the greatest changes and largest level of privatization. It creates a two-tier system. The first tier would provide a maximum flat-rate benefit equal to two-thirds of the poverty line for those who have 35 years of earnings. The second tier would pay benefits based on 5 percent of payroll taxes now redirected into individual accounts that could be invested widely. This last proposed reform is riskiest for those women who are no longer married and are low to moderate income, a group already the most likely to be poor in old age. In part this is because this proposal includes no provision for divorced women to have access to their spouse's private accounts, so such guarantees would have to be made within divorce proceedings, and on a case-by-case basis. Separated women would have no recourse at all. Widows also would not necessarily receive any benefits from the private accounts. In addition, the *maximum* guaranteed income for never-married, separated, or divorced women is only two-thirds of the poverty line; widows would receive at most an amount that would still leave them below the poverty line—$615 a month (Shaw et al. 1998, 13). Finally, among those who are married, the owner of a plan could make the decision concerning lump-sum withdrawal or an annuity without necessarily consulting a spouse at all (Rix and Williamson 1998). Of course, women of high income levels would not be hurt and might in fact benefit from this plan (Rix and Williamson 1998). Thus the effects are not simply gendered, but racialized and class-specific as well.

Although privatization proposals continue to be modified, they still ignore the risks they pose for certain groups, in particular women or people of color with low incomes. Such groups have less to invest and less ability to obtain (i.e., pay for) good financial advice. And, as others have noted, women are more conservative investors so they are not only less likely to lose a lot of money through risky investments, but also not likely to increase their savings very much (Shaw et al. 1998). Beyond this, however, even with the same levels of accumulations as men, women are likely to see smaller monthly benefits, as these may be tied to life tables that differ by gender. All of this ignores the fact that, while stock investments do tend to give decent annual returns in the long run, this "long run" could in fact be very long and one's benefits could be closely tied to factors beyond one's control at retirement (Rix and Williamson 1998, 15). In addition, regardless of race, class, and gender, defined contribution plans are not likely to perform well enough to compensate for any future cuts in Social Security (Atchley 1997); and the median amounts accumulated in defined contribution plans are fairly low, despite the fact that the overall contribution rate has increased (Kennickell and Sunden 1997).

Finally, it is important to emphasize again the structural bases for retirement income. For instance, the individual choices implied by many of the proposals ignore the larger economic and class-based context of the labor market. To cite just one example, those cohorts born in 1951–55 and 1956–60 face lower projected Social Security benefits than previous cohorts. Why? The average earnings of these groups are substantially lower, due to poorer labor market opportunities when they entered the workforce. In addition, real wage growth slowed significantly after 1973. As a result, these present workers will approach retirement with lower expected Social Security benefits (Butrica and Iams 1999). The reasons for this situation are not individual but based instead on such things as the ability of employers to drive wages down in the pursuit of greater profits. Class-based power relations, and not individuals choosing the "wrong jobs," underlie this situation. The same might be expected for those workers employed in the increasing number of poorly paid jobs in the service sector—most likely women, people of color, and the working class.

In all instances, none of the Social Security reform plans address the present inadequacies of retirement income for women (as well as minorities and working-class members) but reinforce or worsen the situation. One lesson to be learned from these proposals is that gendered institutions remain intact. That is, while high-income women might benefit from some of the proposals, this is because of their class position and despite the gendered nature of the policies. None of the proposals in any way alters the gendered inequalities within the family or the workplace and, in fact, these structures are ignored in favor of proposals that emphasize individual choices and options, a circumstance most applicable to White, middle-class men.

To reduce gender inequities, some have suggested giving credits for childcare/bearing years. This might raise the retirement income of some women. However, it does nothing to alter the gendered family relations that led to the problems and indeed would simply create new ones. For example, how would we decide which years to credit? But even more: This solution is race- and class-bound at the very least. Those who can afford the "traditional" model of family, with only one breadwinner (be it a man or a woman), would be rewarded, while families with two earners—or single-parent families, in which one person must do both productive and reproductive labor—would not receive the same benefits. And among dual-earner families, women who can afford to pay for help with care would be privileged relative to working-class or single parents. In fact, women who are forced to engage in *both* forms of labor would become more disadvantaged relative to their more privileged sisters.

A reduction of inequities can only come from policies that disrupt the gendered (as well as racialized and classed) nature of social institutions themselves; they must address the inequities that begin earlier in life and accumulate over time in addition to policies that target age-related issues. These might include subsidized, good-quality childcare; and government funding for such things as housekeeping services for the old to a degree that would allow all old to take advantage of these programs. As a result, women might no longer be the ones primarily responsible for such labor. At the same time, not just policies but organizational structures and ideologies need to change in order for domestic labor to be shared equally. That is, unless both structural opportunities and social expectations reflect an equal division of domestic labor, and such work becomes valued, inequities will persist. Shifting the work of individual women, such as childcare, into the collective labor of, say, a childcare center, does not automatically increase the value of the labor, or those who perform it. The importance of this point will become clearer in chapter 7 as we discuss care work.

CHAPTER 6

Retirement Experiences:
The Continuity of Work

In chapter 2, we noted that prevalent constructions of aging are not only middle-aged, but also based on a White, middle-class, hetereosexual, and male referent. In retirement research, this appears in the focus on "adjustment" to the loss of paid work, predicated on the belief that such labor is central to people's (read: men's) lives. Middle age remains the implicit standard, whether looking at activities or finances in retirement. We equate well-being with feelings of "being useful" or "productive." Recent demographic and marketing trends have also led to retirees being depicted as "consumers"—traveling, golfing, "living the good life"—essentially, a middle-aged, middle-class image. In terms of gender, gerontologists tend to assume family to be of greater relevance to women than to men. Previously, then, they paid little attention to women's adjustment to retirement; more recently, they have assessed "adjustment" as if women were men. In neither instance do theories include work and family as normative or central for both genders (Calasanti 1996b).

Similarly, even though scholars recognize that people move in and out of the workforce (Ekerdt and DeViney 1990), the notion of "careers" with relatively well-defined trajectories still holds sway; other patterns are still viewed as somewhat exceptional. Researchers often ignore the instability of secondary labor force participation characteristic of women, minorities, or some members of the working class.

In this chapter we demonstrate the importance of going beyond these biases in our examination of retirees' lives. We begin by returning to a theme touched upon in the last chapter: the importance of considering the wide array of productive activities in retirees' lives. These productive activities form an intricate mosaic which varies by the intersection of age, gender, race, class, and sexual preference, and which influences their lives. For example, in the last chapter, we showed some ways in which patterns of productive activities, influenced by systems of inequality, shape distributions of economic resources in later life. Knowing retirement income levels does not necessarily tell us what these mean to people, however, as such meanings also differ by social location. Research on very old Blacks, for instance, shows them to be more economically disadvantaged than are similar-aged Whites but to have higher morale (Johnson 1994a). Financial situations constrain some opportunities in this time of life while also encouraging others. In this chapter, we show how patterns of productive activity shape other aspects of retirement, including some of the ways one spends one's time.

Productivity

The last chapter ended with a discussion of Social Security reform, without delving into the reasons why calls for such "reform" have surfaced. Given the reliance of so many of the old on this program, particularly those who are disadvantaged, why instead do people not try to insure greater adequacy of Social Security income, a feasible goal (Smeeding, Estes, and Glasse 1999)? The answer to this question is complex, deriving from the amount of power of different groups defined by age as well as by race, class, and gender. To be sure, concern with the aging of the baby boomers underlies much of this push; but on a deeper level people regard the old as a "burden." As we noted in chapter 2, one stigma that attaches to the old is the belief that they are no longer "productive" members of society. Instead they are "dependent," a status marked, to a great extent, by retirement. How accurate is this depiction?

If, as the above ideology implies, we equate being productive with paid labor, then the vast majority of old people would indeed appear dependent and a burden, as relatively few (less than one in five) of those over age 65 are in fact employed. However, *productive labor* includes both paid and unpaid activity, contrary to the popular notion that only work that earns a paycheck is worthwhile. Volunteer service in betterment of communities, caregiving to the infirm, domestic labor in one's own household—all of these go unpaid yet remain vital to the maintenance, not only of life in general, but also (ironically) of the wage-earners whose toil people usually do recognize as "work." Unpaid work also "adds value to individual and community life" (Brush 1999). Understanding the lives of old people will require that we let go of concepts of productivity that rely on careers and wage-work. Whether or not people earn money for their sweat, hold formal positions in profitable firms, or even draw recognition from family members as "working," they engage in what we define for purposes of this book as *work, or labor*. People work in informal economies in which they barter household items, food, clothes, cars, even homes. They labor in their own homes feeding, cleaning, and preparing children and other adult workers. Recognizing these forms of work allows us to understand how people age. Some groups move through many types of informal and reproductive work central to their position in late life (Estes 1991); such work on the part of some even influences the work lives of others. For instance, in chapter 5 we noted that women's domestic labor facilitates men's engagement in paid work.

When we expand our notion of productive activities, we see that people engage in such labor throughout their lives and that the old perform a vast array of work (Estes 1991). In addition, the kinds and *patterns* of activities undertaken throughout the life course are strongly shaped by the intersection of power relations, including race, class, gender, sexual preference, and age. People often perform a range of work that combines paid and unpaid, or more than one type of each; this array varies by social location, and it changes over time (Stoller and Gibson 2000). For example, in the last chapter, we discussed some of the ways in which gender organizes work: While young and middle-aged adult men and women often engage in both paid and unpaid work, women predominate in unpaid family work even while employed. Workplace and retirement policies assume and reinforce this responsibility. But how do these patterns change over time? How do these gender patterns intersect with other power relations, such as those based on race, class, and sexual preference, and how do they influence retirement experiences?

Although little research has explored the work done by subgroups of elderly persons, we can show some of the ways in which the mix of work types influences retirement and the meaning that this time of life holds (Stoller and Gibson 2000). We illustrate our points with data each of us has collected on retirees in two separate research projects. One study, conducted in a southeastern state, entailed interviews with fifty-seven retirees. The sample, consisting of both men and women, was virtually all White; respondents were both working and middle class (see Calasanti 1987). The second study, conducted in a different southeastern state, focused solely on African American women who were retired professionals. For this research, fifty women were interviewed (see Slevin and Wingrove 1998). We use examples and quotes from these studies to help us demonstrate that retirement does not herald the end of work, and that the continuity of work is very much based on gender, along with race and class.

The Continuity of Work

The idea of a forty-year career followed by permanent labor force withdrawal may have always had a mythical element but, regardless, is increasingly untrue. While many White men live such work lives, presently between one-third and one-half report that they do not permanently leave the labor force when they leave their full-time jobs. Instead, they may reduce their hours, take temporary jobs, or leave and reenter numerous times (Pampel 1998; Quinn, Burkhauser, and Myers 1990).

Because the non-Hispanic White population comprises 85 percent of the old (Siegel 1999), many of the statistics on work and retirement disguise important race differences. The work lives of Mexican Americans, Black men, and American Indians, for example, are far more likely to be characterized by periods of unemployment throughout the life course that belie assertions about continuity of work (John 1999; Zsembick and Singer 1990; Gibson 1987). Similarly, the experience of retirement itself, in terms of the above mythology, varies widely by race. For example, earlier we described Black men's greater likelihood of suffering disability. Their relatively poor health in comparison to Whites' explains much of their lower labor force participation rates in the pre-retirement years (Bound, Schoenbaum, and Waidmann 1996). With their higher mortality rates, Black men appear to spend proportionately more years in the labor market and are more disabled compared to White men. As a result, among men, "[r]etirement is more a White experience than a Black experience" (Hayward, Friedman, and Chen 1996, S9). Similarly, Mexican Americans do not see themselves as retired in the same way as Whites. Further, within this group, gender differences prevail. For instance, men are more likely than women to call themselves retired if they receive retirement income, whereas women see retirement as more of a change in activity status (Zsembick and Singer 1990). Thus, even though our discussion focuses on gender, bear in mind that a confluence of social locations shapes retirement. Retirement is, at best, an attenuated period of life for many men who are disadvantaged by race or class. Further, the intersections of all of these power relations are played out in the lives of many women in ways that are only open to conjecture at the moment, due to lack of research.

Labor Market Reentry

As noted above, many people remain in or return to the labor force in retirement. At the same time, retirees' reasons for and ability to continue to work, as well as what work they do, differs by gender, race, and class. The element of choice is often a good indicator of power, as we see later in the discussion of domestic labor in retirement. In the present context, there is a vast difference between the minority of the more high-profile, "retired workers," whose gender, race, and class privileges allow them to "choose" to continue this activity, and less privileged retirees. Such workers may choose to retire from one job in order to receive a pension, and then enter another to gain supplemental income (Pampel 1998).

These relatively well-educated retirees stand in stark contrast to those who need to reenter the labor force to make ends meet (Han and Moen 1999, 223). As the discussion of retirement income makes clear, working-class retirees, women, and people of color have lowest retirement incomes and as such are most likely to need additional money to survive or at least to maintain some of their prior lifestyle (Boaz 1987; Calasanti and Bonanno 1992). Among those aged 65 and over, earnings from employment comprise nearly one-fourth of the income of Blacks and Hispanics, but only 19 percent of that of Whites (Chen 1999).

Significantly, career paths are gendered. Because intermittent work histories predict greater likelihood of "post-retirement employment" (Han and Moen 1999), women are more likely than men to need and seek re-entry, even among those who have retired due to health problems. Men's work histories allow them greater financial stability and security than women's do. Finally, for women, marital status interacts with race in influencing labor force participation. Given that unmarried women are especially vulnerable to poverty in old age, single old women with low to moderate income may be forced to continue to work for pay to avoid poverty (Shaw et al. 1998). Indeed, the primary reason for divorced retirees' descent into poverty over the course of a nine-year study was a loss of earnings from part-time jobs that had supplemented their Social Security benefits (Shaw et al. 1998, 3–4). These findings vary by race as well. Black women are more likely than White women to be in poor health and out of the labor force as a result. At the same time, if health permits, married Black women tend to continue their higher labor force participation rates, maintaining the economic self-reliance they exhibit at younger ages (Bound, Schoenbaum, and Waidmann 1996; Slevin and Wingrove 1998). Again, as we noted in our discussion of retirement income, among Black women, marital status does not appear to offer an incentive to withdraw from the labor force.

Among men, race and class differences are apparent in motivations for labor force reentry. In one study, working-class men often returned to paid labor to increase financial stability, and thus, like women, are coerced into their labor force activity. However, managerial-class men who reentered were spurred by a desire to be able to purchase "extras" and not by survival needs. In this sense, they were more free to "choose" to work (Calasanti and Bonanno 1992).

Forms of Reentry

Gender, along with race and class, differentiates who will reenter, their motives, and the forms reentry will take. The economic restructuring that began in the 1980s in the United States has created a situation in which forms of post-retirement labor in the formal market tend to be bimodal. Those with greater education appear to have more chances/opportunities to find work (Han and Moen 1999). Thus there are those professionals, for example, who continue employment as consultants. These "working retirees" are often very well paid, but still represent a cost savings to employers who need not pay them benefits. By contrast, women, working-class, and retirees of color are more likely to procure low-paid jobs, especially in the service sector. In fact, some employers look specifically for old people to work in minimum or low-waged jobs to supplement their Social Security (Calasanti and Bonanno 1992). This trend might even accelerate with the recent repeal of the earnings limit set for Social Security recipients under the age of seventy.

Older workers, whether men or women, face problems in the labor market such as job segregation, low pay, and falling rates of salary increases. In fact, contrary to their gender positions earlier in life, both old men and old women are likely to end up in secondary labor market jobs (Dale and Bamford 1988). Gender plays an additional role, however, in at least two respects. First, economic changes have served to push older men out of the market and pull older women in. However, these women must take low-paying service sector jobs (DeViney and O'Rand 1988). Second, women are believed to age and become unattractive sooner than are men. Because of the emphasis placed on their attractiveness in their jobs, women face the problems of age discrimination sooner (Rodeheaver 1990) and perceive more age barriers to employment than do men (Ginn and Arber 1999). Thus, we find that women seeking to reenter the labor market have greater difficulty than do men (Hardy 1991). Because of the racialized nature of the social standards of attractiveness—that is, beauty tends to be based on White women's physical features—non-White women are even further disadvantaged, both earlier in life and later, as they are often seen to age even more quickly (Blea 1992; Rodeheaver 1990). Thus, while older women and men may face similar problems in the labor market, women and racial/ethnic minorities confront different problems that result from the intersection of systems of power. Class has an additional impact. While they are motivated by greater financial need, working-class retirees have fewer opportunities to gain employment (Pampel 1998).

Informal Labor

Those unable or unwilling to secure employment in the formal economy may opt instead to engage in the informal economy—that economic sector not regulated by laws or proceeding through formal channels. Whether paid or unpaid, such as through an exchange of services, informal work has important economic value.

Again, the intersection of race, class, and gender influences the types of informal labor in which a retiree might engage. In general, whether activities are paid or used for barter, the forms of informal labor among all age groups tend to be differentiated on the basis of gender-typed tasks and even spatial locations. Men do more outside work or labor that takes them away from the home, for example, while women engage in crafts, gardening, baby-sitting, sewing, and other activities that can be accomplished in the home and often alongside their domestic labor tasks (Nelson 1999).

The Meaning of Work and Retirement

In many respects, men and women experience work in similar ways. For example, in the paid realm they may lack autonomy on assembly lines, fast food jobs, and other work that is highly defined or "scripted"—in which workers are told what to say and are coached in how to say it. At the same time, women and men may experience these jobs in different ways. For instance, in Pierce's (1995) study, male paralegals are not held to the same gendered expectations as are women. They are not asked to engage in the sorts of "nurturing" behavior that women are asked to perform. Instead, as male "tokens" in a female-dominated occupation, they are assumed to be more qualified for supervisory roles than the women are and in fact are thought to be more intelligent. Similarly, the behaviors of female litigating attorneys are interpreted quite differently than those of men. The same jobs that technically involve the same tasks call forth very different gendered expectations. In this instance, people consider "token" women unfeminine if they engage in the aggressive behavior necessary for their jobs; at the same time, they are dismissed by others as not being good litigators if they do not perform in this manner (Pierce 1995).

We have detailed the ways in which gender, race, and class differences in work result in different experiences of retirement through their impact on such matters as financial security and continued work in formal and informal labor. In this section, we broaden our discussion to look more closely at domestic labor as well as the meaning men and women give to work and, subsequently, retirement. When we examine the gendered nature of domestic labor, we see one more way in which retirement differs for men and women in that women do not "retire"—they do not cease to work.

The Gendered Meaning of Work

Because much research on work and retirement defines work in terms of White, middle-class men's experiences, paid employment is taken to be very different from household work, both in terms of content and in how they might relate to one another. Though many people regard them as different realms of life, female retirees do not. Both employment and their own housekeeping mean *work*, fundamentally differing in terms of pay.

For instance, all of the women in our study of White retirees had been married, and all but two had children. In each case, regardless of the presence of offspring, they had responsibility for domestic duties while also employed. While this is typically unpaid labor, it is work nonetheless, and the inevitable result was that they had, in effect, a minimum of two jobs. Working these two jobs meant doing without "leisure." They simply left one job for another:

> *Cecile:* And I found that . . . I was just so tired when I came home I couldn't, couldn't do anything. And of course I'd worked for 25 years and had raised 5 children, you know. And um, I worked all day long, and of course when the children was younger, I used to come home, even at *lunch* and uh, put a roast or something on in the oven, and fix something for supper where I could just stick it in when I came in before the girls got larger, you know, where they could do it . . . . And it was just when I came home, it was just, go go go right on 'til the end, you know, to go to bed.

Jenny: I raised six children during the time [I was working] too [laugh]. . . . I worked many times 'til 2:00 in the morning, ironing and washing floors and things.

Annie: [I]t was important that we do our jobs and so that had to come first and everything else was built around it. I mean, you have a, you really have a schedule. . . . Like bright and early every morning you're up and you um, get the kids off to school and get your husband off to work and then you get ready to go to work, and you put in your day and stop off on the way home getting groceries, come in, fix supper, do dishes, do a couple loads of laundry, run the sweeper and whatever has to be done. It's um, it was wild [laugh]. I don't know how I ever did it.

Mary: When I was working I, I was tired, I, I didn't have, I wasn't able to do too much [outside of work], you know, you have to fix everybody's supper. But I mean I had to do it, I didn't have nobody else to do it.

These women had primary responsibility for housework and childcare, and they structured their time to try to accommodate both jobs. For them, work, in one form or another, was a constant.

Of course, these women were not alone in working two jobs. A few of the men engaged in farming while they held outside employment; at least one man had a side business. The difference, however, is that these men were engaged in remunerative labor and not daily, unpaid domestic work that continues after paid employment has ceased. For men, work meant paid labor.

Lack of remuneration doesn't change the fact that domestic chores *mean* work to these women. In talking about her present life, Mae, a former inspector at an apparel factory, said that she'd rather be working than retired. What this actually *meant* to her, however, was characteristic of the labor she had undertaken throughout her life:

I enjoy cooking and cleaning and working in a yard or just whatever, anything, and I do. If I was able to do it [work outside the home] I [would] get a lot of satisfaction out of working. I always did like to work. . . .Well, I like to work around the house, too. I know I don't get paid for it, but somebody has to do it. [laugh]

She admitted that she wasn't making a distinction between paid and unpaid labor; to her, both were work, the only difference being wages.

The words and feelings of these women reflect a reality already documented by a number of scholars who have examined women's work. While most research on gender differences in work focuses only on paid labor, "domestic and labor-force activities are two sides of the same coin" (Coverman and Sheley 1986, 413). That is, as we noted earlier, women's unpaid labor enables men's engagement in paid work. The diminution of unpaid work and the relegation of it to women constructs the meaning of womanhood and manhood (Berk 1985; Hartmann 1981). Indeed, unemployed husbands "may affirm their masculinity" by avoiding what they consider to be "women's work" at home (Szinovacz 2000, 78). A gender hierarchy of domestic labor exists such that even among the "inside" chores, men may find some tasks, such as dishwashing, less threatening to masculine identity and thus they are more likely to do them (Twiggs et al. 1999).

We can see the embedded nature of gender hierarchies in the conflating of the meaning of domestic work and family in many women's lives. That is, women's family maintenance activities are synonymous with "family." Where men work for money, women do it for love. Cora's description of her present life in retirement demonstrates this point well:

> When I was working I had to get up to rush off and I wouldn't get back, I wasn't with the family too much. And I enjoyed my work and all that, but still I missed being with the family. Now I got time to do my work. I had to do it in a rush when I was working, I had to work at night late because I raised the two grandchildren.

While she says she missed being with her family, she equates this with performing domestic duties rather than actually spending time with family members.

Claire's sentiments reveal a concrete realization of the importance of women's labor in the home and the fact that it *is* work. She has worked for most of her life—either in the furniture shop she and her husband ran, or, when it became necessary, in a factory. She's also taken care of an ailing husband and raised her children. In her mind, then,

> I've had to be a nurse for 20 years, I've had to work to make a living, I've had to keep a home, so I had three jobs. I think a woman should be able to retire at 55 with full benefits, nothing lacking, in that case, if she wants to.

Class and race may intersect with gender in such a way that some women—White or middle-class—can reduce their domestic burden by turning to the service economy (Cohen 1998). They hire maids, buy convenience foods or eat out, take their laundry to the cleaners and their children to day care. Still, people maintain the myth that household work is divided based on time availability so that, on retirement, women and men will share tasks more equitably. However, research has consistently found that women continue to bear responsibility for domestic labor into the retirement years (Szinovacz and Harpster 1994). Patterns established earlier in a marriage typically remain, despite evidence that a more equitable division of labor increases a wife's happiness and marital satisfaction (Pina and Bengtson 1995).

The fact that the women in this study continued to spend a great deal of time in fulfilling domestic responsibilities demonstrates their realization that, as Mae said, "Somebody has to do it." That this "somebody" is the working wife demonstrates the gender-based power differential within marital relationships (Hartmann 1981).

The Gendered Meaning of Retirement

Research on the movement between employment, unemployment, retirement, and nonparticipation in the labor force documents the "ambiguous meaning of retirement for a significant subset of older workers, particularly women and minorities" (Flippen and Tienda 2000, S26). The ambiguity of retirement for women stems from an additional source, however, one that goes beyond the paid labor market.

The oft-cited maxim "a woman's work is never done" is usually meant to reflect the life of a wife and mother raising a family. In the idealized and romanticized image of "the family," her work was an expression of her love and implicitly justified by the paid labor of the male breadwinner. But this does not cease when paid labor ends. In fact, this is, perhaps, the most critical way in which retirement brings very different experiences for women and men: women's continued domestic labor responsibilities. Common sense tells us that "everyone knows" what retirement is. And because we take it so for granted, we miss the subtle yet important disparities between men's and women's experiences of this time. We miss these differences because they arise in the most taken-for-granted spheres of our lives: gender differences in family roles. The retirees interviewed might be aware of this difference, but both they and some researchers consider it "appropriate" and so do not incorporate it into analyses or hold it up to question.

As the gendered domestic labor influences the experience of work among men and women, so too does it affect retirement. Family obligations that differ by gender do not cease once one has left paid employment. Labor force withdrawal by men effectively ends their work, unless they choose to continue to engage in paid labor. Women, on the other hand, withdraw only from remunerative activities, not from family-related labor.

Retirement, usually defined as a cessation of work, has a different meaning for women. All of the women in the study of White retirees still engaged in domestic labor; in this respect, their lives go unchanged by retirement:

> *Jenny:* Well, I don't think it's [retirement] too much different because I'll always do, the first thing I [always] did was clean up the table and wash the dishes and dry 'em and put 'em away. And then I made the beds. No, I think it's just about the same.

The same notion is similarly illustrated in the words of one of the African American retirees interviewed by Slevin and Wingrove (1998). In describing the "freedom" that accompanies being retired from full-time employment, she comments, " I feel grateful to have the freedom to handle some of the family crises that have been sort of thrust on me."

Men's unearned advantage in relation to work within the family extends into retirement. Typically, both men and women describe retirement in terms of "freedom." But for men, this means freedom from supervision, from punching a time clock, in short, from the constraining activities that are part of paid work. Women, by contrast, often speak of their relief at having the "freedom" to "do laundry any day I like" instead of having to fit such domestic chores into a paid work schedule. In effect, this meant that, for them, retirement was a reduction but not a cessation of work; they went from two (or more) jobs to one. These different retirement experiences rest squarely on women's disadvantaged (and men's advantaged) positions within the home and workplace. Household chores are still women's responsibility unless a husband chooses to help. The element of choice is critical: Men might "choose" to help out, to learn to cook, or to cook special foods; for the most part, women remain responsible for whatever their spouses do not "choose" to do. The ability of some (middle-class, White) men to feel "free" in retirement—to engage in domestic labor, for example, because they choose to do so, or to have the financial wherewithal to enjoy these years—rests upon women's responsibility for housework.

Evidence of how gendered power relations within the family shape retirement experiences can be gleaned from research on the division of household labor in retirement. Early research discovered that most retired people either maintained this unequal division or women's workloads actually *increased*. Only 20 percent of the couples stated that husbands engaged in more domestic work after they withdrew from the labor force—

increases mostly due to the physical impairment of their wives (Szinovacz 1980). Other research found the opposite: that retired men spent more time doing domestic labor (Rexroat and Shehan 1987). Since then, researchers have come to believe that the division of domestic labor might be complicated by a partner's employment status as well as the gender type of tasks involved. Thus, recent studies by Szinovacz and Harpster (1994) and Szinovacz (2000) examined marriages in which one spouse retires while the other remains employed. They found that retired wives with employed husbands take on large portions of the household workload, but that retired husbands do not reciprocate very well. The retired men with employed wives take on a few more "male" tasks, but rarely assume any of the typically "woman's" work. It appears, then, that, "employed wives seem unable to elicit more household help . . . from retired than from employed husbands" (Szinovacz and Harpster 1994, S134). The exception is when a husband's wife is severely disabled. In this situation, he does perform more female tasks. This finding underscores the gendered power differential in the family. Indeed, it appears that when retired men do engage in domestic labor, they are "helping out"; the work remains their wives responsibility (Calasanti 1993).

Interestingly, race appears to have an influence on these gender relations. Among those aged 60 and over, both Black and White women engage in more domestic labor than do men of their race. However, being married significantly increases this burden only for White women (Danigelis and McIntosh 1993), suggesting that Black couples have a somewhat more egalitarian division of domestic labor. Of course, the fact that Black men are less likely than White men to live with their spouses (39.7 percent versus 60.7 percent) matters in this regard (U.S. Bureau of the Census 1998b, table 1). Still, this is in line with other evidence that families of Blacks have tended to be more flexible in their household division of labor (Stoller and Gibson 2000). The comments of a retired school principal in the Slevin and Wingrove study (1998) also illustrate this point:

> I think my husband . . . was a real helpmate when I was working, after our son was born. I think if you ask my son he will see his Mom and Dad as equally important . . . [but] probably his Dad [gave him] more time that his Mom did. So, I think my husband has been a very supportive and encouraging and just an outstanding father.

Women's descriptions and feelings about retirement illuminate the power differentials embedded in gender hierarchies. They talk about "being free" to engage in domestic labor in a more leisurely manner. Among the White retirees studied, Lorraine's comments typify the majority: "[When I was working it was] just rush, rush, rush . . . [Now I] take my time . . . I don't have to rush." The work is not forsaken, but women are "free" to "reshape" it, as Lois' observations demonstrate:

> When I worked I had to do a lot of work at night, housework, laundry, ironing, everything, and now I don't even have a certain day to do my laundry. I do it when I want to and I just don't feel like I'm on a tight schedule.

Similarly, Annie expressed pleasure in the knowledge that if she did not want to do her laundry one day, she could put it off until the next. Doing the laundry is still these women's job, but the strict schedule they adhered to while engaged in remunerative activity is no longer necessary.

Care Work

We can see the fluidity of work/family in women's lives when we consider housework; but retired women are also called upon to perform other tasks, also based on gender expectations, which may or may not be what they wanted or planned for this stage of their lives. The usual notion of "freedom" in retirement also ignores the fact that, for some women, retirement might well mean an *expansion* in domestic labor. The expectations of women, while employed and in retirement, also involve care work. Caring for others extends not only to spouses or parents—their own or their spouse's—but also to their children and grandchildren, and even to communities. In the next chapter, we turn our attention to relationships in later life, but here, we briefly note that such care work, performed far more often by women than by men, can affect retirees' lives in important ways—from the timing of their labor force withdrawal (Quadagno 1999) to the way they spend their time in retirement.

A large number of women take care of grandchildren during the day while parents work. This is not necessarily a source of displeasure, although it can, at times, be confining. Again, we turn to interview data to illustrate our points, beginning with a White, working-class retired woman:

> *Selma:* I thought when you retired you could just do anything you wanted to do, you know, you wanted to get up, you get up. But it hasn't turned out like that, I've got to get up on account of these kids. But that is good for me, it's something to keep me jumping.

A number of the retirees in the Slevin and Wingrove study (1998) also took care of grandchildren, and one widowed grandmother's story was especially noteworthy. She left her own home each Monday morning at 5 A.M. and drove for over three hours to another state to baby-sit her grandson. She did not return to her own home until the following weekend. Many others in both studies report caring for grandchildren and, in some cases, great-grandchildren.

More restrictive, both financially and in terms of one's time, can be the responsibility for helping one's grown children as well as grandchildren. Jenny, a White, retired widow, is a case in point. Her income puts her at the near-poverty level, and she rents her home and so has an additional monthly payment that many retirees do not. Her health is poor and she is frequently tired. Despite her financial and physical conditions, two of her six grown children live with her. One is her divorced son, whose two children stay with them every other weekend. He appears to have no intention of moving, and contributes only a small monthly amount toward his food and shelter. The other is her daughter, in the midst of a divorce. She contributes nothing, but will leave "after her finances are worked out." Some of her grandchildren come to her house to catch the bus for school. The following description of part of her day is replete with care work activities:

> Well, I get up and, my son . . . he lives here and works out at [   ], and um, I get up at 5:00 and fix him breakfast and his lunch, and generally lay back down. Then my grandchildren come about a quarter past six and I sit up until they leave to go to school, and if I don't feel like staying up I'll lay back down. And if I feel like staying up I'll just go on and do some housework. . . . [A]nd I do a lot of sewing, I do sewing all day, and of all my children, none of them like to sew. They bring me blue jeans and everything for me to seam up, you know. . . . [And I run] errands, and then I do my laundry in town because my kitchen's too small . . . for a washer and dryer.

As to whether or not she enjoys having her children live at home, she admitted, "Well, I think I wouldn't have so much to do at home (laugh). I could probably go [out] more." Indeed, Jenny would like to go out with friends more, but her family obligations keep her at home:

> I don't know why I don't get out at night and you know and they [friends] ask me to go out with them and eat and all and I just haven't done it (laugh). Haven't gotten started at it I guess (chuckle). It's because I fix supper here at home for my son and everything when he comes in from work and all, you know . . . then on Sundays when we get home from church I fix lunch

and dinner for 'em and all. If I was just living by myself I'd probably go with [my friends].

Martha, a White retiree who is also widowed, provides yet another example of continued care work. One of her sons, who never married, still lives with her and depends on her for all manner of support. He is unemployed and has been for so long that he doesn't receive any benefits. As a result, they both have to survive on her income—about $400 a month. The fact that the caretaking involved in motherhood does not dissipate once the children are grown is common for these working-class women. They still live in proximity to one another; and neither they nor their offspring have additional economic resources upon which they can call.

Caring for spouses in later life can be especially hard. In addition to time and financial constraints, the age of the retirees means that they face increased likelihood of declining health. For example, Lucy views her retirement in more negative terms now than she did when she first retired. Her husband is bedridden and his entire care is left up to her. She feels tremendous pressure from this responsibility, and she attributes her heart problems to it. Inadequate finances, approximately $500 per month for the two of them, also contribute to her unhappiness; it is possible that, if their income were higher, she would feel less overwhelmed by the burden of his care. As it is, she is confined to the house; she still drives but doesn't feel she can get out much. If it weren't for her husband, she'd rather still be working, although she admits, at age seventy-four, it would be difficult to find something. At the same time, she worked part-time at a laundromat and at a retirement home until she was seventy. But the main reason she would like to work is that it would

> get me out more. See, I sit here all the time. If I run out [it] is to go to the grocery or to go get some medicine. Or we go to the doctor, now he's got an appointment tonight. Sometimes I go down on a Sunday afternoon and they [daughter and children] come to pick me up for about an hour [and we] look at things. Honey, I haven't been in a store downtown for years.

Lucy says she would miss her husband dearly if he were gone; at the same time, the strain of his care takes its toll.

Women's care work is not always restricted by kinship. It may also entail helping neighbors and others within their communities. This gendered ethic of caring for others, even if not blood relatives, has been well documented in studies of African American communities and still exists, albeit at a more reduced level, even in communities that are not as tightly knit as those prior to desegregation (see, for example, Giddings 1984; Collins 1990; Slevin and Wingrove 1998). Two examples illustrate this point—both from interviews with the retired women in the Slevin and Wingrove study. In one case, as we discussed how a retired university administrator spent her time in retirement, she talked about how she enjoyed helping people and she commented:

> [T]here are three women in their eighties that I take to the doctor when they need to go. I fix food for them when they need it and I cook for one of them [every] Sunday.

Her sense of obligation to these nonrelatives is such that, despite the fact that she dislikes cooking, she still does it in order to care for these women who are a few years older than she is. A second example that illustrates the same gendered and racialized ethic of caring for others is one in which a retired educator extensively tutors a young Black boy who is from a severely disadvantaged background. She calls him almost daily to check that he has gone to school and has done his homework; she also regularly calls and visits his school to meet with his teachers and with the principal. Well into her seventies at the point of the interview, she recalls how the night before:

> He called me at ten o'clock. I stayed on the phone with him until quarter of eleven. He named the word and I gave him the definition from the dictionary.

Community and Volunteer Work

Gender, race and class shape the meaning of work and retirement through community work in general, including volunteerism. While women in general engage in more volunteer work than do men, evidence also suggests that Blacks do more than Whites. It is not surprising, then, that national data show that Black women appear to do the most of all (Danigelis and McIntosh 1993). Slevin and Wingrove found, for instance, that among the fifty retirees in their study, only one did not engage in any type of volunteer work and most were heavily committed to multiple projects at the local, regional, and even national level (Slevin and Wingrove 1998). One study of the meaning of work and leisure in the context of the lives of working-class, African American women is illustrative of how community work and paid work merge for this group (Allen and Chin-Sang 1990). They worked throughout their lives, both paid and unpaid, beginning in childhood. In their retirement years, their work included increased service to others and their communities.

Race, class, and gender influence the types of volunteer/community work in which the retired engage. For instance, in a study of retired White women professionals, Wingrove and Slevin (1991) found that the volunteer activities of this group of women stood in contrast to the activities of the Black women they later studied, despite the fact that they shared similar class backgrounds. The women who were White were much more likely to spend their free time and energy on community civic and cultural boards than was the case for the African American women. A key reason given for involvement on the part of the White women was to get out of the house and to meet people, to socialize. Of course, the African American retirees also served on such boards and they too enjoyed socializing and meeting people, but their motivation and focus frequently differed. They were also less likely to spend their time and energy on cultural boards, such as museums. The words of one of these women summarize the approach to volunteer activity that most characterized her African American colleagues:

> Being retired means for me being of service and I don't have time for anything that's not going to help make a difference in this community. Okay? So, that's it in a nutshell: being of service and helping out.

An example of the type of activities that typified those of the African American retirees illustrates this notion of community service and highlights these women's attempts to help those less fortunate than themselves. A retired teacher who was in her late seventies spent considerable time going to two local, inner-city elementary schools and reading to the children, almost all of whom were African American. She recalled how, out of her own pocket, she had in the previous year bought each child (a total of 1,200) a book because she thought it so important that children know what it was like to own their own book. The goal of her efforts is quite straightforward, "I read stories to the children because I'm trying to teach them the importance of knowing how to read." But her own class privilege intersects with race and also shapes her work. Specifically, she is motivated by the notion of "race uplift," as her description of how she approaches her reading exercise with these economically deprived Black youngsters attests:

> When I go to read the stories to the children, I give them a talk first. I explain to them the value of an education and [I] explain to them that they should stay in school . . . and if there is something that they don't understand, to go to the teacher and ask the teacher to help them with it.

[And I tell them] to behave themselves in school, too. And if they have friends who are doing things that are not nice, then you break away from that friend and get another friend who lives a good life. Yeah, and I let them know, I say, "I don't care how poor your parents are, you can be something worthwhile. It's up to you."

Discussion

Gender relations, along with race and class, shape retirement experiences in such a way that the notion of retirement as a time devoid of work amounts to a myth for the vast majority. Women generally continue to work as they maintain their primary responsibility for household labor and caring for others. In addition, many women, people of color, and members of the working class continue to participate in the formal or informal economy, even while receiving Social Security benefits. Thus, the popular notion of retirement ignores the way gender relations, along with race and class, structure domestic labor as well as the interactions between domestic and market labor, on the one hand, and retirement, on the other.

Retired women continue to work in a variety of ways. While higher class status may intervene to lessen the burden by allowing people to engage paid help, women usually continue domestic labor upon retirement, and sometimes expand this work by caring for others—elderly parents, their own children who moved back home, their grandchildren, and the community at large. In addition, women, racial and ethnic minorities, and working-class members must reenter the paid arena, either formally or informally, in order to survive. Retirement, as a time when work ends, does not describe the lives of most people.

How will the increased number of women entering the labor force and the relative rise in the number of old influence women's retirement experiences? We have no reason to expect major changes in, first, retirement incomes and, second, the domestic division of labor. In fact, the economic vulnerability of women and racial/ethnic minorities may worsen. Even with women's increased number of years in paid labor, Social Security "reform" and the increased prevalence of defined contribution pension plans suggest that women's financial security will not strengthen and may even decline, depending on what changes might be made to Social Security. Women's wages have not changed significantly in recent years, and still stood at 73 percent of men's in 1998. Further, the gender gap in wages increases with age so that there is little reason to suspect a rosier financial picture for near-future retired women (U.S. Bureau of the Census 1999a).

Similarly, little change in division of household labor has occurred since the 1960s outside of some aspects of childcare. Between 1951 and 1997, married women's labor force participation has nearly tripled, to 62 percent (U.S. Bureau of the Census 1998a), but this has not led to any significant change in the division of or responsibility for household labor (Press and Townsley 1998; Calasanti and Bailey 1991; Coverman and Sheley 1986). This may have come as a bit of a shock to some of the White women who have entered the labor force in the last few decades; the extent of inequity in this division of labor, more that the overall amount per se, has the greater impact on an employed woman's psychological well-being (Bird 1999). We have little reason to suspect that women's responsibility for domestic labor in retirement will change substantially, either.

It is important to note that, aside from some of the more obvious effects of living below poverty level, gendered experiences of retirement are not inherently positive or negative. In fact, most retirees—men and women, regardless of race/ethnicity, class, and sexuality—say that they are satisfied with their retirement. Instead, what we have tried to show is that the experience of retirement—what one is actually doing—is shaped by social locations. Women who are used to housework need not experience lower retirement satisfaction if they engage in this labor. Indeed, most express happiness in retirement based on the fact they now have time to perform these tasks. The Black women whose words we used were glad to be giving back to their communities; they gained enormous satisfaction from this. Similarly, care work can be a positive experience. Thus, our point is not that these gender differences necessarily lessen or enhance satisfaction but rather that the concepts of work and retirement do not encompass the experiences of the majority: most women as well as men of racial and ethnic minority groups or working class.

The importance of gender and racial/ethnic relations in shaping retirement experiences and, indeed, aging in general are apparent in Danigelis and McIntosh's (1993) national study of productive activities of those aged 60 and over. Past research has found that a variety of resources is important in helping one engage in work, including physical ability, age, education, income, assets, and measures of personal support—marital status and household size. Based on these, they found that White men have the greatest number of resources. Yet, they also engaged in the fewest productive activities. In addition, Blacks in general engage in more work than do Whites. How is it possible that those who have the greatest resources to engage in work do the least? Only by understanding the intersection of power relations do these findings make sense. That is, pointing to gender relations is not enough. Black men are not as able to translate their "manhood" into the same amount of resources as White men are, nor are they able to engage in less paid and unpaid work in comparison to White men. These findings also go against some notions Americans hold concerning meritocracy or fairness; those doing the least, White men, are the most rewarded. However, if we looked at paid labor only, we would miss much of this.

In addition, ignoring the way in which paid and unpaid labor come together over the life course leads to faulty conclusions about the "productivity" and "dependence" of particular populations. Not recognizing the unpaid, productive work performed by the old of both genders increases fears about the rise in the number of old people in comparison to the "working" populations (Calasanti and Bonanno 1986). Further, we obscure the ways in which diverse experiences of retirement may represent strengths or resources in old age when we do not go beyond traditional notions of work and retirement. For example, we have noted some of the ways in which gender relations constrain women's paid labor and retirement income. At the same time, women's "nurturing" may decrease their "dependence" in later life. Caring for grandchildren, for instance, contributes to the well-being of the extended family. Such activities can thus be a part of a larger exchange across generations, wherein each is seen to be contributing, with no one party being more "dependent" than the other.

The issues of diversity in retirement in relation to different types of work take us into the realm of interpersonal relations in later life and family work. In the next chapter, we explore some of these relations further, demonstrating how attention to diversity changes some of our conceptions of caregiving/care work and "family" and the wide array of resources old people draw upon in later life.

CHAPTER 7

Gender, Care Work, and Family in Old Age

The previous chapters have shown that work continues throughout the lives of the old, and that the form and prevalence of such activity is critical for understanding how people age. In this chapter we examine further one type of unpaid labor within families: caregiving,[1] or what we refer to as *care work*. We explore how gender relations interact with other power relations to influence two types of unpaid care work that the old, and especially old women, are likely to engage in—eldercare and grandparenting. We place this labor in the broader context of gender relations within families that also vary by race, ethnicity, class, and sexual orientation.

Our discussion reveals that care work in old age goes beyond eldercare and beyond stereotypic White, middle-class, and heterosexual notions of "family." When we both consider diversity and take off our ageist blinders, we expand our view of family in old age and raise questions about the assumed dependence of the old. Providers of care work and other forms of social support are not necessarily close blood relations. Social location can influence families to encompass a wider array of people, including more distant kin, friends, neighbors, church members, and other community members. A closer look at gender and care work in old age also reveals that the old are not passive care recipients and, further, that they are involved in many reciprocal relationships, within and across generations.

We begin our discussion broadly, first defining care work and then reviewing the types of care work women and men do. We then ask why

---

[1] We use the term "care work" rather than caregiving for reasons we explain shortly.

women do most of the care work, and we explore how gender relations affect the nature of care work and its meaning. We next discuss diverse experiences of care work in old age, and show how consideration of the intersections of gender relations with other social hierarchies in relation to care both revises our notions of "family" in old age and influences the receipt of care. Recognizing family diversity also leads us to explore the important care work that the old provide to younger generations, especially through grandparenting. Finally, we summarize what a gender lens on care work tells us about diverse experiences and inequalities in old age, and about possible sources of change.

What Is Care Work?

Though most people have a general sense of what care work is, its definition is complicated. Does it include any activity that helps others, wanted or not? What if one does it at a distance? How often must one help for this to be considered care work—sometimes, a lot, rarely? What we count as care work shapes our knowledge and consequent actions. If we count housework help but not lawn mowing, then we leave out stereotypical "men's work." If we devalue work when it flows from "love" or "attachment" and thus consider it not really "work," the term itself can erase much of women's work.

What "counts" as care work for the old varies across studies. It can be defined according to the type of care provided; its frequency, duration, or intensity; or the characteristics of the recipient (Martin Matthews and Campbell 1995). The more inclusive the definition of care, the more care men appear to provide (Martin Matthews and Campbell 1995). Thus, our definition of care will influence what, if any, gender differences we find in research, as well as the significance of these for policies. In a nutshell, how we define a problem—indeed, whether or not we see a situation as a problem—influences our solutions. Drawing from strands included in recent feminist discussions, we depict caring as both "providing for the needs of well-being of another person" (Glenn 2000, 86) and one's feelings of affection and responsibility for another's needs. Care work involves rendering physical and emotional care, as well as instrumental or mechanical services. Although such services can be provided for a fee, in this chapter our focus is on unpaid care work. Finally, while there is debate on this point, in our view paying for care supports care work, but does not count as caring per se (Glenn 2000; Cancian and Oliker 2000; Hooyman and Gonyea 1999).

This definition reveals two components that comprise care work. First, it involves "caring for"—the activities of seeing to another's needs. Second, it includes "caring about"—the affective dimension, or the "ethic" of care, to use Glenn's (2000, 86) term—the thoughts and feelings involved in feeling responsible (Glenn 2000; Cancian and Oliker 2000; Hooyman and Gonyea 1999; MacRae 1998). Understanding care in this way has several important ramifications. First, it includes care work for all people, and not only the old and the very young, whom people traditionally define as dependent. Younger marital partners, for example, do care work for one another. Second, caring is a relationship. Different people, in various locations, may perform it, but it always involves at least one caretaker and one care recipient. While the caregiver may sometimes have greater power, the "success" of the activity may rest with the recipient's reactions (Cancian and Oliker 2000; Glenn 2000). This may be more apparent in the case of the young marital partners, but it applies to the old as well. For instance, being able to calm a demented elder may define success to a caregiver; in this situation the recipient's responses matter. Of course, the recipient also might have more power, such as the ability to terminate a paid care worker's employment. In any case, when we see care work as a relationship we see the rights of care recipients along with those of the carers (Rose and Bruce 1995). Third, our definition of care recognizes both the physical labor and the emotion work involved (Rose and Bruce 1995), a fact often hidden by the term "caregiving" (Ray 1996). In keeping with our discussion of domestic work, we recognize the often unpaid labor of supporting others as *work*. Women do work more than men do, and often do it without recognition. Thus, we adopt the term "care work" in this chapter.[2]

---

[2] We also sometimes use the term "eldercare" to reflect the age of care recipients. However, we acknowledge Martin Matthews and Campbell's (1995) critique of this term, which assumes it is parallel with childcare. They note that the two—elder- and childcare—are actually far more different than alike. First, eldercare is far more unpredictable and describes far more heterogeneous relationships than does childcare. Second, the type of care, intensity, and other aspects of eldercare may change directions over time in relation to health, loss of spouse, and so on, and in ways not parallel to childcare. Third, the number of carers involved in each situation may differ and become more complex in eldercare. Fourth, crisis episodes vary: In childcare, most illnesses are of short duration, whereas in eldercare they can be far more serious and can require longer periods for recuperation. Fifth, the care recipients themselves differ, for instance in terms of autonomy typically granted elders versus children. Finally, the integration of community services is also very different for eldercare than for childcare; for instance, the informal care worker for the old must often coordinate the formal services across providers and fill in gaps. Moreover, the term eldercare "promotes and reinforces an image of older people as inherently dependent" (Martin Matthews and Campbell 1995, 131).

Care Work for the Old

Why is care work for the old relevant to our discussions of gender and age? Much public and scholarly attention has focused on care work, with good reason. Among the old, the most rapid growth is among those aged 85 and over, the age group most likely to need care. However, when attention turns to the old and care work, people often forget that many care workers are themselves old. Although the average age of care workers is 46, 12 percent are over age 65, and these latter care workers carry the heaviest and most intensive load of the work involved. The average age of care recipients is 77 (National Alliance for Caregiving and AARP 1997), and most care workers and recipients are women. Care for the old affects people throughout their lives: positively, through satisfaction in providing care and in building support networks, and negatively, through social and economic costs, such as lost social contacts and financial strains—all of which influence their quality of life in old age. We show how the gendered nature of care work makes these outcomes especially important to women.

Gender and Eldercare Work

Care work is a life-course process; women and men engage in it throughout their lives. Women are called upon to do both more and different kinds of caring than are men. Although both genders do care work throughout their lives, women do far more. Approximately 35 years, or one-third, of women's lives are devoted to care for children and later for the old, as well as children and grandchildren (Adams, Nawrocki, and Coleman 1999; Hill 1997), and the costs of doing so much more of that work accumulate over time. Women comprise three-fourths of informal carers of the old and four-fifths of those who provide constant care—40 or more hours of care per week. This gender differential cuts across all racial and ethnic groups, though among Asians the number of female and male care workers is almost even (National Alliance for Caregiving and AARP 1997; Martin Matthews and Campbell 1995). Women are also the most likely to receive care in old age (Hooyman and Gonyea 1999).

While research has not yielded consistent results in relation to gender differences in the number of caring tasks performed, overall, women spend more time in care work than do men and are more likely to be the primary care workers (Yee and Schulz 2000; McNeil 1999; Neal, Ingersoll-Dayton, and Starrels 1997). A national study by the U.S. Census Bureau in 1998 found that women were almost twice as likely to be providing care than were men.

While the study included all forms of care to persons with a long-term illness or disability, the data reveal that the likelihood of giving care does rise with the age of the care worker because of the increased likelihood of having a parent or spouse in need of care. The relationship was curvilinear, however; the peak for care work occurred among those aged 55 to 64, with a slowly decreasing rate in higher ages, partly due to the death of care receivers. At the same time, the amount of time spent providing care increases with age. Those aged 55 to 64 averaged 29 hours a week in care work, while those aged 65 to 74 provided 38 hours and those aged 75 and over worked a full 43 hours a week (McNeil 1999). Taken together, these numbers suggest that while the incidence of care work decreases slightly in old age, the burden, at least in terms of time, grows.

Indeed, when we focus only on primary care workers, we find that half are over age 65 (Administration on Aging 2000). On top of that, in the 1980s, 5 percent of spouse carers reported a significant degree of functional impairment (Dwyer and Seccombe 1991). Recent national data show that married disabled women are still likely to be the primary care worker for their disabled husbands. Further, married disabled women receive many fewer hours of informal care than do married disabled men (14.8 hours versus 26.2 hours) (Katz, Kabeto, and Langa 2000). Women do more care work than men and suffer more chronic health problems and so endure more when they are old. At the same time, as we show, time spent in care does not necessarily equate with feelings of burden or stress, and important variations by race/ethnicity and class exist.

Employment does not change the gendered division of care. Martin Matthews and Campbell (1995) found that, of the more than 5,600 employed men and women they surveyed, approximately equal numbers reported that they were engaged in providing care. However, women spent more time and were almost twice as likely to be providing personal care than were men who reported providing care.

A spouse is likely to be the primary care worker, regardless of gender. Of course, because women tend to marry men older than themselves and men have lower life expectancies, men are usually the recipients, and not givers, of spousal care (Thompson 2000). When no spouse is available, however, gender remains the important determinant. Adult daughters are generally next in line. In fact, daughters-in-law tend to engage in care more than sons, and sisters more than brothers. Family structure also matters; men who have no siblings or no sisters are more likely to be involved in care work of all types (Hooyman and Gonyea 1999; Dwyer and Seccombe 1991). At the same time, men who perform care work for their spouses tend to be just as involved in care tasks, including personal care, as their female counterparts (Martin Matthews and Campbell 1995; Thompson 2000).

Why Do Women Do More Care Work than Men?

Most of the numerous explanations for the gendered nature of care are either psychological or sociological. Many discussions posit that women are more relational than men; because of their socialization and connection to others, women are more caring and nurturant. Thus women engage in more care work either because they have greater attachment to the care recipients, or because it is central to their identity. However, many women are not nurturant while many men are; and research suggests that women do not experience greater feelings of filial responsibility than do men (Alexis Walker 1992). By focusing on nurturance as an indicator of attachment or closeness, researchers have honed in on women but have ignored men's emotional attachments. While women learn the skills that care work requires more often than do men, such skills can and have been learned by men as well (Risman 1987). In addition, evidence among men and women employed in comparable jobs indicates that they give care in very similar ways, and differently from women not engaged in these forms of paid labor (Gerstel and Gallagher 1994). This suggests that care work is not an inevitable result of socialization or personality.

Also inadequate are explanations that note that women's labor market position is not as strong as men's and that they are, therefore, the more logical "choice" as carers. As we noted in chapters 5 and 6, women tend not to leave the labor market when they take on eldercare. In fact, among more recent cohorts of women, employed women are as likely to end up as care workers as are women who are not employed (Moen et al. 1994). In examining the relationship between gender and employment, research finds that virtually all daughters become care workers when needed, regardless of employment status. By contrast, just over half of unemployed and one-third of employed sons take on this role (Noelker and Townsend 1987, reported in Dwyer and Seccombe 1991). Research has failed to demonstrate that labor force differences by gender, time availability, task specialization, or conflict with other roles explain why eldercare is gendered (Stoller 1993; Finley 1989). Indeed, it appears that employment hours and flexibility do not increase men's eldercare (Gerstel and Gallagher 2001).

When we begin to examine these questions in terms of power relations rather than socialization and labor market position, we see that women do not freely choose care work. Macro- and microlevel factors propel far more women than men into this role. The responsibility for care work is "structured by the gender-based division of domestic labor, the invisibility and devaluing of unpaid work, occupational segregation in the work force, and an implicitly gendered work place." (Stoller 1993, 166). It may seem "natural" and a "choice," but what are the alternatives?

The ideological component of care work is evident in the meanings embedded in the concept:

> the term "caregiving" . . . includes at least two assumptions: that the activity involves intimacy and connection ("care"), in addition to the meeting of physical needs, and that this care is offered freely ("given"). Simultaneously, the term excludes a view of care as hard work performed, in the case of service workers, for pay or, in the case of some family members, out of a sense of duty and responsibility. (Ray 1996, 677)

"Care" implies a social connectedness, a sense of emotional attachment, usually identified with women, home, and family. This popular connection can be seen in the fact that "family members know that formal caregiving is not really 'care' because it lacks the commitment and affection that define caregiving by mothers [and] wives," i.e., women in the family (Alexis Walker 1992, 41). Further, women have no real choice—there are few, if any, structural or ideological alternatives available. In industrialized societies, what would happen if an old person was neglected, or considered to be so? Who would be "blamed"—a daughter or a son? As explained by female care workers themselves, "Who else is going to do it?" (Aronson 1992).

As an emphasis on power relations reveals, people define and experience care working relationships in the context of shifting power relations. The larger or different support networks of Blacks, for example, do not result from "natural" racial differences but instead stem from support networks that have grown in relation to power differences and (the culture and economic reality shaped by) the dominant group. The state is one critical actor in this construction of women as care workers.

The public/private split that emerged with industrial capitalism in the nineteenth century relegated middle- and upper-class White women to the private sphere and domestic labor. Their roles within this newly constructed private realm of home included caring for family; reproductive labor was valorized as a mission (Hooyman and Gonyea 1995). At the same time, "the private realm of . . . care [was] defined not only as separate from, but also in opposition to citizenship. The private realm encompasses emotion, particularity, subjectivity, and the meeting of bodily needs" (Glenn 2000, 84–85).

Overall, while men earned money for their own work in the newly created "public" sphere, they got their needs met at little cost to themselves in a culture that declared women to be motivated by love and thus willing to work hard in the home for free. Care work policies fashioned by the state take this gender division of labor in the family for granted; they tend to assume that family care translates into women giving care (Alan Walker 1996, 278). Indeed, the popular term "family care" disguises the gendered nature of this work (Hooyman and Gonyea 1999; Dwyer and Seccombe 1991).

We can see the state's impact on gendering care work across the life course, from younger women's situation in the labor force up to old age. For example, women average lower pay than men, in general as well as for the same jobs that men hold. This situation limits their financial resources as both caregivers and, later, as care receivers. Such workplace inequities reflect laws that include not only those dealing with equal pay, comparable worth, sexual harassment, or unfair job qualifications, but also laws dealing with parental leave, childcare, or family leave policies, retirement income, and health coverage that influence the experiences of women and men in later life and, ultimately, care working. For example, in nations such as the United States and Great Britain, the assumption of women's economic dependence upon men has historically meant women had less access to retirement incomes.

The state has also made paid care work either too expensive, too limited, or both to be accessible to most people (Glenn 2000; Hooyman and Gonyea 1999; Stoller 1993). Policies have steadily moved care work from the federal to the local level while privatizing care in part through federal funding cutbacks. That is, the number of public providers of care services has decreased while the for-profit sector has grown as the government has retreated. Changes in federal reimbursements for health care mean that women do much of the work, without pay, that health care professionals used to do (Glazer 1990). And because corporations prefer the greater profits to be made from more high-technology, acute care services, more and more chronic care has been left to the family and community—i.e., to unpaid women (Hooyman and Gonyea 1999).

The Meaning of Care Work

As we explore what care work means to those who do it, we should first distinguish between two main types of tasks: personal and instrumental. Personal care tasks include help with basic activities of daily living:

getting around within the home (including into and out of a bed or chair), bathing, dressing, eating, and toileting. Instrumental care might include helping another prepare meals, take medications, do housework, get around outside the home (such as providing transportation), and providing financial management help. If we look at type of care provided by non-spouses, then women appear to be overwhelmingly involved in personal care, whereas men are likely to be involved more in instrumental than personal care (Martin Matthews and Campbell 1995).

Distinctions also emerge within instrumental care tasks. For example, daughters tend to perform more housekeeping tasks than do sons, and women also appear to fulfill more shopping, meal preparation, transportation, and laundry needs than do men. Men more often help with financial management and home maintenance work (Yee and Schulz 2000; Martin Matthews and Campbell 1995). On a practical level, then, women not only spend more time in care overall than do men but they do tasks that arise on a daily basis as well, rather than periodic tasks (Yee and Schulz 2000).

Research on care work sometimes takes a "gender difference approach" that treats women's experiences of care work as the norm, and compares men's experiences to them (Alexis Walker 1992). As a result, that research misses much of what men do that might in fact be care work (Matthews 1995). By using women's experiences as the standard, we end up not understanding men's, including the meaning of care work to men (Thompson 2000). For instance, because men tend to perform instrumental work rather than the personal tasks that women more often do, their contributions tend to be devalued by themselves and others, including researchers (Matthews 1995). In addition, we do not really know what men mean when they say they are "involved" in personal care (Martin Matthews and Campbell 1995; Kirsi, Hervonen, and Jylha 2000). Do they help their spouse or partner in this task or do they have primary responsibility? Do they "identify with the responsibility but not with the actual execution of the tasks"? As one man who identified himself as a carer then went on to say, "'My wife does most of it. It is a joint effort'" (Vonhof 1991, 18, in Martin Matthews and Campbell 1995, 143).

Gender interacts with family relationships to influence the meaning of care. In their thought-provoking research, Dwyer and Seccombe (1991) hypothesized that, given gender stratification within families, women would see much of the care work they perform for spouses as a part of their usual domestic labor. As a result, they would not see care work as requiring as many *extra* hours of care work as would husbands, who generally are involved in little to no domestic labor. By contrast, both daughters and sons who engage in care work for parents would perceive any such tasks as additional care work. Using national survey data and questions that specifically asked about how many *extra* hours of work providing care for a disabled adult required, these researchers found that husbands reported spending more hours of care than did wives, whereas daughters reported spending more hours than did sons. This study highlights the importance of understanding what elder care work *means* to men and women, and how this meaning varies not only by gender but also by kin relationship. Ignoring these differences means that many of the studies on care work are not really looking at the same phenomena if they don't understand how and why wives might underreport the care they give. Importantly, however, while Dwyer and Seccombe included Blacks and Whites in their analysis, they did not examine the impact of race, so it is unclear whether the same patterns concerning gender and marital expectations of care work hold for both groups.

In another recent project examining the meaning of care, Kirsi, Hervonen, and Jylha (2000) find the care working stories written by fifteen men point to diverse experiences. They present evidence of a gendered notion of care in these men's writings—that there are "sensitive" and "less sensitive" styles of care work, with the former being more "female" so that men who ascribe to this style—as did one of their respondents—must justify it along other ideological lines (in this case, he refers to Christian norms of love and charity). Through their analysis of the narratives, they also find an implicit tension for some men between being a care worker and being a man. For instance, one man felt a need to explain how one can be both a sensitive carer and still a man; another sought to explain how he was able to express emotions that are not typically "masculine." Research on men care workers in both the United States and Japan finds a similar tension between caring and masculinity (Harris and Long 1999). Interestingly, Bowers (1999) finds that men carers score higher on masculinity scales than men not providing care. She speculates that these men focus on the managerial aspects of care—the need to organize, take charge, and invest time and energy—traits all reflected on masculinity measures. Too, such scores could also represent a type of over-compensation, again as a way to justify what might appear to be "non-masculine" behavior.

Interactions with Race, Ethnicity, Class, and Sexuality

To a great extent, up to this point we have focused on gender, in part because research on other forms of social inequality, let alone their intersections, is rare. Still, race and ethnicity play important roles. For example, Whites are more likely to receive help from a spouse than are Hispanics or Blacks (Shirey and Summer 2000), a situation that may reflect the lower life expectancy of minority groups. However, support networks can vary across racial and ethnic groups such that others step in to provide care. Indeed, recent data suggest that more than half of the care workers for Hispanics are adult children, a larger percentage than among either Blacks or Whites. One in ten care workers for Blacks are adult grandchildren, and one-third are people outside the family, both higher proportions than among Hispanics or Whites (Shirey and Summer 2000).

Gender also interacts with class in distinguishing whether and what type of caring men do. Some studies have found that working-class men are more likely to do personal care than are other men, suggesting that they have fewer financial resources with which to resist this form of care. Among the employed men and women in the research reported above, Martin Matthews and Campbell (1995) found that there was a relationship between class and care for men, but that both working-class and highly educated (post-graduate levels) men were more likely to be involved in personal care than were middle-class men.

Race and ethnicity are also critical: While White, Black, and Hispanic men remain underrepresented as care workers, Asian men are almost as likely to be a carer as Asian women (National Alliance for Caregiving and AARP 1997)—though this last figure does not differentiate between primary and secondary care workers. In the paid sphere, women of color are most likely to be involved in direct, hands-on care of the old— who are predominantly White women (Glenn 2000, 1992; Diamond 1992). Old people of color are less likely to partake of formal care service or be institutionalized than are Whites, despite the fact that, for instance, a much higher percentage of Blacks than Whites suffer severe functional limitations (Dilworth-Anderson, Williams, and Cooper 1999). Why is this the case?

Other racial and ethnic differences also play a part. For instance, many minority groups appear to have more sources of social support available than do Whites. Among both American Indians and Blacks, family includes both blood and non-blood kin (Burton, Dilworth-Anderson and Bengtson 1992). Thus, we find that while kin, including the extended family, provide for elderly American Indians on reservations who need care, other members of the community also participate. As with other racial groups, women do most of the work (John 1999).

The notion of family among Blacks in the United States is much broader than that among Whites, and includes extended family members as well;

old Blacks are significantly more likely to receive care from grandchildren than are Whites (Peek, Coward, and Peek 2000). Family also includes many non-kin members of the community including fictive kin, who might include friends, neighbors, church members, and co-workers (Barker, Morrow, and Mitteness 1998; Taylor and Chatters 1991; Hatch 1991). In particular, studies show that church members provide more social support—both affective and instrumental, including financial—than might be expected (Barker et al. 1998; Lockery 1992; Hatch 1991). Thus, while children are important sources of social support for old Black women, church involvement decreases the amount of help received from offspring (Hatch 1991). Further, one in three Black elders receives care from "others"—those who are neither spouses, children, nor grandchildren (Shirey and Summer 2000).

Blacks' greater breadth of social support relates partly to the oppressive context in which they have lived in the United States; widening support networks and notions of family have been a means of survival (Slevin and Wingrove 1998). As a result, Blacks have more collectivist care work structures (involving two or more carers). However, this may be changing slowly as Blacks become more isolated by class (Barker et al. 1998).

Similarly, research conducted among four different Hispanic communities by Magilvy et al. (2000) reveals that family includes not only immediate and extended family members, but may also include others based on religious connections, or others regarded as "brother" or "sister." Care for their family members is a strong cultural value among Hispanic families, and Hispanic leaders are also more likely to receive care from grandchildren than are Whites (Shirey and Summer 2000). Hispanic elders are valued for their wisdom, including transmitting culture. Caring for elders is thus a strong obligation and value, and it is expected that employment opportunities will be passed by, if need be, in order to provide care. Among these communities, the strong desire to care for their own leads to lower incidence of institutionalization, so that Hispanic elders who go to hospitals are generally sicker than comparable Whites. In the face of economic difficulties and increased geographical mobility, families have employed "creative" means to help keep elders at home—spreading the care across family members, incorporating neighbors or others in their network, and the like.

Magilvy et al. (2000) also document the growing perception among these Hispanics that things are changing: Economic problems are leading children to leave the community and thus making it more difficult for them to care for elders; in addition, attitudes among younger folk are changing as well. For example, in Facio's (1996) study of older Chicanas, the majority of her respondents chose to live alone in order to preserve their independence. They placed great value on family networks but also struggled to maintain their own lives, apart from familial obligations.

This brief discussion of research on some racial and ethnic minorities points to the importance of not taking the family care of these elders for granted. While particular ethnic groups may be viewed as very family-centered, significant variations in family among groups, structural changes, and the passage of time may exert a strong influence on the extent to which elders can and do receive care within families (as well as their own levels of satisfaction with such care and with their lives) (Sokolovsky 1997b; Antonucci and Cantor 1994). In addition, glorifying the "familism" of some racial and ethnic groups ignores women's oppression within, for instance, Latino families (Wallace and Facio 1992).

Later in this chapter we return briefly to family diversity among the old. For now, let us note that we cannot just apply "what we know"—that is, knowledge based on the experiences of the majority—to another group. For example, scholars, who are predominantly White, "know" there is a hierarchy of care worker preferences wherein spouse is the most preferred carer, followed by adult child, with daughters being preferred over sons (Lawton et al. 1992; Alan Walker 1996). The last choice is, generally, a nonrelative. One would assume, then, that those nonrelatives who care for elders would also find it the least rewarding. They are not preferred and, according to traditional notions of familism, they are not expected to provide care. However, for the most part, this "knowledge" concerning both preferences and familism appears to be based on research by and among Whites. In examining care workers' appraisals of their activities, Lawton et al. (1992) found, first, that Black carers of demented elders were far less likely than Whites to be spouses. In fact, Black care workers were almost five times more likely than Whites to be a nonspouse and a nonchild, the "least preferred" choice. Yet, Black carers were as likely as Whites to report positive well-being. Even more, Blacks reported more favorable appraisals of their care working experience than Whites on several indices, including greater care working mastery, less feeling of burden, and greater satisfaction in care working, and perceived care work to be less intrusive on their lives.

Similarly, a focus on "traditional" family ties, including the preference for a spouse carer, obfuscates the situation of gay and lesbian old people. A heterosexist conclusion would be that old gays and lesbians are likely isolated, lonely, and without help when they need care. In the introduction, we discussed the wide diversity among gays and lesbians based on cohort and life course differences in addition to social location (Kimmel 1995). Taken together, these make generalizations difficult. Still, research has shown that old gays and lesbians do not seem to lack informal social supports despite their inability legally to claim a spouse (Berger and Kelly 1996). In fact, many old gays and lesbians do have children, and varying relationships with them. Further, although defining gay and lesbian families remains both difficult and controversial (Allen and Demo 1995), many old gays and lesbians are in long-term committed relationships. In addition, social support networks composed of some biological family members and friends constitute another family type. In fact, the strength of supports derived from "fictive kin" such as friends has spurred researchers to advocate redefining the concept of family to include "friendship families" (Dorfman et al. 1995; Berger and Kelly 1996). Thus, not only do old gays and lesbians not appear to lack supports, but understanding the existence and development of such "families of choice" may help us reconceptualize some of our ideas concerning care work, a topic we will return to later in this chapter.

Consequences of Care Work: Gender and "Caregiver Stress"

Most people not only devalue women's work, they also fail to acknowledge the costs to women. Although women might learn the skills of care work more than men so that their performance seems more "natural," they still perform work, however devalued (Glenn 2000). Societies tend to see women's unpaid labor in care work as relatively "low cost," because they ignore the difficulties and costs (Stoller 1993). People fail to consider the total financial costs to carers, for instance. Carers often take lower pay when their care work forces them to reduce employment hours or productivity. Towns receive less taxes, and workers face lower retirement income through their public plans or private pensions. People also ignore the psychological costs (Alexis Walker 1992) including the stress involved in managing emotions (MacRae 1998).

A recent review of studies on gender differences in care work reveals that female care workers report more anxiety, depression, physical strain and health problems, and lower life satisfaction than do men, and wives who give care report higher levels of depression than do husbands (Shirey and Summer 2000; Yee and Schulz 2000). If women are nurturers and have more "caring skills" than do men, then why are they so stressed?

For the most part, the many reasons gerontologists offer implicitly or explicitly point to gender relations. First, this gender difference could be due to what has been termed men's more "managerial style" of caring (Thompson 2000). Maintaining that this style has been devalued by an implicit bias toward women's modes of caring, Thompson notes "limited but suggestive evidence" that men approach care work as "work"; they seek "control" in the situation, attempting to provide care "in the most efficacious manner with the least engulfment" of the self (2000, 337). In seeking to care "for" the elder, men are able to separate caring for and caring about. They preserve themselves by withdrawing emotionally and taking time for themselves, maintaining outside interests. This "distancing from the demands of caregiving may well assist men temporarily to forget the heavy responsibilities and thereby reduce the distress of caring *for* and increase the perceived gains of caring *about*" (338).

This argument makes some sense but does not go far enough. First, some literature has suggested that men cope better because of their lower levels of connectedness to the person they care for, a suggestion Rose and Bruce (1995, 126) refer to as men's "coping better but caring less." They found some evidence that men are less distressed by caring for their demented wives in part because they could enjoy the accomplishment. They felt useful and able. By contrast, women appeared to grieve for the lost relationship. Rose and Bruce do not dispute the men's suffering or dedication to their care work, but note that

> we began to think of men's caring as a pet rabbit relationship. A pet rabbit's survival requires conscientious care; indeed its condition is a source of pride for its carer, and the well cared for pet, or rather its owner, receives much admiration. For women, the husband with Alzheimer's fails to become an equivalent pet, so they grieved. Their equally conscientious care . . . produced little of the real, if subdued, sense of pride that the men displayed. (Rose and Bruce 1995, 127)

Women did not find the same sense of comfort from providing care, perhaps because such care had always been expected of them, whereas for the men, such care was "extraordinary" and thus brought them attention and respect. In addition, the task of caring gains value when men perform it. Interestingly, the tasks themselves were seen as feminine, or at best gender-neutral; they were never seen as masculine. Thus even when men performed them, caring tasks remained women's realm (Rose and Bruce 1995). More recent research on care work performed by men in Japan and the United States confirms that husbands receive more praise and recognition for their activity than do women due to the perception in both cultures that the work is more "natural" for women (Harris and Long 1999).

Second, when Thompson (2000) asserts that men's style may be more "efficacious" and "professional/managerial" because of their work experience, he implies that women's labor, which often involves at least two "jobs," including paid employment, is less "efficient." Yet women in fact have to juggle far more tasks in many realms.

Third, the ability to take time for oneself is mediated not only by the ideology surrounding what gendered care "should be"—are the same standards used to judge men and women carers?—but also by the financial ability to take advantage of respite and similar services, or rely on the help of others in more informal networks. For example, Yee and Schulz (2000) conclude that many of the gender disparities found in studies of stress and depression result from differences throughout the care working process. Women are less likely to receive informal support from other family members or friends than men are. Overall, men appear to have larger support networks in such situations; sons receive more help from their spouses than daughters do from theirs. Differences in formal service support are not conclusive, though several studies have found men also using more formal services (Hooyman and Gonyea 1999; Yee and Schulz 2000). Carers who can draw upon more community resources, be they formal or informal, generally experience less stress (Neal et al. 1997).

Thus, it appears likely that men who do care work experience less burden and depression because of their generally more privileged position in later life. Generally, old men have more income at their disposal than do old women. This means that in addition to perhaps receiving more help from family, friends, and neighbors, old men may purchase more services that will aid in care work. In addition, taking on devalued work brings more esteem to the tasks themselves. As Rose and Bruce noted, to point to their privilege in no way devalues men's care work, dedication, or commitment; instead it demonstrates the ways in which such commitment and dedication may be differently expressed and experienced by men and women, based on gender relations.

At the same time, what are taken to be gender differences are likely shaped by the intersection of multiple power relations, a reality obscured by research that considers only gender. For instance, when we describe men's style of care work as "managerial" and more like their "work," whose work are we talking about? Embedded within this depiction is an image of a White, professional, heterosexual man, an image which surely leaves out the majority of men, never mind women.

Research on care worker stress among racial and ethnic groups is sparse, but it does point to important similarities and differences. For example, Latinas who provide care to demented elders appear to experience more stress and depression than Blacks, and similar levels as Anglos. Why? Some of the answer might relate to the fact that Latinos are at greater risk for specific diseases, such as diabetes, that present particular challenges to care; tend to become disabled earlier in life and with higher levels of disability; yet have less access to information about illnesses such as diabetes as well as health services (Aranda and Knight 1997, 344–45). In addition, Latino care workers themselves are in much poorer physical health than are Whites (Aranda and Knight 1997).

Different *aspects* of care work may also be the source of stress among various racial and ethnic populations. For example, in one study, Latinos seemed to be more bothered than Whites by performing tasks such as feeding or toileting, and dealing with "problem" behaviors, yet both groups reacted similarly to dealing with dangerous behaviors. Similarly, in another study, Blacks seemed more burdened by the provision of personal care, like toileting, while Whites felt more burdened by instrumental care, such as shopping or money management (Aranda and Knight 1997, 345–346). Finally, John et al. (2001) suggest that American Indian care workers may be more concerned about how stress influences the family or tribe than personal needs.

Further, the *expression* of stress may vary across gender and racial/ethnic groups. Exploring the experiences of Puerto Rican, Black, and White men and women carers, Calderon and Tennstedt (1998) find that while all groups report strain, they articulate it very differently. As a result, measures of stress may underestimate its prevalence among different groups. For example, even though the Whites cared for old people with the lowest levels of impairment, they expressed strong feelings of burden; White women were more likely than other women to express feelings of anger. Interestingly, Whites also had the smallest support networks. By contrast, the racial/ethnic minority care workers had larger support networks while also caring for more impaired old people. In terms of their experiences of caring, Puerto Rican women felt isolated by their care work while Black men and women felt their care work was very time-consuming. Both Puerto Rican and African American care workers, especially men, expressed frustration.

Along these lines, recent research on care workers for Alzheimer's patients uncovers the intense emotion work involved when one must "manage feelings"—in themselves and in the other (MacRae 1998)—and gives us some insights as to how social locations might interact in producing stress. Exploring this emotion work, MacRae (1998) shows that carers are aware of the "feeling rules" that govern interaction. That is, they are conscious of the expectations concerning how one ought to feel, or the range of emotions one has a "right" to feel in a particular context, and they experience stress when they deviate from these norms. Carers who fail to manage their emotions appropriately experience negative self-evaluations. Importantly, however, those who "succeed" also do so at a cost. By controlling or suppressing their emotions in order to cope, "they are at risk of becoming estranged from them and of perhaps even losing the capacity to feel" (MacRae 1998, 157).

Drawing from this research, we might ask: Do male carers experience less stress because they have greater latitude in the emotions they are "allowed" to feel? Or, because care work is not "supposed" to be a part of their identity, can they circumvent the guilt and consequent stress for not managing their feelings appropriately? How might such feeling rules vary by race, class, and sexual orientation, and in relation to different masculinities? How do expectations of care work among racial and ethnic minority groups vary by gender and class, and how might these also influence feeling rules?

Answers to such questions must also consider care work as a process, one that can be contradictory. It can be oppressive—stressful and entailing high costs in many ways; reinforcing gender inequities within families; and used to justify women's inferior position in society at large. At the same time, it can also be rewarding, generating connectedness and reciprocity (Abel 1991; Alexis Walker 1992). Because it is dynamic, care work can be either or both of these at different times or the same time and in varying contexts; it is subject to changes in meaning and duration.

Finally, underlying explorations of the stresses of informal care are notions about "family." As we have already noted, power relations influence what constitutes a family such that what may prove helpful or disruptive in terms of care work differs. Thus, for instance, racial and ethnic variations in family forms can shape how care work is performed and consequent sources and levels of stress. At the same time, cultural norms can be shaped very differently by the historical and socio-economic context. For instance, the restrictive immigration laws of the early twentieth century meant that many of the Chinese men now old remained single due to a lack of Chinese women in the United States and the assumption of intra-racial marriage (Amott and Matthaei 1996). As a result, they lack family and traditional sources of support and care, and have had to turn to outside assistance sooner than might have been the case otherwise. By contrast, many of the Japanese who immigrated in the early twentieth century were able to do so in family units. Consequently, they have been able to maintain cultural norms concerning family roles and care (Lockery 1992).

Similarly, while there are important differences between Blacks and Hispanics, to a large extent they have cultivated fictive kin and community in response to discrimination and its consequences. The potential disintegration of these systems also relates to their disadvantaged labor market position, and the need to relocate in order to secure jobs and their economic survival (Magilvy et al. 2000; Barker et al. 1998). Class mediates these experiences. For instance, research among Black care workers shows that those with higher incomes report greater burden than those with lower incomes, while the opposite is true for Whites (Lawton et al. 1992). This might well be related to the fact that if Blacks have to move in order to acquire employment, they lose social support even as income goes up. Research on Black and White women as carers lends support to the belief that Whites more often give care individually and Blacks collectively. For instance, that Black women tend both to have larger households and to maintain employment more than White women (Hatch and Thompson 1992) suggests family structures in which care work might be spread out across more members. Indeed, Blacks and Asians are more likely to report caring for more than one person than are Whites or Hispanics (National Alliance for Caregiving and AARP 1997).

The receipt or loss of social support and informal care networks also has gender implications. For example, the relatively high numbers of Black and Hispanic women who are widowed, poor, and in bad health and thus need care may result in even greater strain on their social support networks, creating the conditions for increased incidence of institutionalization (Lockery 1992). At the same time, Black men often rely on their wives to such a degree that widowhood or divorce can leave them isolated and more vulnerable to institutionalization (Barker et al. 1998).

The dynamics of the care relationship have been implied throughout our discussion, but the focus has been on who provides care and their experiences. The care receiver is present, for instance, when we discuss sources of informal family care. Missing, however, has been an exploration of the *experiences* of care receiving. We turn to this aspect of eldercare below.

Receiving Eldercare

Beginning with their impact on care workers, care recipients play a role in the gendering care. For instance, women's predominance as care workers results in part from recipients' preferences. Although elders in need of care take the specific situations of their children into account—who lives closest, seems most able to help, and the like (Peek et al. 1998)—they generally prefer to rely upon their daughters (Matthews 1995).

Recipients of care can also shape the experiences of those who nurture them, giving emotional or material "rewards" to the care workers. "Successful" care work depends in large measure on the responses of receivers; and many studies have documented the importance of the pride, love, fulfillment, or accomplishment felt by those doing care work, be they adult children or spouses, and regardless of gender (Kirsi et al. 2000; Abel 1991; Rose and Bruce 1995; Harris and Long 1999).

How one receives care certainly depends on personal and individual factors; but by viewing caring as a relationship, we see the importance of social structure (Gibson 1998). For instance, the negative sense of "inadequacy" (Reissman 1990) often associated with receiving care depends on our larger organization of age relations. Such negative assessment does not hold for the care that children receive. Different cultures, such as the Ju/'hoansi of Botswana, both demand and value help for the old, and do not associate it with diminished autonomy (Rosenberg 1997). In Japan, expressions of gratitude for care can stave off labels of "dependence" (Akiyama, Antonucci, and Campbell 1997).

Aronson's (1990) research among White, middle-class Canadian women demonstrates that receiving care is neither passive nor easy, especially since the social context may also be contradictory in itself—the need for care in conflict with the desire for independence, for instance. These women, none of whom needed extensive care, lived in a context defined by contradictory ideologies reflected in social policies: familism, in which people regard kin, particularly women, as the appropriate care workers; and individualism, which resulted in a strong need to "not be a burden" to one's children. Thus, frail elderly women may experience receiving care as simultaneously satisfying and warm on the one hand, and marked by shame and conflict on the other (Evers 1985, in Aronson 1990).

The old often speak of their fear of being "burdens to children." Many of the White middle- and working-class men and women in the study described in chapter 6 expressed this as their primary worry about their futures. Each of the White middle-class elders interviewed by Minichiello et al. (2000) stated they would rather depend upon others than accept care from, and thus burden, their children:

> My daughter-in-law said "I'll look after you." I said I don't believe in having anyone look after me like that. They've got their own lives to live. (Minichiello, Brown, and Kendig 2000, 265)

> I do know that I will try . . . [a home for the aged] rather than going to live with my daughter. I don't want to do that, I don't want to put any extra burdens on her. (Aronson 1990, 239)

> I think it's very important to people to have their own life and their own lifestyle, because children, no matter how good they are, don't appreciate having somebody to be saddled with. (Aronson 1990, 242)

This sense of "being a burden," and the bases for resisting it, varies by social location. For example, Aronson discovered that White middle-class women who receive care must "relinquish their lifelong identities as carers and nurturers and [hand] over responsibility for self-care to other, younger women" (Aronson 1990, 237). By contrast, the typical division of domestic labor might lead us to believe that similarly situated old men would not have the same difficulties receiving many of the same types of care that old women do. For example, having meals prepared or housework performed would not violate their self-identity as much. They likely did not perform these tasks before and do not see it as a part of themselves being given up or taken away. At the same time, old men might resist help with tasks they had previously performed that require more masculine demonstrations of strength or decision-making.

Racial/ethnic variations in feeling like a "burden" have not been extensively studied either. Still, we have seen that some minority groups have a more collectivist orientation; these may not define independence in terms of individualism so common among Whites. As a result, the same helping behaviors or need for care may not result in similar feelings of dependence. For instance, Hispanics see the old as having wisdom to impart, and a role to play, and so do not readily apply the label of dependence (Magilvy et al. 2000). The co-residence rates of old people with their children, quite prominent among Blacks, can enhance economic well-being for many Black families as well as provide aid with childcare (Waehrer and Crystal 1995). The families base their co-residence more on family closeness and connection than on economic need (Dilworth-Anderson et al. 1999). Both the economic and emotional ties may enhance Black elders' ability to receive care in a more positive manner; and research finds that people attach fewer negative assessments to help when help is mutual—both given and received (Roberts et al. 1999). For instance, Blacks expect that grandchildren raised by grandmothers will engage in care work for them when needed (Burton 1996). It appears likely, then, that the ways in which old people receive some types of care work vary with their race/ethnicity, class, and gender.

Resistance to receiving care varies in the same ways. The old White women in Aronson's (1990) study were marginalized by their age and constrained by ideals of appropriate behavior for "old women." As a result, they felt tensions and tended to hide their needs for support and security. Still, they resisted the potential assaults on their self-identity by trying to prevent their daughters from overextending themselves in the provision of care. In this way, they not only exert some control over the amount of care they receive, but they also might extract "satisfaction from their continued position in mothering and caretaking" (Aronson 1990, 239). In effect, by attempting to protect their daughters, they could still act in a nurturing and caring manner.

Although receiving help can be difficult, a number of factors can ease the receipt of care. We reduce the stigma when we do care work for old people universally rather than for specific groups labeled "dependent," or when we allow the old to control the way in which others help them (Reissman 1990). In this regard, Gibson (1998) notes that frail elders are in a vulnerable position, one that depends on the level of need for care; alternative sources of care; and the extent to which the services are at the discretion of the provider. Those with great need but little control over when, how, or by whom they receive care remain in powerless and vulnerable positions (Gibson 1998). Receiving care under such circumstances can prove difficult and leave one feeling burdensome and dependent.

Power relations have obvious impacts on such vulnerability. The economic resources that vary by race, ethnicity, class, and gender intersections influence all three dimensions. For instance, women more likely lack the financial resources that might keep them from having to rely on family members. While women outlive men in the United States, they also suffer more chronic conditions and more disability than do men and hence are likely to require some type of care. At the same time, however, women may have greater social resources than men, a situation which may help them receive care. Being able to afford appropriate medicines or aids—which may allow a greater retention of abilities—also influences the type and amount of care needed. And of course, a financial cushion will ease tensions caused by the economic strain of care working. Similarly, both social and economic resources influence the availability of alternatives for care, and the control one may have over when and how care is provided. The ability to pay for personal care, for instance, gives one greater say in how it will be provided. Likewise, having multiple care workers removes the need to rely on only one person.

Thus, the old who look for care from those outside of their families may be seeking greater control. These respondents may feel that family care diminishes their autonomy:

> Ironically they perceive the option of entering a formal care situation as the retention of their decision-making power, individuality and choice. However, talk about nursing home care is in reference to needs for physical, not emotional, care and there is an underlying assumption that when in a nursing home current social relationship networks will be maintained. (Minichiello et al. 2000, 265)

From the scant literature on lesbians and gay men, we also learn some constructive lessons about care options for the old. Gays and lesbians often cannot assume that they will receive support from their biological families, many of whom alienate anyone who comes out of the closet. As a result, they often learn self-reliance and skills that serve them well in old age. First, same-sex couples are less likely to adopt male and female divisions of household labor; both partners often perform both kinds of tasks (Berger and Kelly 1996). This reality may also prepare them to engage in care work with both greater ease and competence. Second, lesbians and gay men are often more aggressive about choosing their own caretakers. This coping mechanism has far-reaching consequences worth some discussion.

Kimmel (1995) notes the fear with which many people view advancing age, particularly in relation to being "old and alone." Such fears may be especially compelling for those without children. Whereas parents might say to themselves, "we need a guilt-obligated daughter, or daughter-in-law, to take care of us" (Kimmel 1995, 300), not everyone can default to unpaid women's work within the family. Indeed, "lesbians and gay men who do not have children must realize that care in old age is not automatic and plan accordingly." Many adopt a strategy of maintaining an age-mix in their friendships and plan care work arrangements as they age. Because "guilt . . . is not the most effective motivation for high-quality care at any age," Kimmel believes that there may be "an advantage to choosing one's caregiver, for the 'automatic' care by children is of no higher quality in general than the 'automatic' care of children by parents" (Kimmel 1995, 300–301).

We do not know how many people deliberately plan this way; but we do know that gays and lesbians enjoy levels of social support in old age comparable to those of heterosexuals. Kimmel's theory that necessity can spur planned care provides a plausible explanation as well as a suggestion for all of us. *Choice*—on the part of both care worker and care receiver—affects the receipt of care, which might not smack of the obligation and dependence often observed among heterosexual families. An eighty-five-year-old lesbian describes the situation:

> My family is very important to me, but I'm not very important to my family. It's not because I'm gay; it's because they have children and they're preoccupied with them. . . . I have friends who come by and cook me dinner every now and then and I have friends who take me to my doctors' appointments. These are new and younger gay friends. . . . [N]ow all these gay people are helping me. It's not my family that is taking care of me; it's my gay friends. They have been wonderful to me. (Adelman 1986, in Kimmel 1995, 301)

Until now, we have considered only care work in which the old are the receivers of care. An increasingly important type of care work in old age, however, involves that provided for younger generations. As we discuss below, gender, race, ethnicity, can class shape grandparenting in terms of levels and types of care work involved.

Care Work from Old to Young

Care work is intergenerational. Contrary to popular belief, the old give care to, rather than simply depend on, younger family members (Lockery 1992). Among some American Indians, an ideology of interdependence among extended family members *and* the tribe appears in studies conducted among the Potawatomi, located on Midwest reservations, and Pueblo Indians (John 1999). The old, grandmothers in particular, play central roles as teachers and childcare providers (John 1999). Similarly, old Black women serve as centers of broad kin networks in which intergenerational exchanges are common. Old women give support, services, and information to younger generations (Conway-Turner 1999; Slevin and Wingrove 1998). Hispanic families provide emotional and social support based on a network of mutual obligations across generations, and grandmothers are particularly obligated to engage in childcare (Magilvy et al. 2000; Facio 1996). Chicanos see grandmothers as integral members of the family, a position based upon their performance of gendered tasks within the family, such as taking care of grandchildren (Facio 1997). By contrast, while White men, for instance, often provide help to their children, their tasks, such as repair or yard work, are not as directly involved in care.

As we have noted throughout this chapter, then, gender differences in old age have been shaped by the division of care work over the life course. In old age this takes the form of eldercare but also childcare, through parenting and grandparenting. As we saw in chapter 6, it is not uncommon for the White, working-class retired women to have their children move back home after divorce or bouts of unemployment. These women were again engaged in providing care for their offspring. However, among this group, grandparenting is even more common; and, because of the rise in certain kinds of very involved care work, grandparenting has become a focus of research. Thus, in our discussion of care work given by the old to the young, we focus on the increasing levels of care work that grandparenting can entail.

Grandparenting and Care Work

A gender lens recognizes the diversity of parenting and grandparenting. And sure enough, although women's identities are often taken to be intricately bound up with their roles as wives and mothers, recent research suggests that a sizable minority of women do not "place exclusive emphasis on their maternal role or on relationships with offspring" (Roberto, Allen, and Blieszner 1999, 81). For another example, grandchildren tend to be closest to their maternal grandparents because their mothers are (Chan and Elder 2000). This generalization, however, does not tell us what such "closeness" entails, or how gender, race, class, or sexuality might shape grandparenting relationships. Thus, while Black grandmothers tend to have very strong ties to grandchildren (Conway-Turner 1999), this does not mean that Black grandfathers, as men, do not. In fact, research among rural old men also suggests that Black grandfathers provide more help and feel closer to their grandchildren than do White grandfathers (Kivett 1991). Looking at the intersection of social locations helps us understand how grandparenting occurs across generations, and what it means for those involved.

Our discussion of grandparenting focuses on those who are heavily involved in care work for grandchildren on a daily basis. Such grandparenting relationships tend to come in three forms shaped by social location. The first two include households headed by grandparents. The first includes the "pure" grandparent care-working households, where no other adult resides (Minkler 1999). Such households are also often referred to as "skipped generation families." Whether or not the grandparent has legal custody (an important issue, as custody allows grandparents rights to make certain decisions and be eligible for aid), this grandparent is still engaged in surrogate parenting. The second type includes grandparent-headed households in which the grandchild's parent may also reside. Following available research, we focus on these two types of care work. The third form of grandparenting relationship involves an increasingly important role as a daily childcare provider. The number of mothers in the paid labor force means that, for many, childcare becomes an important issue. As we saw in the last chapter, retired grandparents are often called on to provide such care even when they do not reside with the grandchild.

In terms of grandparent-headed households, it is sometimes difficult to know how many old people are involved, as grandparenting is a social role that people can, and often do, begin to play before they reach age 65. Thus, our discussion is complicated by the fact that the research we draw from does not always distinguish between grandparents based on age. In particular, younger custodial grandparents may still be working, a situation that creates additional problems for them. They must find childcare, if the grandchildren are young; and failing that may have to quit their jobs or reduce their hours in order to care for these children. As we show below, many of these families are poor to begin with, a fact that not only can make childcare prohibitive but also makes job loss or reduction all the more problematic.

Grandparent-Headed Households

As of 1997, 5.5 percent of all children in the United States live in a household maintained by a grandparent (Bryson and Casper 1999). This percentage has been growing rapidly, with the biggest increase being among the "skipped generation families." The number of grandparent-maintained households with no parent present increased 53 percent between 1990 and 1998, and in 1999, a total of 1,417,000 children lived in such households (U.S. Bureau of the Census 2000; Beltran 2000; Bryson and Casper 1999; Fuller-Thomson, Minkler, and Driver 1997). More than one in ten grandparents have cared for a grandchild for 6 months or longer; half of these continued care for at least 3 years (Fuller-Thomson et al. 1997). A full 10 percent report more than 10 years of care (Pruchno 1999).

As presented in table 7.1, nationally, more than three-fourths of grandparents raising grandchildren are women; 43 percent are grandmothers without a spouse (Fuller-Thomson et al. 1997; Bryson and Casper 1999). [3] Almost one-fourth (23 percent) of grandparent families are over age 65; another 29 percent are aged 55 to 64. Race makes a difference in all of this, of course. Although the largest group—almost half—are White non-Hispanic (46.9 percent), Black non-Hispanics (27.8 percent) and Hispanics (17.7 percent) are disproportionately likely to be caring for grandchildren (7.6 percent identify themselves as other, non-Hispanic). As many as one-eighth of Black grandchildren live with their grandparents, predominantly grandmothers (Pruchno and Johnson 1996). Nationally, Black grandparents have twice the odds of Whites of raising grandchildren (Fuller-Thomson et al. 1997); among those households headed by a grandmother only, just over half are Black.

Although one might ascribe much of this racial difference to the strong kinship ties among African Americans, class also plays an important role. Grandparent-headed households are disproportionately poor (Minkler 1999). Almost one-fourth of all such households live below the poverty line (Fuller-Thomson et al. 1997). Among skipped-generation families, the median income is only $18,000; 41 percent are below the poverty line or just above (Chalfie 1994). The likelihood of such poverty is also related to gender and race: Co-resident grandmothers are twice as likely to be poor as similar grandfathers. Further, more than half (57.2 percent) of grandmothers raising grandchildren alone are poor compared to only one in five (19.9 percent) similarly situated grandfathers. In addition, partly because Black grandmothers are more likely to have no spouse present (due to higher chances of widowhood and divorce), they are also more likely to be poor (Bryson and Casper 1999).

That grandparent-headed households are disproportionately female, Black, and poor is important for a variety of reasons. First, the contradictions within care work that mothers experience are also apparent in what Minkler (1999) terms the "profound ambivalence" with which such

---

[3] In our discussion, we include all grandparents involved in surrogate parenting, whether or not they are legal guardians. Grandparents often do not attempt to get legal guardianship (e.g., Beltran 2000).

Table 7.1

Characteristics of Grandparent-Maintained Households

	No Parents Present			Some Parents Present			
	Both grandparents		Grandmother only	Both grandparents		Grandmother only	Grandfather only*
% of all grandmothers' households	17%		14%	34%		29%	6%
Race/Ethnicity	Grandmothers	Grandfathers		Grandmothers	Grandfathers		
Women/Non-Hispanic	62.8	63.6	27.9	56.7	59	38.6	63.6
Black/Non-Hispanic	18.8	19.5	53.5	16	16.2	45.4	19.5
Hispanic	15.3	14.6	15.8	20.5	19.2	12.5	14.6
Other/Non-Hispanic	3.2	2.2	2.8	6.8	5.6	3.5	2.2
Age							
Under 45	14.8	11	6.9	22.9	16.9	24.2	11
45–54	35.2	23.7	34.1	42	38.4	30.1	23.7
55–64	36.4	38.8	36.9	26.5	29.9	25.4	38.8
65+	13.6	26.5	22.2	8.6	14.8	20.3	26.5
Marital Status							
Married, spouse present	100		0.9	100		4.8	8.6
Divorced/Separated			50.3			50.4	56
Widowed			36.1			32.9	29
Never married			12.7			11.9	6.4
Poverty							
Poor	14.4		57.2	10		26.9	19.9
Not poor	85.6		42.8	90		73.1	80.1

* Grandfather-only maintained households are too few to separate into categories.

Source: Casper and Bryson 1999, Table 2 and Figure 3.

grandmothers are treated. As she notes, grandmothers have both been praised "as 'silent saviors' and berated . . . for their perceived failure in raising their own children." Courts have often behaved similarly, "with judges in custody and child support cases not infrequently citing a grandmother's 'duty' to care for her family 'out of love,' and/or her 'failure' as a mother in rendering their verdicts" (Minkler 1999, 202). These women are also disproportionately members of minority racial/ethnic groups, such as Hispanics and particularly African Americans and this, in combination with their poverty, further influences their social policy treatment. The "deservingness" of such groups is at the heart of many debates concerning, for instance, whether such grandmothers should be exempt from the stringent time limits imposed on welfare receipt (Minkler 1999).

Similarly, the intersections of race/ethnicity, gender, and class also help explain the recent increase in surrogate parenting. That is, the middle, "missing" generation has been decimated by the social ills poverty creates: drug addiction, AIDs, incarceration (especially due to drug use), and the like (Fuller-Thomson et al. 1997). Being Black and female increases the likelihood of such poverty and these problems. For instance, AIDS is the number one killer of Blacks aged 25 to 44. Similarly, mandatory drug sentencing is one cause of the six-fold increase in women's imprisonment over the past 15 years, and grandparents are the surrogate parents for over half of the children left without mothers (Minkler 1999).

The Experience of Grandparental Care Work

While substitute parenting may have its rewards, it also produces considerable stress. Whether and to what extent a grandparent experiences more stresses or rewards is still open to debate. While many studies have documented negative influences on such life areas as physical or mental health or social contacts, samples have tended to be small, drawn disproportionately from disadvantaged populations, or procured through support groups for grandparents. At the very least, parenting at this time of life strains relationships with peers and spouses as well as expectations one had for "retirement" and their later years. As one White custodial grandmother poignantly notes,

> It's something that I've been trying very hard to overcome but I've been feeling . . . very hurt and self-pitying. . . . This is what we had planned and so forth, and it's just not fair for this to happen to us. And I'm not taking anything away from the children . . . but it's just a feeling that we have. . . . We

know now if we're going to have any of it, we're going to have to try harder, and there are some things which are just not going to happen. (Jendrek 1996, 303–4)

But our discussion of Sally in the last chapter also reveals that the change in lifestyle that unexpected childcare may entail is not entirely negative. Providing regular daycare means she lost the freedom she had anticipated having in retirement, but she also feels that having to get up to take care of the grandchildren is "good for me." Similarly, a White custodial grand-mother says

> I really enjoy doing little things with [my granddaughter]. We go out and play in the yard and do a little bit of yard work and play in the leaves. We go to the library . . . and I'm really enjoying it. (Jendrek 1996, 297–98)

To be sure, the types of rewards from grandparenting also reflect one's so-cial location. This woman does not appear to be living in poverty, and has a house to share and time for playing in the yard and going to the library. Benefits accruing to custodial care among other subgroups may take a somewhat different tone, for instance, broadening support networks such that one's future care is also insured (Burton 1996).

Stress also rises in grandparent-headed households if one is not a le-gal custodian, as this can involve high levels of responsibility without authority, or can enhance tension between parent and grandparent (Jendrek 1996). Lacking a legal tie creates other obstacles as well. For example, the grandparent may be unable to secure social services or financial assistance, or cover the grandchild/ren on their health insurance. By the same token, suing for legal custody also threatens family ties if, for instance, the grand-parents hope that the parents will be able to care for their child/ren in the future (Beltran 2000).

We must bear in mind different grandparenting types here. In general, those whose grandchildren live with them feel the larger impacts—both positive and negative. While day-care grandparents report that they have less physical and emotional energy, less time to get things done, have to alter their routines, and are more likely to be edgy than before, each of these consequences is more prevalent among co-resident grandparents. Day-care grandparents are also more likely to believe that grandparenting is fun (Jendrek 1996). Caring for a grandchild only part of the day appears to have different impacts than does full-time care. This partial responsibility may also help explain some of the gender differences in grandparental care work, a topic to which we return shortly.

Most research on mental and physical health outcomes finds that grandparents who raise grandchildren report higher levels of depression and poorer physical health than do other grandparents (Minkler 1999). White, custodial grandparents are especially likely to report feeling emotionally drained (Jendrek 1996), a situation which may reflect smaller support networks. In terms of social impacts, all three types of grandparenting can lead to decreased contact with friends among Whites, but this is especially true for co-residential carers (Jendrek 1996). Not having friends in a similar situation can also create problems. The ability to cope with the strains of parenting may vary when raising a child occurs "off-time"—at an unexpected time in one's life. Among White grandparents, friends are generally done with child-rearing and are in a different life stage, and they feel isolated as a result. By contrast, Black grandmothers are more likely to have peers in similar situations and thus experience less stress (Pruchno 1999).

Social isolation can also have an additional, racialized and class-based twist. That is, grandparents whose care work results from stigmatized conditions such as AIDS or drug abuse may also feel the direct or indirect sting of this label. Thus, both Black and Hispanic grandparents "have reported that the frequent failure of their communities and particularly their churches to openly acknowledge the extent of AIDS or crack use in their midst have contributed to a sense of isolation" (Minkler 1999, 209). Similarly, the general failure of social institutions, like schools, to recognize that children might not be raised by parents can leave a child or grandparent feeling "apart" because s/he cannot take part in "parents' night" activities (Minkler 1999).

As already apparent, gender affects the experience of raising grandchildren. Life expectancy differences make it more likely that grandmothers both will be alive to raise grandchildren while also being widowed; and women's positions as primary care workers reflects the gender division of labor in families (Fuller-Thomson et al. 1997). In most cases, grandfathers move into day care or surrogate parenthood as spouses. As a result, they have fewer responsibilities and less diminishment of their social lives than grandmothers have. This may be reflected in recent national survey data that reveal a small decrease in well-being among grandmothers but increased social life among grandfathers. The latter are likely to visit bars and taverns more than before, perhaps as an escape or simply because they believe that grandmothers should and will do the work. Grandfathers also appear to benefit more from the experience of custodial grandparenting, perhaps through companionship; by contrast, grandmothers who take the burden of care experience greater stress, especially early on (Szinovacz, DeViney, and Atkinson 1999).

Black and White surrogate grandparents do not appear to differ in terms of well-being, but this does not mean that they experience caring for grandchildren in the same way. Although African American grandparents may undertake such parenting under more difficult circumstances such as lower incomes, they are more likely to receive social support from others to aid their parenting (Szinovacz et al. 1999). Looking only at grandmothers, Pruchno (1999) also finds similarities in the experiences of Blacks and Whites. On the positive side, both groups derive satisfaction from their care work. On the negative side, care of grandchildren makes their paid work more difficult. Important racial differences also arise, however. Black grandmothers are more likely to be single, working, and have more grandchildren living with them. But they are also more likely to have peers in similar situations, to have prior experience with multigenerational households, and thus to experience less stress—just as we have seen in relation to eldercare among this group.

Among Puerto Rican and Dominican grandparents, norms concerning shared child-rearing and extended support networks result in assistance for surrogate parents. However, the number seeking help from formal services and from those outside the family suggest that such informal support falls short of meeting grandparents' needs. In addition, the high level of poverty among these grandparents (nearly all of whom are women) also suggests that social support networks can only do so much. Class shapes the performance of these roles (Burnette 1999).

Many American Indians give to the old a "cultural conservator" role, in which grandchildren live with grandparents for extended periods in order to learn more about the Native American way of life (Weibel-Orlando 1997, 149). Thus, cultural norms concerning grandparents—particularly grandmothers—make surrogate parenting easier for this group. The opportunity to be a custodial grandparent, while often resulting from instability in the parental household, can also be an advantage for American Indian grandparents (John 1999; Weibel-Orlando 1997). At the same time, the poverty among this group makes childcare responsibilities difficult.

The responsibility of grandparenting—especially among old women of particular class and racial/ethnic groups—comes at a time in which they are increasingly called on to engage in care work for spouses or parents

(Conway-Turner 1999). In chapter 6 we noted that women's experiences tend to be characterized as "serial caregiving"—women must care for both young and old but generally not at the same time. However, this notion rests, first, on the experiences of the numeric majority of women, who are White. Because significant caring for grandchildren or other relatives has not been a modal experience for most middle-class White women, the main concern of investigators has been with the possibility of caring for one's own children and one's parents at the same time. But substantial numbers of grandmothers, particularly old women of color, now shoulder care for grandchildren more than in the past. Their extended kin networks give them greater responsibility for the care of sick relatives and friends. As a result, the old women engaged in simultaneous care work, especially among those disadvantaged by race, ethnicity, and class, warrants concern and consideration.

Examining patterns of care work for the old and the young reveals the wide diversity in "family" throughout the life course and into old age. When we look at custodial grandparenting we see that, for increasing numbers of children, "family" involves a much wider network of relatives than the White, ideal-type "family" contains. We need to recognize these variations for many reasons. First, the rhetoric of familism ignores women's work and fails to describe the majority or even the "best" situation for old or young people, with its emphasis on individual families—especially women—as the best sources of care work. Further, this norm obscures not only differences by social locations but also the strengths of diverse family forms. Finally, prevalent myths concerning the dependence of the old fall by the wayside once we examine their care work and aid to others.

Discussion

In this chapter, we have used a gender lens to explore some care work experiences in old age. Our discussion has highlighted the gender, class, and racial/ethnic bases of such care work and hence the diversity in family forms in old age. Emotional and instrumental support is a two-way street that can and often does come from many, varying sources. To be sure, as the old become frail they receive care from "traditional" family sources, beginning with spouses. At the same time, many carers are distant relations or are not blood relatives at all; often, they are still considered family. Further, regardless of the relationship, the vast majority of both carers and receivers are women, a situation unlikely to change in the near future without alterations in the social bases for this gender inequity.

An understanding of care work in later life reveals many grandparents, and primarily grandmothers, who not only provide regular childcare, but who are increasingly involved in surrogate parenting—raising grandchildren for short or extended periods. This reality again underscores the diverse family forms in later life and the problems with assuming old age, and grandparenting, to be a time characterized by a White, middle-class ideal of leisure and love at a distance. Understanding the variations in family forms points to both unmet needs—such as financial assistance for low-income grandparents—and previously hidden sources of strengths—such as broad support networks. Indeed, research on old gays and lesbians documents both their adjustment to aging as well as strong family and friend networks (Dorfman et al. 1995; Friend 1991). Such research also serves as an important challenge to the assumption that being partnered is better than being single (Boxer 1997). In fact, recent research has shown that the widowed and never married have larger care work networks than do old people who are married (Barrett and Lynch 1999); unmarried, childless old people also have support available to them, with women still at an advantage in this regard (Wu and Pollard 1998).

A gender lens on elder care work broadens our understanding of the old as care workers and as care recipients. Understanding how social inequalities govern caring experiences changes how we view the "problems" and solutions associated with caring. For example, it would be a mistake for us to see the main source of stress in eldercare as occurring between (women) care workers and the old. Rather, "the primary division is between both carers and older people on the one side and the (patriarchal) state, which is failing to ensure adequate support for either, on the other side" (Alan Walker 1996, 281). In terms of policy, this assertion does not ignore "caregiver stress" but rather than pointing to the care working *relationship* as the *primary* site for intervention, it directs our attention to state policies that can establish viable alternatives to various aspects of care work. It tells us to look to underlying structures—such as inadequate and gendered social policies—to understand and ameliorate the negative aspects of care work, rather than individual-level causes and solutions (Harrington Meyer 1997), such as coping styles. In fact, solutions to care worker stress that do not alter structural arrangements ultimately serve to reinforce that burden. For example, Stoller (1993, 164–66) notes that the expansion of respite care and other services might relieve stress, but only in allowing women to cope a little longer than they might otherwise. In her words, these "bandaid approaches . . . leave untouched a division of labor which obligates women to assume responsibility for caring for others in the private sphere while at the same time limiting their access to resources within the public sphere."

Thus, old women's care work is intensifying as women's responsibilities continue to grow, but not for the reasons usually indicated. Although many people point to demographics—the fact that people are living longer and thus are more likely to confront disability while at the same time having smaller families and thus fewer children to provide for them—we now see the structural roots to this situation. Of critical importance are the value placed on care work in society and public responses to care, particularly through government policies (Glenn 2000; Hooyman and Gonyea 1999). Necessary supports to facilitate care in the public realm have not grown commensurate with the increase in need. Further, sensitivity to power relations allows us to see how the variations in care work experiences relate to lifetime inequities. For example, race and class differences across the life course come together in old age such that racial and ethnic minority women have higher rates of disability, and thus need care more than other groups. At the same time, they are more likely to lack access to formal care services and thus rely more heavily on family and social support networks (Hooyman and Gonyea 1999).

The *choice* to provide care or not—for women and for men—is critical to gender equity (Hooyman and Gonyea 1999). Among other things, such a choice would require that there actually *be* other options—within the community, through policies, that would insure equal access to care, regardless of power relations, and would not penalize women for not opting to provide care work. This would also require that care work be valued—not just verbally but economically (Glenn 2000; Hooyman and Gonyea 1999). Unpaid care work provided in 1997 is estimated to equal $196 billion, compared to $32 billion and $83 billion for home health and nursing home care, respectively (Shirey and Summer 2000). Yet, these dollars do not make their way down to care workers, directly or indirectly. If they did, women—or men—who do provide care would not be penalized by such outcomes as lowered retirement income. In addition, it would ensure that paid care providers are adequately compensated for their work. Both would signal a change in ideology that would assume that care work is important, should be supported socially, and should be shared by men and women (Hooyman and Gonyea 1999).

The ways in which care work appears to be more valued when performed by men also suggest an avenue for structural change. Drawing from researchers who ask why it is that we do not see the work men do as care work (Matthews 1995), we might think about ways in which we could both normalize men as carers while simultaneously raising the value of care work. That is, although we cannot maintain that men do as much care work as women do, by acknowledging, making visible, the work that men *do* in fact engage in, we might create conditions whereby they can also define themselves as care workers, and not see this as only the realm of women.

Finally, we want to emphasize the often unrecognized strengths of women's participation in care work for aging experiences. That is, women's lifelong care work can have negative economic and psychological outcomes but can also give women advantages in old age that exclusive focus on "victimization" would miss, including feelings of connectedness (Abel 1991) or larger support networks in old age including help provided by the grandchildren they helped raise (Conway-Turner 1999). Women's possession of daily life skills that are a part of care work can also help explain why widowers face a greater risk of institutionalization than do widows (Blieszner 1993). While widows' greatest source of vulnerability appears to be economic, old women also generally have requisite domestic skills, more confidants, and more diverse social support networks than do men (Wu and Pollard 1998; Barker et al. 1998). By contrast, men tend to rely on wives for both domestic labor and social connection. As a result, death of a spouse can sever instrumental and emotional support for men (Barker et al. 1998), making them more vulnerable to isolation and eventual institutionalization.

A gender lens on care work in old age thus broadens our understanding in important ways. Attending to diversity and power relations reveals the wide range of inter- and intra-generational care work and how these relate to different family forms. Gender, race, ethnicity, class, and sexuality influence the type, amounts, and overall experiences of the work involved, as both a provider and a receiver. A gender lens allows us to see the complexities of care work such that the old are not regarded as passive or as dependents, nor are all sources of disadvantage in old age seen as inherently negative. Ultimately, it challenges us to transform concepts and theories to be more inclusive. In this way, we can view diverse experiences on their own and also in relation to one another, linked to social inequalities across the life course as well as age relations, a topic we take up in the next chapter.

CHAPTER 8

A Gender Lens on Aging and an Aging Lens on Gender

In this concluding chapter we come full circle in a way that pushes us to question where we began. Our goal in this book has been to use a gender lens to see how this changes the way in which we see old age. This gender lens is grounded in feminist approaches that are sensitive to the intersection of power relations rooted in gender, racial/ethnic, sexuality, and class hierarchies. Consideration of power relations, the old, and ageism, however, leads us to turn the gender lens back on itself.

Our focus on old age has an impact similar to feminist scholars' earlier focus on women. That is, just as the latter led scholars and activists to see the importance of examining not just women but gender relations, so too has our study of old age led us to see that we must also place old people, and *age relations*, at the center of our work. Similar to gender relations, our notion of age relations contains three aspects. First, age serves a social organizing principle; second, different age groups gain identities and power in relation to one another; and third, age relations intersect with other power relations. An appreciation of the implicit ageism within our culture and scholarship points to the importance of examining the underlying age relations. In addition, just as we needed an examination of gender relations in order to understand not only women but men as well, so too do we need a focus on age relations in order to learn more about how all of our positions and experiences are linked to and rest upon power relations based on age.

One thread throughout this book has been an interest in ageism, and what a gender lens tells us about how various groups of old people experience this phenomenon. In this chapter, we use this gender lens to build on the discussion in chapter 2 concerning ageism in social gerontology and then examine the ageism in feminist scholarship. Despite the concern with old age in the case of the former and with power relations in the case of the latter, we maintain that both areas have incorporated ageism into their theories by not examining the old on their own terms and by not theorizing age relations. After turning the gender lens back on itself in this manner, we speculate about some of the ways in which considering age relations might change feminist theories, our gender lens on old age, and our understanding of diverse old people. We conclude by drawing on what we learned throughout the book in order to suggest new ways to approach the study of old age.

Social Gerontology, Ageism, and Age Relations

As we noted in chapter 2, a gender lens has continued to be absent from much aging research, even that dealing with old women. Newly published textbooks often do not mention feminist theories at all and talk about gender in more of the add-and-stir method (e.g., Cox 2001). Similarly, recent work dedicated to the theoretical advancement of gerontology (Wellin 1999) pays scant attention to feminist theories of aging (Cutler 2000).

At the same time, feminist theories and other critical approaches have raised researchers' awareness of the importance of diversity, such that some textbooks do not assume that the old are White, middle-class, heterosexual men (e.g., Hooyman and Kiyak 1999; Quadagno 1999), and some writers are explicitly concerned with diversity and the inequalities that shape aging experiences (e.g., Pampel 1998; Stoller and Gibson 2000). Ironically, however, most social gerontologists remain blind to/disinterested in power relations based on *age*, particularly in relation to how these might intersect with other social inequalities. To be sure, gerontologists recognize that societies tend to assign tasks on the basis of age. Still, only age stratification theory addresses resultant power differences and even here, age does not intersect with other power relations (McMullin 2000).

Age Relations in Theories of Aging

McMullin (1995) argues that theorists of aging have not challenged mainstream sociological approaches for their neglect of age relations. As a result, aging theories tend to adopt these dominant perspectives with their ageist biases intact; for example, they often still depict the ideal family "unit" as socializing agent and "haven" for family members. Thus, older families' "deviations" or distance from this norm—for example, children leaving home or childlessness among the old—appear as a problem (McMullin 1995).

Yet, research shows that most older couples enjoy the "empty nest" (McMullin 1995) and that childlessness need not present problems of support in old age (Barrett and Lynch 1999; Rubinstein et al. 1991). McMullin (1995) also notes that examinations of marital satisfaction in later life often proceeds along the same lines as research among younger couples, even though the bases for couples' feelings/assessments may shift. Finally, she maintains that family theories ignore other issues that are of perhaps greater importance to older families, including relationships with grandchildren and extended family.

Similarly, Kohli (1988) challenges sociological theorizing itself on the basis that traditionally it has mostly focused on the notion of a "work society" organized around the world of paid labor. However, the aging of our population means that our society now includes ever-increasing numbers of persons who have left the arena of paid work. Merely assuming continuity from work to retirement does not address this challenge. If, for example, people do maintain their class positions or activities, we need to explore how this occurs, and what class even means for the old. While some social gerontologists have examined such things as class position in later life, only a few (e.g., Estes 1991; McMullin 2000) have noted the necessity of reformulating the concept itself.

It is also apparent that gender, race/ethnicity, class, and sexuality intersect with age relations in ways that further challenge many existing central theoretical assumptions and demonstrate how such approaches fall short of helping us understand current realities. For instance, Arber and Ginn (1991a, b) take Kohli's argument concerning the centrality of paid labor further still, challenging these core assumptions of sociological theorizing for their relevance to women's lives, whose experiences, for instance, may be influenced more by unpaid labor within families. Similarly, as our discussion in chapter 7 suggests, the extent to which relationships with grandchildren become intrinsic to "normal" family life varies according to the intersections of race/ethnicity, class, gender, and sexual orientation.

Perhaps because social gerontologists spend so much time trying to ameliorate or contradict the vision of old age decline, they do not theorize old age as a political location—both on its own, as well as one that intersects with other social inequalities. In addition, the fact that social gerontologists have not theorized age relations means that, however un-wittingly, they adopt theoretical perspectives based upon midlife experiences that may not adapt well to studying old age. As a result, we lose much of what the old experience, and wind up implicitly treating old people as "deviant." As a consequence, and as we discussed concerning the effects of "adding in" women to theories developed to understand men, "adding in" the old to social theories developed on the basis of younger groups' experiences also renders the old deviant. We can tell whether and how they conform to these depictions, but have much less knowledge about their lives. We just know that they are more or less "different." Thus, even though social gerontologists study old age, they can inadvertently exclude aspects of the lives of the old from analysis by not beginning with their experiences and using these to broaden their concepts. Further, by not ques-tioning the age relations underlying much of their thought, social gerontologists implicitly treat old bodies as deviant and so reinforce age-ism. In order to illustrate these points we examine two specific examples of ageism within gerontological thinking. By revisiting the issues of suc-cessful aging and the mask of aging, we hope to expose how ageism undergirds even those theoretical perspectives designed to focus on old age itself.

Successful Aging

Gerontological theorizing tends to promote a notion of successful ag-ing which has at its central premise the necessity of staying *active* (Andrews 1999). As we previously noted, social gerontologists have, for the most part, turned away from the 1940s and 1950s emphasis on individual adjustment to old age. Still, the effect of those early investigations lingers on such that "active" adjustment to old age is promoted "as an antidote to pessimistic stereotypes of decline and dependency" and this active engagement has taken on the aura of a moral imperative (Katz 2000, 135, 137–38). Thus, the old must stay busy and "need to remain both physically and socially ac-tive" (McHugh 2000, 112). Of particular value in contradicting notions of dependence is productive activity, and many advocates for the old have therefore touted "productive aging" in particular. However, important but generally hidden power relations are embedded in this approach.

First, as we noted in chapter 2, the dictate to age successfully by re-maining active is ageist. It rests upon age relations that implicitly devalue the old in relation to the middle aged. It encourages us to define an old person "by what she or he is no longer: a mature productive adult" (McHugh 2000, 104), that is, someone of middle age. Of course, class, race, and gender assumptions about productive middle age are built into these depictions as well. The goal of remaining active is to show that one is not really old. In this sense, successful aging means *not* aging, not being *old*: "The unspecified but clearly preferred method of successful ageing is, by most accounts, not to age at all, or at least to minimize the extent to which it is apparent that one is ageing, both internally and externally" (Andrews 1999, 305). In light of the physical changes that do occur over time, many of the old must therefore develop strategies to preserve their "youthfulness" so that they will not be seen as old. As one old woman explains her strategies:

> "Well, I think, for me, the most important thing is not to be locked away with my own generation, and to be able to stay around all age groups, and . . . having mental stimulation and intellectual challenge is still important, still being able to drive my car, and I suppose also feeling useful. I feel useful in this household . . . and it's give and take and feeling as though I still count." (Miss Phillips, in Minichiello et al. 2000, 274)

The old, and their bodies, have become subject to a kind of discipline *to* activity (Katz 2000). In particular, research among rather well-to-do, White old people in a retirement community finds that "[p]roductive activity is the route to happiness and longevity; to live otherwise is tantamount to a death wish. Retirement communities, then, provide the ultimate script of successful aging, as seniors rush about as if their very lives depended upon it" (McHugh 2000, 112). This emphasis on productive activity means that those who are chronically impaired or who prefer to be contemplative are considered to be "problem" old people (Katz 2000; Holstein 1999).

Second, the command—and ability—to remain active is also conditioned by intersections with other social locations as well. To begin, there are multiple interpretations of "productive aging," and even those who advocate a "productive aging society" often recognize that this refers to more that just paid work. However, the dominant one equates it with paid work. Although Holstein (1999) only focuses on the gendered results of this depiction, many people are already disadvantaged in relation to paid work in old age. Women, people of color, and members of the working class may have intermittent paid work histories, making it unlikely they would secure any labor in their older years other than low-paid work. In addition, the diverse kinds of economic contributions of women and people of color, for instance, tend to be ignored at worst and devalued at best. And finally, the emphasis on productivity hurts the old as it can serve as an argument against continued social policies or benefits for the old. Those already disadvantaged in old age, then, face an expectation to work despite the low quality of available jobs, as well as an increased need to work to compensate for declines in or absence of benefits.

Third, to "fight aging"—and ageism—by promoting "productive" or "active" aging fits, of course, with our consumer culture (Katz 2000; McHugh 2000) which represents the other side of the production coin. Further, the images of the "active elder" promoted in marketing and advertising are themselves bound by gender, race, class, and sexuality. Perhaps this is most obvious in one of the most commercialized images, the marketing of Sun City, Arizona, and similar retirement communities geared toward "middle-class Whites with sizable pensions and large automobiles" (McHugh 2000, 110). The sorts of consumption and lifestyles implicated in this depiction of "'imagineered' landscapes of consumptions marked by 'compulsively tidy lawns' and populated by 'tanned golfers'" (McHugh 2000, 110), assumes a sort of "active" lifestyle available only to a select group: men whose race and class make them most likely to be able to afford it, and their spouses.

Mask of Ageing

In recent years, a "mask of ageing" theory (Featherstone and Hepworth 1989; Featherstone and Wernick 1995) has emerged in response to two trends. First, as we noted in chapter 3, a variety of technologies allow consumers to alter their bodies in any number of ways, including hiding many signs of aging. Second, old people commonly report feeling that their outer appearance does not reflect their inner youth (I may *look* old but I *feel* young). However, bodies are limited and their capacities to change are not endless. By contrast, the inner "self" is not similarly constrained. The "mask of ageing" results when bodies become less able to hide signs of ageing, and individuals are thus subjected to ageist attitudes and behaviors that contradict their sense of identity (Biggs 1997).

However, in positing that "a youthful self [is] trapped inside an ageing mask" (Biggs 1997, 566), this theory unintentionally may reproduce ageism itself. That is, the notion of a "mask" assumes a dichotomy of body and mind: "between what is shown and what lies beneath the skin" (Andrews 1999, 305) and a tension between these (Irwin 1999; Andrews

1999). The theory can reinforce this dualism—rather than seeing the language old people may use about "being young inside" as a reflection of ageism within the wider culture. This does not mean that we should not listen to the words of the old and place them at the center of our analysis. Instead, we need to go one step further: to situate these words by exposing the cultural contexts that shape them.

For example, interviews with those who are chronologically old indicate that in fact the negative cultural depiction of "old" has taken root. Thus,

> oldness . . . is not about chronological age, but about a state of being. . . . Once defined by the self or others as old, a person is then categorized as belonging to the negative stereotypical image of old age.
>
> Being old to the informants, then, is about loneliness, loss of things that were meaningful, being unimportant and irrelevant, or having no role. (Minichiello et al. 2000, 260)

These people see aging as a loss of activity, symbolized in part by bodily declines that are not culturally "acceptable":

> "If all those things that you enjoy are behind you and you're not enjoying the latter years of life because you're lonely, then I think you're old. My impression of getting old is physical frailty, or mental slow down." (Mr. King, in Minichiello et al. 2000, 259)

Mr. King's sentiments demonstrate the context in which people are aging. For him, as for others, "oldness" is in fact something to be avoided as it is entirely negative. Thus, the sense of denial of old age that is expressed in the words of old people reflects this reality.

Certainly, old people may speak negatively about their aging. But empirical research has not shown the old to actually feel like they are trapped behind an ageing mask (Oberg and Tornstam 1999). Importantly, we describe ourselves in terms given by our society (Oberg 1996); and theories should not report such sentiments by the old uncritically. By doing so, gerontologists ignore the fact that the old are part of a culture in which "old" has little, if any, positive content. In fact, because old is negative and because people generally assume old people must "feel old," elderly respondents will describe themselves as not old on those grounds: "'I know I look older, but I don't feel old. I haven't arrived at the feeling of feeling old.'" (Mrs. Smith, in Minichiello et al. 2000, 260). Furthermore, an ageing mask approach implies that old people rightly see their minds and bodies as separate parts of themselves, as though it was bad that bodies age, and good if minds do not. Such a theory implies that mind and body do not age together—as if mind did not have physical properties, or that physical changes did not affect mental powers.

This is the heart of ageism: We deny that we are aging, and when we are forced to confront it, we treat it as ugly and tragic. As Andrews (1999, 305) suggests, the mask of ageing theory is itself

> a manifestation of the very splitting Simone de Beauvoir identified: "*that* will never happen to us—when *that* happens it will no longer be ourselves that it happens to." Although I may look like someone that *that* has happened to, in fact I am not, for though you cannot see it, inside I am still young.

In addition to splitting the old within themselves, this also promotes a division of the old into two camps (Andrews 1999). On the one hand are those whom we value and accept because they have "aged successfully"; who look or otherwise act like the middle aged. Certainly race and especially class privilege make it possible to prolong this middle-aged façade. And of course, ultimately this is only a delaying tactic that will eventually fail, unless they die first. On the other hand are the chronically ill or frail, for example, who thus cannot "act" younger; those whose bodies show obvious signs of old age—gray hair, deep wrinkles, stooped posture; or those who might prefer the more contemplative or less "active" paths to personal growth.

People also use notions of inner and outer selves to deny stereotypes of old age by promoting a sense of continuity and "agelessness" that rests upon ageism. However, as Andrews (1999) warns, ongoing life is not "agelessness." Indeed, such a depiction denies the realities of aging bodies, our unique histories, and the value of the differences between young and old. Further, recent research among Swedish women and men fails to support the idea that the old see themselves as ageless (Oberg and Tornstam 1999). Andrews (1999) argues that a closer examination of the words of the old reveals a tension between continuity and change. She found that her respondents' "self-identities were both durable and dynamic" (Andrews 1999, 313). As she puts it, "Old age can be . . . a growing into ourselves. We are still the same people who we always have been, but we are more deeply so. This is not agelessness, but a radical reconstruction of successful aging" (Andrews 1999, 311).

In addition, regarding "old age" as a *mere* social construction also depends upon an ageist bias. Andrews observes that all life cycle stages are social constructions, but "there is not much serious discussion about eliminating infancy, adolescence, or adulthood from the developmental landscape. It is only old age which comes under the scalpel" (1999, 302).

Feminism, Ageism, and Age Relations

In chapters 1 and 2 we discussed the ageism that permeates our knowledge, our culture, and our daily lives. That this ageism appears among scholars should surprise no one. However, some might assume that those of a more critical bent, particularly feminist scholars, would be more aware of age-based oppression. Nevertheless, feminists are not necessarily any more attuned to ageism than are other scholars. Despite their attention to power relations, their work, for the most part, also ignores age relations. On those relatively rare occasions when they do mention age, they either avoid old age or fail to theorize age relations as a unique inequality. Indeed, age-based oppression is treated as a given, mentioned in a way that is meant to indicate some level of shared understanding that "we all know what that is"—a black box to be taken for granted rather than opened and understood. Such theories of inequality imply but never declare who benefits from the oppression faced by the old.[1]

Let us briefly consider the ageism within feminist scholarship. In order to accomplish this we take the gender lens with its foundation in feminist approaches and turn it back on itself. That is, we use this same sensitivity to power relations in tandem with our knowledge about aging to help us better understand old age and age relations. Thus, by including the importance of theorizing old age and age relations we can speculate about some of the ways in which this approach might transform feminist theories.

Historically, feminism has paid scant attention to older women's concerns. Among the reasons for this oversight is the fact that the women's movement of the 1960s was dominated by younger women (Arber and Ginn 1991a). Additionally, feminist concerns with women's productive and reproductive rights inevitably led to a concentration on the lives of younger women. Further, and perhaps much like the effects of White, middle-class women's racist assumptions for women of color, old women, faced with

---

[1] D. Gibson (1996), however, provides a partial exception by implying that the middle aged benefit by taking their experiences as the standard and thus treating the old as deviant.

the ageism of younger women, also felt unwelcomed (Arber and Ginn 1991a, 28), further ensuring that their issues were not taken up: "Ageism was branded onto the women's movement with the word 'Sisterhood.' When we accepted Sisterhood we . . . dismissed mothers and grandmothers as outsiders to the action. . . . Once we had accepted the brand of Sisterhood, we could not even see how we had dismissed and excluded older women" (Rich 1983b, 104).

Whatever the historical genesis that helps explain the lack of attention to older women's issues, it is also the case that, even in the ensuing decades, old women's concerns have still not come to the fore. Some two decades later in 1985, activist Barbara Macdonald, then over 65, sought to address her exclusion from the Women's Movement at a national Women's Studies conference. According to Browne (1998), Macdonald tried to get attendees to see and confront their ageism. Maintaining that ageism is a critical feminist issue, she accused younger feminists of stereotyping old women into familiar dichotomies: either weak or strong; childlike or wise; "cute" and funny or boring; sweet or cantankerous. Whether they viewed the old with pity or with honor, she noted that none of these depictions are based on the diverse reality of old women. Despite her speech, however, little has changed since 1985, and the ageism in the women's movement is reflected in the lack of feminist theorizing on old age or age relations.

Typically, feminists' focus on younger and middle-aged women, and early work on "the life cycle" rarely includes women over 65 (Rose and Bruce 1995). More recently, discussions of menopause have emerged as aging feminists themselves faced this event (e.g., Greer 1991; Pogrebin 1996). For example, Friedan (1993) provides an analysis of the medicalization of menopause and how the money to be made by treating menopause as a "disease" has lead to the widespread attention that this "problem" has received. This medicalization represents a step away from the feminist ideal that women not be defined by their reproductive functions.

As useful as such analyses of menopause can be, however, they fall short of providing examinations of old age. For the most part they equate menopause with the outer limits of "generation" (Rose and Bruce 1995, 114–15) and with the upper limit of "old age." More recently, some concern has centered on care work (Cancian and Oliker 2000). By contrast, care receiving has been virtually ignored—a telling omission.

In theorizing bodies, some feminists have discussed bodies in relation to aging. Generally, such work focuses, however, on either menopause or on body projects geared at helping one "pass" as young. Consequently, attention is again centered on middle-aged or "young-old" women. Old women—for instance, those over age seventy, let alone those not White, middle-class, and heterosexual, have little to do with such expensive cosmetic overhauls. By contrast, old women's body projects, pertaining more to matters of health, receive little attention in feminist thought. Similarly, old women's sexuality is widely ignored. Finally, the work that does discuss bodies or sexuality retains the middle-aged bias in terms of physical appearance or bodily function. Women in their seventies, eighties, nineties, and older—some frail, some not—remain out of sight.

Feminists have argued for the incorporation, and not just addition, of women's experiences. The transformation of theories, feminist theories included, requires that scholars not just "add" age on to gender hierarchies; gender inequities "are *both* patterned throughout the life course and are related to age" (McMullin 1995, 37).

There is some irony then in the fact that feminist theories have, for the most part, assumed but not theorized age relations. At best, age relations are "tacked on" in a rather commonsensical way to their list of oppressions. It has become, in effect, the "great et cetera," at the end of a string of listed inequalities such as gender, race, ethnicity, class, and sexual orientation. Sometimes age appears at the end of this list. More often it does not.

Until very recently, the only feminists who questioned ageism were among the most marginalized: lesbian feminists who have questioned the use of the term "older" instead of "old"; who have challenged the ageism within the lesbian community; and who have challenged exclusion from the Women's Movement (Copper 1986; Cruikshank 1991; Macdonald 1983; Rich 1983a). What is noteworthy is the general silence by which most feminists have greeted these charges, a response that powerfully suggests discomfort or indifference. At least challenge shows some sign of being heard, of being important enough to even warrant response. The invisibility of old women in general, then, appears to be no less the case among feminists (Arber and Ginn 1991a).

The dearth of attention to old age cuts across feminist frameworks, even those that might seem more open to inclusion. For example, feminisms that explicitly rest on notions of "interlocking systems of oppression" such as Black feminism (e.g., Collins 1990) and multicultural feminism (Baca Zinn and Dill 1996) tend to ignore age relations too—though sometimes they do consider old women and their positive contributions. Liberal and cultural feminists also ignore old age despite the understanding that we cannot speak of women as a universal category; and radical feminists ignore the sexual matters facing old women in the workplace as well as at home, both during and after menopause (Browne 1998). While Friedan (1993) and Greer (1991) have written more about aging as they themselves have grown older, they are among the very few; and neither actually theorizes old age or age relations.

Thus, the ageism that leads us to ignore age relations suffuses our culture and our scholarship, and feminist scholarship is not immune. As Rose and Bruce (1995, 115) state in explaining the shortcomings of feminists approaches, "feminism, unaware of its own 'race,' able bodiedness and age, had in its desire to cease to be the Other constructed Other Others." Put differently, feminists who continue to be unaware of their own privileges based on age (i.e., being "not old") also render old women deviant. The invisibility of their privilege blinds them to the oppression that old women face, and that, ironically, they themselves will face. Indeed, it is this last point that makes ageism different from other systems of oppression, and presages our discussion on the importance of theorizing old age and age relations, below.

Theorizing Old Age

Does old age, based on age relations, constitute a unique form of oppression? Few theorists have addressed this question, but the general consensus among those who have appears to be affirmative.[2] As we have shown, the old are not homogenous. For instance, if we focus on the old we see that it matters if you are an old *woman* or an old *man*. By the same token, when we focus on women, we find differences between the experiences of *young* women and *old* women. What we are saying is that age matters. Old age is a unique time of life; "many older people are not just like middle-aged people, only older" (Holstein 1999, 368), nor are they treated just like middle-aged people, only older. As should be apparent by

---

[2] Irwin (1999) argues that what matters are life course processes rather than life course divisions into what she refers to as youth, independent adulthood, and old age. While a discussion of her argument is beyond the scope of this chapter, we believe that her emphasis on life course processes does not differ substantially from the processes involved in reproducing other forms of inequality. Further, the differences she points to between age relations and gender and class hierarchies—the two forms of inequality she discusses—do not detract from the impact that old age itself has on loss of power.

now, ageism toward the old is a reality and does not simply represent a slight change from when people were middle aged. Because one does not arrive at old age devoid of race/ethnicity, class, gender, and sexual preference clearly one's old age is shaped by these particular social locations. Still, old age does in fact confer a loss of power, even for those advantaged by other social positions. The "old" jokes made about President Reagan at the height of his political power are one public indicator of this, as is the ideological disdain with which old age is held in general. Thus, we agree with McMullin (2000) who maintains that, while gender and other relations influence old age, age relations carry with them an additional, unique form of oppression that intersects with gender, race, ethnicity, class, and sexual preference.

Certainly, the variations in when one is seen as "old" relates to the intersections of various social locations. At the same time, if a well-to-do white woman can afford plastic surgery in order to make herself look younger, her life is still shaped by ageism. In other words, being able to "pass" still implies that there is a form of oppression she is trying to avoid. Her actions imply the realization that she will be treated differently—excluded—if she looks old. The same is true in how people assess the "value" of those who have a physical condition that cannot be easily hidden. That is, an old person whose arthritis is disabling is evaluated negatively (Minkler 1990), as not having "aged well." Thus, to argue that old age and age relations do not constitute an independent form of inequality ignores several realities. First, bodies grow old. Second, the old confront unique forms of exclusion. Third, the old find themselves in unique circumstances; for example, the experience and consequences of widowhood is different early versus later in life.

We tend to not see the importance of age relations in part because we are privileged when we are "not old"—even if we are disadvantaged in other ways. Often, it is when we begin to lose privilege that the importance of age relations—slowly or suddenly—becomes apparent. Old age can even override other marginal statuses. For example, an essay by Barbara Macdonald, a lesbian activist in the women's movement, makes this point. She describes how her life had changed when, at age sixty-three, she met her present partner and moved to a new city:

> Again I was outside, again I was 'other.' Again I lived with the never-knowing when people would turn away from me, not because they had identified me as a lesbian, since I was no longer thought of as a sexual being, but because they had identified me as old. I had lived my life without novels,

movies, radio, or television telling me that lesbians existed. . . . Now nothing told me that old women existed, or that it was possible to be glad to be an old woman. Again the silence held powerful and repressive messages. Again I had to chart my own course, this time into growing old. (Macdonald 1983, 5)

This quote suggests a number of important issues. First, being old is a different and unique oppression. Certainly, the experience of this oppression may have a familiar ring to it as in the case of Ms. Macdonald who has felt before the silence that often accompanies marginal status. Second, how and when we lose privilege is intimately tied to our race, class, gender, and sexuality. Third, in trying to understand age relations, it is important that we begin with the experiences of those who are oppressed: the old.

The Importance of Understanding Age Relations

Age relations are unlike race/ethnicity, gender, and class in critical ways. Age is *fluid* and thus the same individual can be advantaged or disadvantaged by age over the course of the life-span. Certainly, other social locations can be malleable, too. That said, such changes are, in fact, relatively uncommon. By contrast, we all must age or die. Where individuals stand in relation to old age, then, must change, whereas other social locations may never change. Everyone must get old (or die) and when this (becoming old) occurs varies by the intersection of other power relations.

The fluidity of age relations in an individual's life reveals the social construction of old age in ways that differ from the construction of other social locations. Thus, those whose advantage keeps them unaware of their privilege and how power relations work for them throughout their earlier lives may respond differently to the loss of privilege as they grow old. Those whose lives have been most shaped by advantage may be most surprised by a loss in power, even if this decline is softened by economic privilege. As a result, they may come to see how precarious their position actually is, and power relations may become more apparent. This consciousness may provide the potential for change. By contrast, those who have been disadvantaged in their earlier lives and have faced relative powerlessness are often aware of their lack of power and may actually deal with some aspects of growing old more easily as a result (Slevin and Wingrove 1998). Even if they had not considered the disadvantages that accrue to old age, they will have dealt with powerlessness before.

These differences between age relations and other oppressive relations suggest the emancipatory potential of understanding age relations. The fact that age is fluid, and that everyone will grow old or die means that ageism is the *one* oppression that we will *all* face. Thus, an understanding of age-ism, if coupled with an exploration of the underlying age relations, can help us understand other social inequalities (see also Browne 1998). Since ev-eryone will eventually experience it, it can give insight to those who have never been really conscious of their own or others' privilege or oppression. Moving from a more privileged status—from "not old" to "old"—entails a loss of power that is eventually apparent. Rich (1983a) describes this loss of privilege in a very concrete way, using as an example a quote taken from Matthews' (1979) interviews of old women: "'You know about young people. . . . Go over here to Kmart and they take up the whole sidewalk. And the way they look at you, they wouldn't get off that sidewalk. You have to go around them'" (Matthews 1979, in Rich 1983a, 61).

Because age relations differ from other power relations in this regard, it is possible to also think about the ways that we see/feel ourselves losing privilege, and when and how that occurs. Much of this is in relation to the body. First, we can see privilege dissipating in relation to visible physical signs of aging. These outward signs both strike and matter to individuals at different times in their lives based on the intersection of power relations. For example, for women, depending on their race, class, and sexual orien-tation, physical signs (such as gray hair or wrinkles) will have a negative impact sooner. Further, their ability to forestall such signs also varies by social location. By contrast, gray hair for a white, middle-class, heterosexual man may cause him to be viewed positively—he may be see as "distin-guished." Vary his race/ethnicity and class and this evaluation may be radically altered.

What becomes apparent in such an analysis is how we come to pass into marginal status that we ourselves actively and obviously construct. That is, no matter who we are, and no matter how privileged, to the extent that we reproduce age relations in our daily lives, we also shape our own future oppression. For all these reasons, then, it may be that enhanced pos-sibilities for social change rest on listening to the old, and understanding their oppression and how this intersects with other inequalities.

Finally, we need to consider what we mean by age relations. That is, when we talk about ageism, do the "oppressed" include both the old and the very young? Each group faces discrimination, but in different ways. As we've noted, we all become the "other" if we live long enough, and we never transcend that status. This fluidity of age relations means that the young experience a discrimination fundamentally different from the old: youth is seen, even by the majority, to be temporary, almost as a rite of passage to attaining power. The young are certainly constrained in certain ways but, because of their status as "future adults," they face eventual liberation. Indeed, one can also argue that because youthfulness is so highly valued in our culture the oppression that the young may experience is tempered in important ways by the positive regard in which being young in and of itself is generally held. By contrast, for the old (and other oppressed groups), the exclusion is permanent; they are marginalized as "forever other."

Age Relations and Social Inequalities: Freedom and In/Dependence

At the center of much theorizing about social inequalities is a concern for equality, often assessed by reference to notions of independence and freedom from exploitation. By not considering the critical role of age relations in shaping life experiences, a gender lens approach falls short by not exploring comprehensively the myriad realities that constitute and shape oppression, emancipation or even empowerment. Attention to the notion that independence/autonomy is a critical component of liberation/freedom allows us to see the ways in which dependence—lack of independence—is structured by the intersection of age relations with other social inequalities. In the following sections, then, we will suggest some ways in which considering age relations might broaden our understandings of such things as freedom and dependence in just a few areas often taken to be central to feminist theories and a gender lens: sexuality, family, and wage work and in/dependence.

Sexual Exploitation versus Cast-offs

Many feminist scholars begin with women's experiences of objectification and exploitation by men. As a result they focus their theories and actions on breaking the dependence of women on men: as sex workers, as wives, as targets of sexual aggression. For instance, the issue of voluntary plastic surgery highlights the patriarchal sentiment that aging means decline and that women, in order to remain attractive to men, must actively resists signs of old age. However, feminist considerations of plastic surgery often ignore the ageism within it. That is, recognition of the gendered double standard that requires women to remain youthful longer than men still ignores the fundamental ageism inherent in the dictate to "remain young." Missing is a critique of looking old itself, and why "old" is viewed negatively, especially in women. Thus, much of the argument against such surgery centers on its male-defined nature rather than also recognizing that aging *itself* has been male-defined and constitutes its own political issue for feminists to consider.

Given the negative sexual imagery and (lack of) power of old women, a more salient issue than sexual exploitation for them might be that of being *cast aside*—of being invisible altogether. Such invisibility is not only in relation to men, but to women as well, including younger members of the Women's Movement and lesbian communities (Holstein 1999; Copper 1986; Macdonald 1985). The nature of this invisibility calls forth a different set of issues and dependence than that experienced by younger women.

The sexualization of women occurs not only at the intersections of race, class, and sexual preference, but also age. This means that feminists need to attend to the variety of ways such objectification occurs and to the critical role of age in this process. Although feminists have noted the growing invisibility of women as sexual beings through the aging process (the disappearance of the male gaze, for instance) this recognition falls short of putting old women's sexuality at the center of theorizing. How might our theories change if we explore the lives of old heterosexual women who are "interested" in men, who still see themselves (or might want to) as sexual? These women are not the same as middle-aged, post-menopausal women. The latter, for example, may find menopause freeing and allow for greater sexual expression. They may still be seen as sexual, at least to a degree. But are eighty-year-old women seen this way? By whom? Themselves? How is this similar or different by race/ethnicity, class, or sexuality? For example, why is it that many Black retired professional women appear to have an appreciation for themselves as sexual beings, in contrast to similar White women (Slevin and Wingrove 1998; Wingrove and Slevin 1991)?

Age relations intersect with other social inequalities to shape old women's de/sexualization. For instance, younger women benefit from this "casting aside" of old women, in much the same way that white women have benefited from the subordination of women of color (Hurtado 1989). Younger (i.e., "not old") women are relatively advantaged by their ability to be sexual partners and to align with those with power—men, especially those with class, race, and heterosexual privilege. Depending of course on their race/ethnicity, sexual orientation, and class, younger women may also benefit from the depiction of old women as less/undesirable, as this would enhance their opportunities with privileged men.

In relation to sexuality and gender identity, feminist approaches might also begin asking how taking age relations and old age into account would redefine notions of femininity and masculinity, especially in relation to bodies. What happens when natural, age-related changes in bodies not only affect appearance, but also strength? What is the impact of decreased mobility or less common changes, such as the loss of ability to walk? While some feminist approaches already consider masculinities and femininities (e.g., Connell 1999), such questions would further broaden notions of gender identity. For example, in old age femininity and masculinity might encompass different forms of expression beyond the typical ideas about appearance for women, or performance for men. Indeed, it is possible, as we suggest below, that for some old women, femininity may be more about "doing"—for example, performing feminine tasks, such as housework—than appearance. If we consider age relations, one question we might ask is, who benefits from these changes, and how?

Family

Although we hear about differences between "second" and "third wave" feminists, these "generational" differences still refer to those middle aged and younger. Within these debates, we find little consideration of women (or men) in their seventies or eighties, whose ideas about "family" and "liberation," for instance, may be quite different. Women of color have long maintained that the White feminist insistence on family as a source of conflict (Hartmann 1981) may not adequately characterize their experiences (e.g., Glenn 1985; Thornton Dill 1983), and feminist approaches to family have become more nuanced as a result. Now, if we take age relations seriously, we begin to question much of what feminists have theorized and advocated in terms of "freedoms" in the workplace and family.

For example, concerns that center around childbearing years and young married life—while they influence later-life situations—are almost meaningless to many old women. Furthermore, other issues still unexplored, may emerge with a shift in focus. For instance, how concerned are old women about gender differences in families when, first, so many are widowed? What are the concerns of widows? Second, what of those who face condescension, loss of autonomy, or abuse at the hands of their children rather than parents or spouses? A wide range of well-intentioned ageist behaviors can limit independence "for their own good." Think, for instance, about a woman of means who spends her money on a man—taking him on a cruise, going out to nice dinners, and the like. Such behavior in a middle-aged woman might draw scorn from relatives and friends (for the inappropriate enactment of gender if nothing else). However, an old woman who indulged herself this way could face legal intervention as children move to declare her "unfit" and seize her assets. Children can also engage in "infantilization" (Arluke and Levine 1984) in which they treat the old as little children and, as a result, lead to them to a greater dependence.

An additional example concerning the impact of age relations can be seen in the division of domestic labor. Many middle-aged (and younger) women may define themselves in traditional terms and say that they prefer to engage in domestic labor rather than having to bear the burden of labor market activity. Thus, women's performance of the vast majority of domestic labor in old age might appear to flow from "traditional" preferences that have little to do with age. Yet, the bases for such work may differ in ways that remain hidden if we do not examine old women more closely. To be sure, such things as food preparation are an integral part of continued feminine identity among old women (Howarth 1993). In addition, however, the preponderance of widows in later life may also mean that some married old women might not experience the unequal division of housework as "oppressive," because they feel lucky to have partners and spouses, or lucky that they the physical ability to work. For old women in an ageist society, whose appearance and sexuality might have lost their currency, any signs of "femininity" and "productivity" can be precious indeed. Still, this ideology related to productivity might be especially oppressive to old women for many reasons, including the fact that, for some this will be the first time in their lives that they are actually free from paid labor as well as domestic labor related to child-rearing (Holstein 1999).

As always, other social inequalities shape the picture presented above. For example, Glenn (1999) discusses some of the ways that women of color were called upon to perform the more difficult or trying aspects of reproductive labor so that White women could be freed from these tasks in order to pursue other, more desirable activities. In a similar manner, we can say that age relations interact with other social inequalities to create situations wherein grandmothers may be called in to care for grandchildren so that their mothers may pursue paid labor or other activities that carry greater social status. In this way, younger women benefit from the exploitation of their elders. Indeed, the "superwoman" may often exist to the extent that she can count on the unpaid labor of mothers/mother-in-law. Just as the "cult of domesticity" for White middle-class women depended frequently upon the exploitation of women of color, so too the "career" woman (who may also be white) with a family may depend on the unpaid labor of an old woman.

To be sure, exploitation through grandmothering may have different bases depending upon the intersection of social inequalities. The need for and extent of such care varies, as we saw in the last chapter. Still, while they may enjoy caring for grandchildren, the grandmother role is also confining (Browne 1998; Facio 1996; Rich 1983b). Among other things, it maintains her position of servitude to others within the (patriarchal) family. It maintains gender relations within the family by reinforcing women's status as domestic laborer. But she is also exploited based on her age; grandmothers' unpaid labor benefits other family members (Laws 1995, 116). Because old women might look forward to greater freedom, and not increased childcare, at this time in their lives, they may resist too much grandmothering. For example, Facio (1996) found that Chicana grandmothers employ a number of strategies to resist the obligations of child care expected of them in order to gain some independence and freedom. Overall, the characterization of old women as grandmothers—perhaps the only positive way we see old women—is problematic: "Each time we see a woman as 'grandmother,' we dismiss the courage of her independence; we invalidate her freedom. We tell her . . . that her real place is in the home" (Rich 1983b, 105).

Finally, our discussion of grandmothering suggests that of greater concern than the gender inequality of housework in later life might well be the gendered nature of care work in old age and how this intersects with age relations. Especially in combination with other social inequalities, gender and age structure both the giving and the receiving of (formal and informal) care. Greater attention to this area can expand further notions of family; power relations across generations previously ignored; gender and age-based differences in the receipt of care; and the value of each.

Waged Work and In/Dependence

What happens when we talk about groups permanently out of the workforce? We might address the issue with the concepts of productivity and dependence. People tend to regard those not in the labor force as "dependent," as opposed to wage workers, who are "productive." This logic underlies the "dependency ratio" that policy analysts use to calculate a society's economic burden. The measures for this figure vary but usually define dependents as those either younger than 19 or over 65. This ratio is meant to reflect the proportion of producers to dependents, and thus how much "burden" a society must bear.

Public debate over such "dependence" and "burden" reveals unarticulated age relations in the different meanings attached to the old and the young. Although the United States sustained a higher dependency ratio in the 1960s than that projected for 2050, the latter predictions have led to a public outcry about the burden of the old that was never heard at the height of the baby boom (Calasanti and Bonanno 1986). And this despite the fact that a child under age five is far more likely to be "dependent" than a person aged sixty-five to seventy. Neither did the large numbers of women who were "dependent" (i.e., without incomes of their own) prior to the 1960s raise public eyebrows. Apparently, only the "over sixty-five" category can cause such public dismay.

Feminist scholars have long been concerned with issues of dependence and support; but only with a grasp of the intersection of age relations with all of the other inequalities can feminist theory understand the current situation. For example, feminists have focused on women's economic dependence on men or the state (D. Gibson 1998) that both results from and reinforces gender inequities in domestic labor as well as pay inequities in the marketplace. But in old age, this dependence changes. Both men and women remain involved in relations of distribution, in ways distinct from those of their younger lives. That is, many old men occupy a relation to the state generally regarded as feminine: They become dependent upon economic resources distributed by the state. Age-based power relations among men can leave some in good positions in terms of, for example, pensions based on race/ethnicity, class, and sexuality. At the same time, they may still be harmed by social policies that target the old. Take, for example, the debate over Social Security reform, which we touched on in chapter 6. Such policy reforms disproportionately affect some groups of old more than others, and discussions vilify all old people by including such politically loaded factors as "dependence," regardless of their social locations. In this way, age relations intersect with other forms of oppression to not only differentiate among groups of old but also unify them in a way unexplored by feminist theories or an age-blind gender lens.

A consideration of old age and age relations suggests some expansion of feminist notions of dependence linked to the production/reproduction debate. That is, confronted with the massive devaluation of women's labor, feminists have spent a tremendous amount of energy demonstrating women's productivity. Women provide valuable labor in the home that re-produces the species and keeps the large economy running. However, because feminists tended to base their work on younger women's lives, these important arguments tend to maintain an assumption that productive is better than "unproductive." This age-based assumption again saddles the old with the requirement that they stay active and "young" in order to be first-class citizens. One could use feminist arguments concerning the value of domestic labor to show that the old are also productive and hence valuable; but such as strategy can result in a sort of tyranny. Old women would then feel shackled to care work; and anyone unable or unwilling to do such work would lose her status as a respectable member of her society. Feminists did not intend such ageism, but their arguments lead in that direction.

The emphasis on the value of reproductive labor makes it all the more difficult for the old to resist being exploited as cheap or unpaid labor. If freedom is about choice, in old age this would mean having the opportunity, rather than the directive, to be productive. By not examining the ageist basis of dependence, feminists have unwittingly undermined potential value in that which—and those who—might be deemed "unproductive."

Finally, there are multiple kinds of dependence—economic, physical, psychological, social—that may or may not be related in any given context. To the extent that this is the case, feminist analyses have been useful in demonstrating that dependence has an ideological component, changing meaning based on historical context (D. Gibson 1998). However, even here, dependence retains a negative cast. For instance, feminists have demonstrated that contemporary assertions of dependence among welfare mothers are misplaced (e.g., Fraser and Gordon 1994), but in so doing they distinguish between their reliance on the state and the more negative dependence on others. To a great extent, we believe this results from their focus on young and middle-aged women and neglect of age relations. We explain this more clearly below.

As we noted in chapter 7, feminists have examined care work extensively, but primarily from the standpoint of the care worker. That is, they have been concerned about the ways in which care work is gendered such that women both bear the "burden" of such care and also, as a result, are more vulnerable to economic dependence in later life. But feminists have been far less interested in the care receiver, or the age relations that might fashion the relationship. Indeed, by focusing on the care worker, and the burden and consequences involved, such research reinforces the status of the dependence of the care receiver—the old—as a "negative" trait. The old person him/herself represents the burden, and dependence—in the negative sense— is left as a characteristic of the individual, rather than the product of a relationship. This, then, is the basis on which analyses of welfare mothers, for instance, are predicated. The care that women provide for those who are dependent lead them to rely on others—men or the state. "Dependency continues to be seen as inherently undesirable here, but in this sense it is undesirable not for the primarily dependent person, but for those who carry the 'burden'" (D. Gibson 1998, 201). The notion of dependence itself as a negative condition is never challenged.

What can we learn by focusing on old care receivers? First, as Gibson (1998) aptly demonstrates, care work is relational. As a result, dependence is constructed within the relationship and is not merely a characteristic of an individual. Second, she shows that the real issue, in talking about whether "dependence" is a "good" or a "bad" thing, is power/lessness. She maintains that the problem is not dependence per se; in fact, she notes that we are all involved in some form of dependence in our lives. Examining disabled and frail populations, she demonstrates that one neither can nor need reduce dependency in general. Dependence is inevitable, but not "bad." Instead, the issue is the powerlessness that may accompany it—a powerlessness born of the conditions of the relationship in which one receives care. Having control over one's own care is critical. Gibson (1998, 202) draws from disabled feminist Jenny Morris (1993a, b) who argues that self-determination—independence—involves control of how tasks are carried out, rather than whether or not one can do them oneself. Thus, by understanding the relational aspects of care, we can see ways in which we can reduce the negative aspects of dependence without maintaining that the need for care is negative.

The ideological construction of dependence is still important, however; and here we can again see how a consideration of age relations pushes this argument further. Even in the case of physical dependence, we could posit many babies and children in similar positions as frail elderly people. However, children are not subject to negative notions of dependence in the same way as the old at all. To a great extent, this may be due to the fact that each group stands in a different relationship to middle age: Children are future adults whereas the old will not return to that status.

Conclusion

Taking a gender lens to the study of aging, we have argued that we must understand the ways in which social inequalities shape old-age experiences. Incorporation of these experiences helps us theorize the constructed nature of what we take to be "old age," forces us to expand our concepts to consider context and process, and encourages us to bear in mind the strengths and agency of the old. Together these can lead us to more effective policies and intervention. In this final chapter, we reverse that lens by taking an aging lens to feminist theories of gender inequality. We maintain that feminist theories—the bases of our gender lens—have failed to theorize age relations and their interaction with other systems of oppression.

Just as one cannot merely add women to mainstream theories, one cannot merely add the old, or old women, to feminist approaches. This chapter has identified some areas in need of attention and asked how feminist theories might look when viewed through an *age lens*. In refracting the feminist lens back on itself, we speculated on some of the ways that feminist theories might benefit from attending to the voices of old women at the intersections of social inequalities, and from an examination of age relations. We do not intend to "add to a list of oppressions" that divide people. Instead, theorizing age relations will help us to examine the processes that produce all inequalities, in part by representing one form of inequality that we all face.

We all age, willingly or not; and though the process is dynamic, we all know the crude age categories with which we have divided the population. In this sense, age relations are similar to other social hierarchies in that age groups are both subjective and constructed. Emphasizing their subjective nature, however, does not make age categories any less real; they have real consequences. Bodies—old bodies—matter. We cannot "construct away" or "cure" many of the physical changes that we face. To this extent, the old are not, in fact, just like the middle aged only older. They are different.

Similarly, it is not enough for gerontologists and feminists to put old people at the center of analysis; old age itself must be the focus (Andrews 1999, 316). For instance, scholars need to explore how the changes of old age have been constructed. What meanings do they have? What do we make of old bodies? How do these vary by social location? To be sure, some medical interventions would improve quality of life. But many others do not—nor are they even intended to—except insofar as they hide aging in an attempt to decrease the ageist scorn that the "not old" heap upon the old. The "problem" is not that we age but that we so abuse the old that they want to hide themselves and pass as middle aged. This is our starting point for examining age relations. Borrowing from Schwalbe's (2001) recent work on social inequality, we might ask, how does this process of defining a visible, identifiable group as somehow inferior to the dominant group occur? Who is privileged by such ageism, and how? That is, what advantages, psychic or material, do some people receive from ageism?

We must work to give positive content and power to "old," just as feminists have tried to do to "feminine" and the civil rights/Black power movements did with "Black." We must use the word with respect until we strip it of its negative connotations. "Old," like terms used for other age groups, must encompass positive aspects of this time of life. For instance, even though we know that this overgeneralization does not fit everyone, "young" includes energy *and* immaturity. "Old" could include less energy as well as wisdom. We must also address structural inequities that deny power to subgroups of the old. This involves, among other things, breaking the ethical hold that "activity" and "productive aging" have on our views of aging. Just as feminists have argued for women's emancipation and freedom—specifically for their right to choose on a variety of levels— so too must the old be free to choose lifestyles and ways of being old that suit them. Thus, we might envisage acceptance of a wide variety of ways of being old that include inactivity as well as activity; contemplation as well as physical exertion; acceptance by others and by oneself that the old do not stop being sexual but have the right to be vibrant sexual beings who decide whether (or not) to engage in sexual expression in all its varieties.

We need to examine age relations in order to address ageism in its deepest form. From our perspective, old people will have achieved equality when they feel free *not* to spend so much time trying to be "young" in order to be acceptable, when they don't have to be "exceptional," when they can be frail, or flabby, or have "age spots." They can, in fact, be old, in all its diversity. "Old" will have positive content, and not simply be defined by disease, mortality, or the absence of value.

Lastly, a society where the old are valued and where old age is not seen negatively is a society that likely will pay attention to the diversity of ways in which the old can serve as mentors for those who are younger. Growing old is the one inevitability that all of us share. Consequently, even if only from a pragmatic standpoint, it behooves us to pay attention to the many avenues that the old traverse as they cope with the positives and negatives of old age. We can learn much from examining other cultures, to identify conditions that promote greater or different sources of respect for the old. But the experiences of the old in the United States are also instructive, perhaps especially those whose social locations have resulted in experiences speak directly to dealing with discrimination and stigma. Thus, there is much to learn from old lesbians who have developed a lifetime of strategies to help them confront and resist stigma. We can look as well to old minority women and men who have met and conquered challenges throughout their lives and who now in old age are equipped to survive and create meaningful lives—even in the face of adversity.

AARP. 1999. Modern Maturity Sexuality Survey. Washington, DC: AARP.

———. 1995a. *Images of Aging in America.* Chapel Hill, N.C.: FGI Integrated Marketing.

———. 1995b. "The Sandwich Generation: Does It Really Exist?" *Horizons* 5(1): 5.

Abel, Emily K. 1991. *Who Will Care for the Elderly? Public Policy and the Experiences of Adult Daughters.* Philadelphia: Temple University Press.

Abrams, K., L. Allen, and J. Gray. 1993. "Disordered Eating Attitudes and Behaviors, Psychological Adjustment, and Ethnic Identity: A Comparison of Black and White Female College Students." *International Journal of Eating Disorders* 14: 49–57.

Acker, Joan. 1990. "Hierarchies, Jobs, Bodies: A Theory of Gendered Organizations." *Gender & Society,* 4(2): 139–58.

Adam, Barry D. 2000. "Age Preferences Among Gay and Bisexual Men." *GLQ: A Journal of Lesbian and Gay Studies* 6(3): 413–33.

Adams, Stephanie, Heather Nawrocki, and Barbara Coleman. 1999. "Women and Long-Term Care." Fact Sheet No. 77, AARP Public Policy Institute. Washington, D.C.: AARP.

Administration on Aging. 2000. *America's Families Care: A Report on the Needs of America's Family Caregivers.* Washington, D.C.: U.S. Department of Health and Human Services.

Akiba, Daisuke. 1998. "Cultural Variations in Body Esteem: How Young Adults in Iran and the United States View Their Own Appearances." *The Journal of Social Psychology* 138: 539–40.

Akiyama, Hiroko, Toni C. Antonucci, and Ruth Campbell. 1997. "Exchange and Reciprocity Among Two Generations of Japanese and American Women." Pp. 163–78 in *The Cultural Context of Aging: Worldwide Perspectives,* 2nd ed., ed. Jay Sokolovsky. Westport, Conn.: Bergin & Garvey.

Allen, Katherine R., and Victoria Chin-Sang. 1990. "A Lifetime of Work: The Context and Meanings of Leisure for Aging Black Women." *The Gerontologist* 30(6): 734–40.

Allen, Katherine R., and David H. Demo. 1995. "The Families of Lesbians and Gay Men: A New Frontier in Family Research." *Journal of Marriage and the Family*, 57(1): 111–27.

Altabe, Madeline, and J. Kevin Thompson. 1992. "Size Estimation versus Figural Reactions of Body Image Disturbance: Relation to Body Dissatisfaction and Eating Dysfunction." *International Journal of Eating Disorders* 11: 397–402.

Amott, Teresa, and Julie Matthaei. 1996. *Race, Gender and Work: A Multicultural History of Women in the United States*, revised edition. Boston: South End Press.

Andrews, Molly. 1999. "The Seductiveness of Agelessness." *Ageing and Society* 19(3): 301–18.

Anderson, A. E., and L. DiDomenico. 1992. "Diet vs. Shape Content of Popular Male and Female Magazines: A Does-Response Relationship to the Incidence of Eating Disorders?" *International Journal of Eating Disorders* 11: 283–87.

Antonucci, Toni, and Marjorie H. Cantor. 1994. "Strengthening the Family Support System for Older Minority Persons." Pp. 40–45 in *Minority Elders: Five Goals Toward Building a Public Policy Base*, ed. James S. Jackson. Washington, D.C.: The Gerontological Society of America.

Aranda, Maria P., and Bob G. Knight. 1997. "The Influence of Ethnicity and Culture on the Caregiver Stress and Coping Process: A Sociocultural Review and Analysis." *The Gerontologist* 37(3): 342–54.

Arber, Sara, and Jay Ginn. 1991a. *Gender and Later Life*. Newbury Park: Sage.

Arber, Sara, and Jay Ginn. 1991b. "The Invisibility of Age: Gender and Class in Later Life." *Sociological Review* 39(2): 260–91.

Arendell, Terry, and Carroll L. Estes. 1991. "Older Women in the Post-Reagan Era." Pp. 209–26 in *Critical Perspectives on Aging: The Political and Moral Economy of Growing Old*, ed. Meredith Minkler and Carroll L. Estes. New York: Baywood Publishing Co.

Arluke, Arnold, and Jack Levine. 1984. "Another Stereotype: Old Age as a Second Childhood." *Aging* (August): 7–11.

Aronson, Jane. 1992. "Women's Sense of Responsibility for the Care of Old People: 'But Who Else Is Going to Do It?'" *Gender & Society*, 6(1): 8–29.

Aronson, Jane. 1990. "Old Women's Experiences of Needing Care: Choice or Compulsion?" *Canadian Journal on Aging*, 9(3): 234–47.

Associated Press. 1998. "Poll: Young Fear Aging, Elders Don't." April 5.

Atchley, Robert C. 1997. "Retirement Income Security: Past, Present, and Future." *Generations* 21(2): 9–12.

Baca Zinn, Maxine, and Bonnie Thornton Dill. 1996. "Theorizing Difference from Multiracial Feminism." *Feminist Studies* 22(Summer): 321–31.

Badgett, M.V. Lee. 1998. "The Economic Well-Bring of Lesbian, Gay, and Bisexual Adults' Families." Pp. 231-48 in *Lesbian, Gay, and Bisexual Identities in Families: Psychological Perspectives*, ed. Charlotte J. Patterson and Anthony R. D'Augelli. New York: Oxford University Press.

Barak, Benny. 1998. "Inner-Ages of Middle-Aged Prime-Lifers." *International Journal of Aging and Human Development* 46(3): 189–228.

Barer, Barbara. 1994. "Men and Women Aging Differently." *International Journal of Aging and Human Development* 38(1): 29–40.

Barker, Judith C., Joelle Morrow, and Linda S. Mitteness. 1998. "Gender, Informal Social Support Networks, and Elderly Urban African Americans." *Journal of Aging Studies* 12 (2): 199–222.

Barrett, Anne E., and Scott M. Lynch. 1999. "Caregiving Networks of Elderly Persons: Variation by Marital Status." *The Gerontologist* 39(6): 695–704.

Bartky, Sandra L. 1990. *Femininity and Domination*. New York: Routledge.

———. 1998. "Foucault, Femininity, and the Modernization of Patriarchal Power." Pp. 25–45 in *The Politics of Women's Bodies: Sexuality, Appearance, and Behavior*, ed. Rose Weitz. New York: Oxford University Press.

Belgrave, Linda L. 1988. "The Effects of Race Differences in Work History, Work Attitudes, Economic Resources, and Health on Women's Retirement." *Research on Aging* 10(3): 383–98.

Beltran, Ana. 2000. "Grandparents and Other Relatives Raising Children: Supportive Social Policies." *The Public Policy and Aging Report* 11(1): 1, 3–7.

Bengtson, Vern L., Elisabeth O. Burgess, and Tonya M. Parrott. 1997. "Theory, Explanation, and a Third Generation of Theoretical Development in Social Gerontology." *Journal of Gerontology: Social Sciences*, 52B (2): S72–S88.

Benjamin, A. E. 1999. "Targeted Attention and the Diversity of Aging." *The Gerontologist* 39(1): 111–14.

Beren, Susan E., Helen A. Hayden, Denise E. Wilfley, and Ruth H. Striegel-Moore. 1997. "Body Dissatisfaction Among Lesbian College Students." *Psychology of Women Quarterly* 21: 431–45.

Beren, Susan E., Helen A. Hayden, Denise E. Wilfley, and Carlos M. Grilo. 1996. "The Influence of Sexual Orientation on Body Dissatisfaction in Adult Men and Women." *International Journal of Eating Disorders* 20: 135–41.

Bergeron, Sherry M., and Charlene Y. Senn. 1998. "Body Image and Sociocultural Norms: A Comparison of Heterosexual and Lesbian Women." *Psychology of Women Quarterly* 22: 385–401.

Berger, Raymond M. 1982. "The Unseen Minority: Older Gays and Lesbians." *Social Work* 27: 236–42.

Berger, Raymond M., and James J. Kelly. 1996. "Gay Men and Lesbians Grow Older." Pp. 305–16 in *Textbook of Homosexuality and Mental Health*, ed. Robert P. Cabaj and Terry S. Stein. Washington, D.C.: American Psychiatric Press, Inc.

Berk, Sarah Fenstermaker. 1985. *The Gender Factory: The Apportionment of Work in American Households*. New York: Plenum Press.

Bielby, Denise D., and William T. Bielby. "She Works Hard for the Money: Household Responsibilities and the Allocation of Work Effort." *American Journal of Sociology* 93: 1031–59.

Biggs, Simon. 1997. "Choosing Not To Be Old? Masks, Bodies and Identity Management in Later Life." *Ageing and Society* 17(5): 553–70.

———. 1999. *The Mature Imagination: Dynamics of Identity in Midlife and Beyond*. Buckingham: Open University Press.

Bird, Chloe E. 1999. "Gender, Household Labor, and Psychological Distress: The Impact of the Amount and Division of Housework." *Journal of Health and Social Behavior* 40(1): 32–45.

Blea, Irene I. 1992. *La Chicana and the Intersection of Race, Class, and Gender*. New York: Praeger.

Blieszner, Rosemary. 1993. "A Socialist-Feminist Perspective on Widowhood." *Journal of Aging Studies* 7(2): 171–82.

Boaz, Rachel F. 1987. "Work as a Response to Low and Decreasing Real Income During Retirement." *Research on Aging* 9(3): 428–40.

Bourdieu, Pierre. 1984. *Distinction: A Social Critique of the Judgement of Taste.* London: Routledge.

Bound, John, Michael Schoenbaum, and Timothy Waidmann. 1996. "Race Differences in Labor Force Attachment and Disability Status." *The Gerontologist* 36(3): 311–21.

Bowers, Susan P. 1999. "Gender Role Identity and the Caregiving Experience of Widowed Men." *Sex Roles* 41(9/10): 645–55.

Boxer, Andrew M. 1997. "Gay, Lesbian, and Bisexual Aging into the Twenty-First Century: An Overview and Introduction." *Journal of Gay, Lesbian, and Bisexual Identity* 2(3/4): 187–97.

Braithwaite, Virginia A., and Diane Gibson. 1987. "Adjustment to Retirement: What We Know and What We Need to Know." *Ageing and Society,* 7(1): 1–18.

Brand, P., E. Rothblum and L. Soloman . 1992. "A Comparison of Lesbians, Gay Men, and Heterosexuals on Weight and Restricted Eating." *International Journal of Eating Disorders* 11: 253–59.

Bretschneider, J., and N. McCoy. 1988. "Sexual Interest in Healthy 80–102 Year Olds." *Archives of Sexual Behavior* 17: 109–30.

Browne, Colette V. 1998. *Women, Feminism, and Aging.* New York: Springer Publishing Company.

Brownmiller, Susan. 1984. *Femininity.* New York: Ballantine.

Brumberg, Joan Jacobs. 1998. *The Body Project: An Intimate History of American Girls.* New York: Vintage Books.

Brush, Lisa. 1999. "Gender, Work, Who Cares?! Production, Reproduction, Deindustrialization, and Business as Usual." Pp. 161–89 in *Revisioning Gender*, ed. Myra Marx Ferree, Judith Lorber, and Beth B. Hess. Thousand Oaks, Calif.: Sage.

Bryson, Ken, and Lynne Casper. 1999. *Co-resident Grandparents and Grandchildren.* Pp. 23–198. U.S. Bureau of the Census: Washington, D.C.

Burnette, Denise. 1999. "Social Relationships of Latino Grandparent Caregivers: A Role Theory Perspective." *The Gerontologist* 39(1): 49–58.

Burton, Linda M. 1996. "Age Norms, the Timing of Family Role Transitions, and Intergenerational Caregiving among Aging African-American Women." *The Gerontologist,* 36(2): 199–208.

Burton, Linda M., Peggye Dilworth-Anderson, and Vern L. Bengtson. 1992. "Creating Culturally Relevant Ways of Thinking about Diversity and Aging: Theoretical Challenges for the Twenty-First Century." Pp. 129–40 in *Diversity: New Approaches to Ethic Minority Aging*, ed. E. Percil Stanford and Fernando M. Torres-Gil. Amityville, New York: Baywood Publishing Co.

Butler, Judith. 1993. *Bodies that Matter: On the Discursive Limits of "Sex."* New York: Routledge.

Butler, Robert. 1969. "Ageism: Another Form of Bigotry." *The Gerontologist* 9(3): 243–46.

Butler, R. N., and M. I. Lewis. 1988. *Love and Sex After 60.* New York: Harper & Row.

Butrica, Barbara A., Howard M. Iams, and Steven H. Sandell. 1999. "Using Data for Couples to Project the Distributional Effects of Changes in Social Security Policy." *Social Security Bulletin* 62(3): 20–27.

Butrica, Barbara A., and Howard M. Iams. 1999. "Projecting Retirement Income of Future Retirees with Panel Data: Results from the Modeling Income in the

Near Term (MINT) Project." *Social Security Bulletin* 62(4): 3–8.

Byer, Curtis, and Louis Shainberg. 1994. *Dimensions of Human Sexuality*. Madison, Wis.: W.C. Brown Co.

Calasanti, Toni M. 1987. Work, Gender, and Retirement Satisfaction. Unpublished dissertation, University of Kentucky, Lexington.

———. 1993. "Bringing in Diversity: Toward an Inclusive Theory of Retirement." *Journal of Aging Studies* 7(2): 133–50.

———. 1996a. "Gender and Life Satisfaction in Retirement: An Assessment of the Male Model." *Journal of Gerontology: Social Sciences*, 51B(1): S18–S29.

———. 1996b. "Incorporating Diversity: Meaning, Levels of Research, and Implications for Theory." *The Gerontologist*, 36(2): 147–56.

———. 1999. "Feminism and Gerontology: Not Just for Women." *Hallym International Journal on Aging* 1(1): 44–55.

Calasanti, Toni M., and Carol A. Bailey. 1991. "Gender Inequality and the Division of Household Labor in the United States and Sweden: A Socialist-Feminist Approach." *Social Problems* 38(1): 34–53.

Calasanti, Toni M., and Alessandro Bonanno. 1986. "The Social Creation of Dependence, Dependency Ratios, and the Elderly in the United States: A Critical Analysis." *Social Science and Medicine* 23(12): 1229–36.

Calasanti, Toni M., and Alessandro Bonanno. 1992. "Working 'Over-time': Economic Restructuring and Class Retirement." *The Sociological Quarterly* 33(1): 135–52.

Calasanti, Toni M., and Anna M. Zajicek. 1993. "A Socialist-Feminist Approach to Aging: Embracing Diversity." Journal of Aging Studies, 7 (2): 117–31.

———. 1997. "Gender, the State, and Constructing the Old as Dependent: Lessons from the Economic Transition in Poland." *The Gerontologist* 37(4): 452–61.

Calderon, Vanessa, and Sharon L. Tennstedt. 1998. "Ethnic Differences in the Expression of Caregiver Burden: Results of a Qualitative Study." *Journal of Gerontological Social Work* 30(1-2): 162–75.

Cancian, Francesca M., and Stacey J. Oliker. 2000. *Caring and Gender*. Thousand Oaks, Calif.: Pine Forge Press.

Cash, Thomas F. 2000. "Women's Body Images: For Better or for Worse." Unpublished manuscript.

Cash, Thomas F., and Patricia E. Henry. 1995. "Women's Body Images: The Results of a National Survey in the U.S.A." *Sex Roles* 33: 19–28.

Cash, Thomas F., and Thomas Pruzinsky. 1990. *Body Images: Development, Deviance, and Change*. New York: The Guilford Press.

Cash, Thomas F., and K. L. Hicks. 1990. "Being Fat Versus Thinking Fat: Relationships with Body Image, Eating Behaviors, and Well-Being." *Cognitive Therapy and Research* 14: 327–41.

Cattell, Maria G. 1997. "African Widows, Culture, and Social Change." Pp. 71–98 in *The Cultural Context of Aging: Worldwide Perspectives*, 2nd ed., ed. Jay Sokolovsky. Westport, Conn.: Bergin & Garvey.

Chalfie, D. 1994. *Going It Alone: A Closer Look at Grandparents Parenting Grandchildren*. Washington, D.C.: American Association of Retired Persons.

Chan, Christopher G., and Glen H. Elder Jr. 2000. "Matrilineal Advantage in Grandchild-Grandparent Relations." *The Gerontologist* 40(2): 179–90.

Chen, Yung-Ping. 1994. "Improving the Economic Security of Minority Persons as They Enter Old Age." Pp. 22–31 in *Minority Elders: Five Goals toward Building a Public Policy Base*, ed. James S. Jackson. Washington, D.C.: The Gerontological Society of America.

———. 1999. "Racial Disparity in Retirement Income Security Directions for Policy Reform." Pp. 21–31 in *Full Color Aging: Fact, Goals, and Recommendations for America's Diverse Elders*, ed. Toni P. Miles. Washington, D.C.: The Gerontological Society of America.

Chen, Yung-Ping, and Thomas D. Leavitt. 1997. "The Widening Gap between White and Minority Pension Coverage." *The Public Policy and Aging Report* 8(1): 10–11.

Choudhury, Sharmila, and Michael V. Leonesio. 1997. "Life-Cycle Aspects of Poverty among Older Women." *Social Security Bulletin*, 60(2): 17–36.

Clements, Mark. 1996. "Sex After 65." *Parade Magazine*, March 17: 4–6.

Cohen, Philip N. 1998. "Replacing Housework in the Service Economy: Gender, Class, and Race-Ethnicity in Service Spending." *Gender & Society*, 12(2): 219–31.

Cole, Thomas. 1992. *The Journey of Life: A Cultural History of Aging in America.* Cambridge: Cambridge University Press.

———. 1995. "What Have We 'Made' of Aging?" *Journal of Gerontology* 50B(6): S341–43.

Coles, Catherine. 1991. "The Older Woman in Hasau Society." Pp. 57–81 in *The Cultural Context of Aging: Worldwide Perspectives*, 2nd ed., ed. Jay Sokolovsky. Westport: Conn.: Bergin & Garvey.

Collins, Patricia Hill. 1990. *Black Feminist Thought: Knowledge, Consciousness, and the Politics of Empowerment.* Boston: Unwin Hyman.

Coltrane, Scott. 1999. *Gender and Families.* Thousand Oaks, Calif.: Pine Forge Press.

Connell, R.W. 1995. *Masculinities.* Berkeley: University of California Press.

———. 1999. "Making Gendered People: Bodies, Identities, Sexualities." Pp. 449–78 in *Revisioning Gender*, ed. Myra Marx Ferree, Judith Lorber, and Beth B. Hess. Thousand Oaks, Calif.: Sage Publications.

Connell, R.W. and G.W. Dowsett, eds. 1992. *Rethinking Sex: Social Theory and Sexuality Research.* Philadelphia: Temple University Press.

Conway-Turner, Kate. 1999. "Older Women of Color: A Feminist Exploration of the Intersections of Personal, Familial and Community Life." *Journal of Women and Aging* 11(2/3): 115–30.

Copper, Baba. 1986. "Voices: On Becoming Old Women." Pp. 46–57 in *Women and Aging: An Anthology by Women*, ed. Jo Alexander et al. Corvallis, Ore.: Calyx Books.

Coverman, Shelly. 1983. "Gender, Domestic Labor Time, and Wage Inequality." *American Sociological Review* 48(6): 623–37.

Coverman, Shelly, and Joseph Sheley. 1986. "Change in Men's Housework and Child-Care Time, 1965–1975." *Journal of Marriage and the Family* 48: 413–22.

Cox, Donna M. 1993. "The Influence of Class on Aging Policy: Why Catastrophic was Repealed." *Journal of Aging Studies* 7(1): 55–65.

Cox, Harvey. 2001. *Later Life: The Realities of Aging*, 5th edition. Englewood Cliffs, New Jersey: Prentice Hall.

Crandall, C., and R. Martinez. 1996. "Culture, Ideology, and Anti-Fat Attitudes." *Personality and Social Psychology Bulletin* 22: 1165–76.

Crystal, Stephen, Richard W. Johnson, Jeffrey Harman, Usha Sambamoorthi, and Rizie Kumar. 2000. "Out-of-Pocket Health Care Costs among Older Americans." *Journal of Gerontology: Social Sciences* 55(1): S51–S62.

Crisologo, SueAnne, Mary H. Campbell, and James A. Forte. 1996. "Social Work, AIDS and the Elderly: Current Knowledge and Practice." *Journal of Gerontological Social Work* 26(1/2): 49–70.

Cruikshank, Margaret. 1991. "Lavender and Grey: A Brief Survey of Lesbian and Gay Aging Studies." *Journal of Homosexuality* 20(3/4): 77–87.

Cutler, Stephen J. 2000. Review of *Handbook of Theories of Aging*, ed. Vern L. Bengtson and K. Warner Schaie. *Contemporary Gerontology* 6(3): 84–85.

Dale, Angela, and Claire Bamford. 1988. "Older Workers and the Peripheral Workforce: The Erosion of Gender Differences." *Ageing and Society* 8(1): 43–62.

Danigelis, Nicholas L., and Barbara R. McIntosh. 1993. "Resources and Productive Activity of Elders: Race and Gender as Contexts." *Journal of Gerontology: Social Sciences* 48(4): S192–S203.

Dannefer, Dale. 1996. "The Social Organization of Diversity, and the Normative Organization of Age." *The Gerontologist* 36 (2): 174–77.

Davis, Kathy. 1995. *Reshaping the Female Body: the Dilemma of Cosmetic Surgery*. London: Routledge.

Davis, Cindy, and Melanie Katzman. 1997. "Charting New Territory: Body Esteem, Weight Satisfaction, Depression, and Self-Esteem In Hong Kong." *Sex Roles* 36: 449–59.

Day, Christine L. 1993. "Older Americans' Attitudes toward the Medicare Catastrophic Coverage Act of 1988." *Journal of Politics* 55: 167–77.

Defey, Denise, Eduardo Storch, Silvia Cardozo, Olga Diaz, and Graciela Fernandez. 1996. "The Menopause: Women's Psychology and Health Care." *Social Science and Medicine* 42(10): 1447–56.

DeViney, Stanley, and Angela M. O'Rand. 1988. "Gender-Cohort Succession and Retirement among Older Men and Women, 1951–1984." *The Sociological Quarterly* 29(4): 524–40.

DeViney, Stanley, and Jennifer Crew Solomon. 1995. "Gender Difference in Retirement Income: A Comparison of Theoretical Explanations." *Journal of Women & Aging* 7(4): 83–100.

Diamond, Timothy. 1992. *Making Grey Gold: Narratives of Nursing Home Care*. Chicago: University of Chicago Press.

Dilworth-Anderson, Peggye, Sharon Wallace Williams, and Theresa Cooper. 1999. "Family Caregiving to Elderly African Americans: Caregiver Types and Structures." *Journal of Gerontology: Social Sciences* 54B(4): S237–S241.

Dinnerstein, Myra, and Rose Weitz. 1994. "Jane Fonda, Barbara Bush, and Other Aging Bodies: Femininity and the Limits of Resistance." *Feminist Issues* 14(3): 3–24.

Dorfman, Rachelle, Karina Walters, Patrick Burke, Lovida Hardin, Theresa Karanik, John Raphael, and Ellen Silverstein. 1995. "Old, Sad and Alone: The Myth of the Aging Homosexual." *Journal of Gerontological Social Work* 24(1/2): 29–44.

Dressel, Paula, Meredith Minkler, and Irene Yen. 1997. "Gender, Race, Class, and Aging: Advances and Opportunities." *International Journal of Health Services* 27(4): 579–600.

Dwyer, Jeffrey W., and Karen Seccombe. 1991. "Elder Care as Family Labor: The

Influences of Gender and Family Position." *Journal of Family Issues* 12(2): 229–47.

Ekerdt, David J., and Stanley DeViney. 1990. "On Defining Persons as Retired." *Journal of Aging Studies* 4(2): 211–29.

Elias, Norbert. 1978. *The History of Manners*. New York : Pantheon Books.

Ericksen, Julia A., and Sally A. Steffen. 1999. *Kiss and Tell: Surveying Sex in the Twentieth Century*. Cambridge, Mass.: Harvard University Press.

Estes, Carroll L. 1983. "Austerity and Aging in the United States: 1980 and Beyond." Pp. 169–85 in *Old Age and the Welfare State*, ed. Annemarie Guillimard. Beverly Hills: Sage.

———. 1991. "The New Political Economy of Aging: Introduction and Critique." Pp. 19–36 in *Critical Perspectives on Aging: The Political and Moral Economy of Growing Old*, ed. Meredith Minkler and Carroll Estes. New York: Baywood Publishing Co.

Estes, Caroll L., and Elizabeth A. Binney. 1991. "The Biomedicalization of Aging: Dangers and Dilemmas." Pp. 117–34 in Critical Perspectives on Aging: The Political and Moral Economy of Growing Old, edited by Meredith Minkler and Caroll L. Estes. NY: Baywood.

Estes, Carroll L., Karen W. Linkins, and Elizabeth A. Binney. 1996. "The Political Economy of Aging." Pp. 346–61 in *Handbook of Aging and the Social Sciences*, fourth edition, ed. Robert H. Binstock and Linda K. George. San Diego: Academic Press.

Estes, Carroll L., and Martha Michel. 1999. "Fact Sheet on Women and Social Security." GSA Task Force on Women. Washington, D.C.: The Gerontological Society of America.

Facio, Elisa. 1996. *Understanding Older Chicanas: Sociological and Policy Perspectives*. Thousand Oaks, Calif.: Sage.

———. 1997. "Chicanas and Aging: Toward Definitions of Womanhood." Pp. 335–50 in *Handbook on Women and Aging*, ed. Jean Coyle. Westport, Conn.: Greenwood Press.

Fallon, A. 1990. "Culture in the Mirror: Sociocultural Determinants of Body Image." Pp. 80–109 in *Body Images: Development, Deviance and Change*, ed. Thomas Cash and Thomas Pruzinsky. New York: Guilford Press.

Farkas, Janice I., and Angela M. O'Rand. 1998. "The Pension Mix for Women in Middle and Late Life: The Changing Employment Relationship." *Social Forces* 76(3): 1007–32.

Featherstone, Mike, and Andrew Wernick, eds. 1995. *Images of Aging: Cultural Representations of Later Life*. London: Routledge.

Featherstone, Mike, and Mike Hepworth. 1989. "Ageing and Old Age: Reflections on the Postmodern Life Course." In *Becoming and Being Old: Sociological Approaches to Later Life*, ed. Bill Bytheway, T. Keil, P. Allatt, and A. Bryman. London: Sage.

Featherstone, Mike, Mike Hepworth, and Bryan S. Turner, eds. 1991. *The Body: Social Process and Cultural Theory*. London: Sage.

Feingold, Alan, and Ronald Mazzella. 1998. "Gender Differences in Body Image Are Increasing." *Psychological Science* 9(May): 190–95.

Feldberg, Rosalynn, and Evelyn Nakano Glenn. 1979. "Male and Female: Job Versus Gender Models in the Sociology of Work." *Social Problems* 26(5): 524–38.

Finch, C. B. Jr. 1991. Sexual Orientation, Body Image, and Sexual Functioning.

Unpublished master's thesis, Old Dominion University, Norfolk, Va.

Finley, Nancy. 1989. "Theories of Family Labor as Applied to Gender Differences in Caregiving for Elderly Parents." *Journal of Marriage and the Family* 51(1): 79–86.

Flippen, Chenoa, and Marta Tienda. 2000. "Pathways to Retirement: Patterns of Labor Force Participation and Labor Market Exit among the Pre-Retirement Population by Race, Hispanic Origin, and Sex." *Journal of Gerontology: Social Sciences* 55(B): S14–S27.

Flynn, Kristin, and Marian Fitzgibbon. 1996. "Body Image Ideals of Low-Income African American Mothers and their Preadolescent Daughters." *Journal of Youth and Adolescence* 25: 615–30.

Franzoe, Stephen L., and Virginia Koehler. 1998. "Age and Gender Differences in Body Attitudes: A Comparison of Young and Elderly Adults." *International Journal of Aging and Human Development* 47: 1–10.

Fraser, Nancy, and Linda Gordon. 1994. "A Genealogy of Dependency: Tracing a Keyword of the U.S. Welfare State." *Signs* 19(Winter): 309–36.

Friend, Richard A. 1991. "Older Lesbian and Gay People: A Theory of Successful Aging." *Journal of Homosexuality* 20(3/4): 99–118.

Friedan, Betty. 1993. *The Fountain of Age*. New York: Simon and Schuster.

Fronstin, Paul. 1999. "Retirement Patterns and Employee Benefits: Do Benefits Matter?" *The Gerontologist* 39(1): 37–47.

Foucault, Michel. 1979. *Discipline and Punish: The Birth of the Prison*. New York: Vintage Books.

Fuller-Thomson, Esme, Meredith Minkler, and Diane Driver. 1997. "A Profile of Grandparents Raising Grandchildren in the United States." *The Gerontologist* 37(3): 406–11.

Fullmer, Elise M., Dena Shenk, and Lynette J. Eastland. 1999. "Negating Identity: A Feminist Analysis of the Social Invisibility of Older Lesbians." *Journal of Women and Aging* 11(2/3): 131–48.

Garner, David. 1997. "The 1997 Body Image Survey Results." *Psychology Today* (January/February): 30–44, 75–80, 84.

Gerike, Ann E. 1996. "On Gray Hair and Oppressed Brains." Pp. 155–63 in *Aging for the Twenty-First Century*, ed. Jill Quadagno and Debra Street. New York: St. Martin's Press.

Gerschick, Thomas J., and Adam Stephen Miller. 1994. "Gender Identities at the Crossroads of Masculinity and Physical Disability." *Masculinities* 2(1): 34–55.

Gerstel, Naomi, and Sally Gallagher. 1994. "Caring for Kith and Kin: Gender, Employment, and the Privatization of Care." *Social Problems* 41(4): 519–39.

———. 2001. "Men's Caregiving: Gender and the Contingent Character of Care." *Gender & Society* 15(2): 197–217.

Gibson, Diane. 1996. "Broken Down by Age and Gender: 'The Problem of Old Women' Redefined." *Gender & Society* 10(4): 433–48.

———. 1998. *Aged Care: Old Policies, New Problems*. New York: Cambridge University Press.

Gibson, Rose C. 1987. "Reconceptualizing Retirement for Black Americans." *The Gerontologist* 27(6): 691–98.

Giddens, Anthony, and Mitchell Duneier. 2000. *Introduction to Sociology* (third edition). New York: W. W. Norton.

Giddings, Paula. 1984. *When and Where I Enter: The Impact of Black Women on Race and Sex in America*. New York: Bantam Books.

Ginn, Jay, and Sara Arber. 1999. "Changing Patterns of Pension Inequality: The Shift from State to Private Sources." *Ageing and Society* 19(3): 319–42.

Glasse, Lou, Carroll L. Estes, and Timothy Smeeding. 1999. "Older Women and Social Security." GSA Task Force on Women. Washington, D.C.: The Gerontological Society of America. http://www.geron.org/Updates.htm. Accessed March 5, 1999.

Glazer, Nona Y. 1990. "The Home as Workshop: Women as Amateur Nurses and Medical Care Providers." *Gender & Society* 4(4): 479–99.

Glenn, Evelyn Nakano. 1985. "Racial Ethnic Women's Labor: The Intersection of Race, Gender and Class Oppression." *Review of Radical Economics* 17(3): 86–108.

———. 1992. "From Servitude to Service Work: Historical Continuities in the Racial Division of Paid Reproductive Labor." *Signs* 18:1–43.

———. 1999. "The Social Construction and Institutionalization of Gender and Race: An Integrative Framework." Pp. 3–43 in *Revisioning Gender*, ed. Myra Marx Ferree, Judith Lorber, and Beth B. Hess. Thousand Oaks, Calif.: Sage Publications.

———. 2000. "Creating a Caring Society." *Contemporary Sociology* 29(1): 84–94.

Goldsmith, Ronald E., and Richard A. Heiens. 1992. "Subjective Age: A Test of Five Hypotheses." *The Gerontologist* 32(3): 312–17.

Gonyea, Judith G. 1994. "The Paradox of the Advantaged Elder and the Feminization of Poverty." *Social Work* 39(1): 35–41.

Gough, J. 1989. "Theories of Sexual Identity and the Masculinisation of the Gay Man." Pp.119–35 in *Coming on Strong: Gay Politics and Culture*, ed. Simon Shepherd and Mick Wallis. London: Unwin Hyman.

Gould, Ketayun. 1989. "A Minority-Feminist Perspective on Women and Aging." Pp. 195–216 in *Women as They Age: Challenges, Opportunity, and Triumph*, ed. J. Dianne Garner and Susan O. Mercer. New York: Haworth Press.

Graebner, William. 1980. *A History of Retirement: The Meaning and Function of an American Institution*. New Haven, Conn.: Yale University Press.

Graham, Avy D. 1994. "Coordinating Private Pension Benefits with Social Security." *Monthly Labor Review* 117(3): 35–38.

Gray, Heather, and Paula Dressel. 1985. "Alternative Interpretations of Aging among Gay Males." *The Gerontologist* 25(1): 83–87.

Greenwood, S. 1992. *Menopause Naturally: Preparing for the Second Half of Life*. Volcano, Calif.: Volcano Press.

Greer, Germaine. 1991. *The Change: Women, Aging, and Menopause*. New York: Fawcett.

Grogan, Sarah. 1999. *Body Image*. London: Routledge.

Gross, David, and Normandy Brangan. 1999. *Out-of-Pocket Health Spending by Medicare Beneficiaries Age 65 and Older: 1999 Projections*. Public Policy Institute, AARP. Washington, D.C.: AARP.

Gupta, Sanjiv. 1999. "The Effects of Transition in Marital Status on Men's Performance of Housework." *Journal of Marriage and the Family* 61(3): 700–11.

Haber, Carole. 1983. *Beyond Sixty-Five: The Dilemma of Old Age in America's Past*. New York: Cambridge University Press.

Haber, Carole, and Brian Gratton. 1994. *Old Age and Search for Security*. Bloomington: Indiana University Press.

Han, Shin-Kap, and Phyllis Moen. 1999. "Clocking out: Temporal Patterning of Retirement." *American Journal of Sociology* 105(1): 191–236.

Hardy, Melissa A. 1991. "Employment After Retirement: Who Gets Back In?" *Research on Aging* 13(3): 267–88.

Harrington Meyer, Madonna. 1996. "Family Status and Poverty among Older Women: The Gendered Distribution of Retirement Income in the U.S." Pp. 464–79 in *Aging for the Twenty-First Century*, ed. Jill Quadagno and Debra Street. New York: St. Martin's Press.

———. 1997. "Toward a Structural, Life Course Agenda for Reducing Insecurity Among Women as They Age." *The Gerontologist* 37(6): 833–34.

Harris, L., and Associates. 1995. *The Myth and Reality of Aging in America*. Washington, D.C.: The National Council on the Aged, Inc.

Harris, Mary B. 1994. "Growing Old Gracefully: Age Concealment and Gender." *Journal of Gerontology: Psychological Sciences* 49(4): 149–58.

Harris, Phyllis Braudy, and Susan Orpett Long. 1999. "Husbands and Sons in the United States and Japan: Cultural Expectations and Caregiving Experiences." *Journal of Aging Studies* 13(3): 241–67.

Harris, S. 1994. "Racial Differences in Predictors of College Women's Body Image Attitudes." *Women and Health* 21: 89–104.

Hartmann, Heidi. 1981. "The Family as the Locus of Gender, Class, and Political Struggle: The Example of Housework." *Signs* 6(3): 366–94.

Hatch, Laurie Russell. 1991. "Informal Support Patterns of Older African-American and White Women." *Research on Aging* 13(2): 144–70.

Hatch, Laurie Russell, and Aaron Thompson. 1992. "Family Responsibilities and Women's Retirement." Pp. 99–113 in *Families and Retirement*, ed. Maximilliane Szinovacz, David J. Ekerdt, and Barbara Vinick. Thousand Oaks, Calif.: Sage Publications.

Hayward, Mark D., Samantha Friedman, and Hsinmu Chen. 1996. "Race Inequities in Men's Retirement." *Journal of Gerontology: Social Sciences* 51B(1): S1–S10.

Heidrich, Susan M., and Carol D. Ryff. 1993. "The Role of Social Comparison Processes in the Psychological Adaptation of Elderly Adults." *Journal of Gerontology: Psychological Sciences* 48(3): 127–36.

Heinberg, L. J. 1996. "Theories of Body Image Disturbance: Perceptual, Developmental, and Sociocultural Factors." Pp. 27–47 in *Body Image, Eating Disorders, and Obesity*, ed. J. K. Thompson. Washington, D.C.: American Psychological Association.

Hendley, Alexa A., and Natasha F. Bilimoria. 1999. "Minorities and Social Security: An Analysis of Racial and Ethnic Differences in the Current Program." *Social Security Bulletin* 62(2): 59–64.

Hendricks, Jon. 1995. "The Social Construction of Ageism." Pp. 51–68 in *Promoting Successful and Productive Aging*, ed. Lynne A. Bond, Stephen J. Cutler, and Armin Grams. Thousand Oaks, Calif.: Sage.

Herdt, Gilbert, Jeff Beeler, and Todd W. Rawls. 1997. "Life Course Diversity among Older Lesbians and Gay Men: A Study in Chicago." *Journal of Gay, Lesbian, and Bisexual Identity* 2(3/4): 231–46.

Herzog, A. Regula, R. L. Kahn, John N. Morgan, James S. Jackson, and Toni Antonucci. 1989. "Age Differences in Productive Activities." *Journal of Gerontology* 44(4): S129–S138.

Hill, Shirley A. 1997. Book Review of *Feminist Perspectives on Family Care: Policies and Gender Justice*, by Nancy R. Hooyman and Judith Gonyea. *Gender & Society* (1): 133–34.

Hite, Shere. 1976. *The Hite Report: A Nationwide Study on Female Sexuality.* New York: Macmillan.

Hodson, Diane S., and Patsy Skeen. 1994. "Sexuality and Aging: The Hammerlock of Myths." *The Journal of Applied Gerontology* 13(September): 219–35.

Holstein, Martha. 1994. "Changing Concepts: Visionary or Short-Sighted?" *Ageing International* 11(2): 20–22.

———. 1999. "Women and Productive Aging: Troubling Implications." Pp. 359–73 in *Critical Gerontology: Perspectives form Political and Moral Economy*, ed. Meredith Minkler and Carroll L. Estes. Amityville, N.Y.: Baywood Publishing Co.

Hooyman, Nancy R. 1999. "Research on Older Women: Where is Feminism?" *The Gerontologist* 39(1): 115–18.

Hooyman, Nancy R., and N. Asuman Kiyak. 1999. *Social Gerontology: A Multidisciplinary Perspective.* Boston: Allyn and Bacon.

Hooyman, Nancy R., and Judith Gonyea. 1995. *Feminist Perspectives on Family Care: Policies and Gender Justice.* Thousand Oaks, Calif.: Sage Publications.

———. 1999. "A Feminist Model of Family Care: Practice and Policy Directions." *Journal of Women & Aging* 11(2/3): 149–69.

Howarth, Glennys. 1993. "Food Consumption, Social Roles, and Personal Identity." Pp. 65–77 in *Ageing, Independence, and the Life Course*, ed. Sara Arber and Maria Evandrou. London: Jessica Kingsley Publishers.

Huffine, Christopher. 1991. Body-Image Attitudes and Perceptions Among African Americans and Whites as a Function of Socioeconomic Class. Unpublished dissertation, Virginia Consortium Program in Clinical Psychology, Virginia Beach, Va.

Hurtado, Aida. 1989. "Relating to Privilege: Seduction and Rejection in the Subordination of White Women and Women of Color." *Signs* 14: 833–55.

Irwin, Sarah. 1999. "Later Life, Inequality, and Sociological Theory." *Ageing and Society* 19(6): 691–15.

Jackson, Jacquelyne Johnson. 1988. "Aging Black Women and Public Policies." *Black Scholar* 19 (May/June): 31–43.

Janus, S. S., and Janus, C. L. 1993. *The James Report on Sexual Behavior.* New York: John Wiley and Sons.

Jendrek, Margaret Platt. 1996. "Grandparents who Parent Their Grandchildren: Effects on Lifestyles." Pp. 286–305 in *Aging for the Twenty-First Century*, ed. Jill Quadagno and Debra Street. New York: St. Martin's Press.

Jenike, Brenda Robb. 1997. "Gender and Duty in Japan's Aged Society: The Experience of Family Caregivers." Pp. 218–38 in *The Cultural Context of Aging: Worldwide Perspectives*, ed. Jay Sokolovsky. Westport, Conn.: Bergin & Garvey.

John, Robert. 1994. "The State of Research on American Indian Elders' Health, Income Security, and Social Support Networks." Pp. 46–58 in *Minority Elders: Five Goals toward Building a Public Policy Base*, ed. James S. Jackson. Washington, D.C.: The Gerontological Society of America.

———. 1999. "Aging Among American Indians: Income Security, Health, and Social Support Networks." Pp. 65–91 in *Full Color Aging: Fact, Goals, and Recommendation for Americas' Diverse Elders*, ed. Toni P. Miles. Washington, D.C.: The Gerontological Society of America.

John, Robert, Catherine Hagan Hennessy, Timothy B. Dyeson, and Mario D. Garrett. 2001. "Toward the Conceptualization and Measurement of Caregiver Burden among Pueblo Indian Family Caregivers." *The Gerontologist* 41(2): 210–19.

Johnson, Colleen L. 1994a. "Introduction: Social and Cultural Diversity of the Oldest-Old." *International Journal of Aging and Human Development* 38(1): 1–12.

———. 1994b. "Differential Expectations and Realities: Race, Socioeconomic Status and Health of the Oldest-Old." *International Journal of Aging and Human Development* 38(1): 13–27.

Johnson, Richard W., Usha Sambamoorthi, and Stephan Crystal. 1999. "Gender Differences in Pension Wealth: Estimates Using Provider Data." *The Gerontologist* 39(3): 320–33.

Katz, Stephen. 2000. "Busy Bodies: Activity, Aging, and the Management of Everyday Life." *Journal of Aging Studies* 14(2): 135–52.

Katz, Steven J., Mohammed Kabeto, and Kenneth M. Langa. 2000. "Gender Disparities in the Receipt of Home Care for Elderly People with Disability in the United States." *Journal of the American Medical Association* 284(23): 3022–27.

Katzko, Michael W., Nardi Steverink, Freya Dittmann-Kohli, and Ramona Rubio Herrera. 1998. "The Self-Concept of the Elderly: A Cross-Cultural Comparison." *International Journal of Aging and Human Development*, 46(3): 171–87.

Kellett, J. M. 1991. "Sexuality and the Elderly." *Sexual and Marital Therapy* 6: 147–55.

Kennickell, Arthur B., and Annika E. Sunden. 1997. "Pensions, Social Security, and the Distribution of Wealth." Board of Governors of the Federal Reserve System. Finance and Economics Discussion Series. No. 1997-55 (Nov.).

Kimmel, Douglas C. 1995. "Lesbians and Gay Men Also Grow Old." Pp. 289–303 in *Promoting Successful and Productive Aging*, ed. Lynne A. Bond, Stephen J. Cutler, and Armin Grams. Thousand Oaks, Calif.: Sage.

King, Mary C. 1992. "Occupational Segregation by Race and Sex, 1940–1988." *Monthly Labor Review* 114(7): 30–36.

Kinsey, Alfred C., Wardell B. Pomeroy, and Clyde E. Martin. 1948. *Sexual Behavior in the Human Male*. Philadelphia: W. B. Saunders Co.

Kirsi, Tapio, Antti Hervonen, and Marja Jylha. 2000. "A Man's Gotta Do What a Man's Gotta Do: Husbands as Caregivers to Their Demented Wives: A Discourse Analytic Approach." *Journal of Aging Studies* 14 (2): 153–69.

Kivett, Vira R. 1991. "Centrality of the Grandfather Role among Older Rural Black and White Men." *Journal of Gerontology: Social Sciences* 46(5): S250–S258.

Klem, M. L., R. C. Klesger, C. R. Bene, and M. W. Mellon. 1990. "A Psychometric Study of Restraint: The Impact of Race, Gender, Weight, and Marital Status." *Addictive Behaviors* 15: 147–52.

Kohli, Martin. 1988. "Ageing as a Challenge for Sociological Theory." *Ageing and Society* 8(3): 367–94.

Korczyk, Sophie. 1996. "Pre-Retirement Pension Distributions in a Lifetime Perspective." Washington, D.C.: American Association of Retired Persons.

Laumann, E., J. Gagnon, R. Michael, and S. Michaels. 1994. *The Social Organization of Sexuality: Sexual Practices in the United States.* Chicago, Ill.: University of Chicago Press.

Lavine, Howard, Donna Sweeney, and Stephen H. Wagner. 1999. "Depicting Women as Sex Objects in Television Advertising: Effects on Body Dissatisfaction." *Personality and Social Psychology Bulletin* 25(August): 1049–58.

Laws, Glenda. 1995. "Understanding Ageism: Lessons From Feminism and Postmodernism." *The Gerontologist* 35(1): 112–18.

Lawton, M. Powell, Doris Rajagopal, Elaine Brody, and Morton H. Kleban. 1992. "The Dynamics of Caregiving for a Demented Elder among Black and White Families." *Journals of Gerontology: Social Sciences* 47(4): S156–S164.

Lee, John Alan. 1987. "What Can Homosexual Aging Studies Contribute to Theories of Aging?" *Journal of Homosexuality* 13(4): 43–71.

Leiblum, Sandra. 1990. "Sexuality and the Midlife Woman." *Psychology of Women Quarterly* 14: 495–508.

Levy, Judith. 1994. "Sex and Sexuality in Later Life Stages." Pp. 287–309 in Sexuality across the Life Course, ed. Alice Rossi. Chicago, Ill.: University of Chicago Press.

Lillard, Lee, Jeannette Rogowski, and Raynard Kington. 1997. "Long-term Determinants of Patterns of Health Insurance Coverage in the Medicare Population." *The Gerontologist* 37(3): 314–23.

Lockery, Shirley A. 1992. "Caregiving among Racial and Ethnic Minority Elders: Family and Social Supports." Pp. 113–22 in *Diversity: New Approaches to Ethic Minority Aging,* ed. E. Percil Stanford and Fernando M. Torres-Gil. Amityville, N.Y.: Baywood Publishing Co.

Lopez, Ester, Glen Garry Blix, Arlene Gray Blix. 1995. "Body Image of Latinas Compared to Body Image of Non-Latina White Women." *Health Values* 19: 3–10.

Loprest, Pamela. 1998. "Retiree Health Benefits: Availability from Employers and Participation by Employees." *The Gerontologist* 38(6): 684–94.

Lorber, Judith. 1999. "Embattled Terrain: Gender and Sexuality." Pp. 416–48 in *Revisioning Gender,* ed. Myra Marx Ferree, Judith Lorber, and Beth B. Hess. Thousand Oaks, Calif.: Sage.

Lynott, R. J., and Patricia P. Lynott. 1996. "Tracing the Course of Theoretical Development in the Sociology of Aging." *The Gerontologist* 36(6): 749–60.

Macdonald, Barbara (with Cynthia Rich). 1983. *Look Me in the Eye: Old Women, Aging and Ageism.* San Francisco: Spinsters, Ink.

MacRae, Hazel. 1998. "Managing Feelings: Caregiving as Emotion Work." *Research on Aging,* 20(1): 137–60.

Magilvy, Joan K., Joann G. Congdon, Ruby J. Martinez, Renel Davis, and Jennifer Averill. 2000. "Caring for Our Own: Health Care Experiences of Rural Hispanic Elders." *Journal of Aging Studies* 14(2): 171–90.

Malkin, Amy R., Kimberlie Wornian, and Joan C. Chrisler. 1999. "Women And Weight: Gendered Messages on Magazine Covers." *Sex Roles* 40: 647–55.

Martin Matthews, Anne, and Lori D. Campbell. 1995. "Gender Roles, Employment and Informal Care." Pp. 129–43 in *Connecting Gender & Ageing: A Sociological Approach,* ed. Sara Arber and Jay Ginn. Buckingham, UK: Open University Press.

Masters, William, and Virginia Johnson. 1966. *Human Sexual Response.* Boston: Little Brown and Co.

———. 1970. *Human Sexual Inadequacy*. Boston: Little Brown and Co.

Matthews, Sarah H. 1979. *The Social World of Old Women*. Beverly Hills: Sage.

———. 1995. "Gender and the Division of Filial Responsibility between Lone Sisters and Their Brothers." *Journal of Gerontology: Social Sciences*, 50B(5): S312–S320.

Matthias, Ruth, James Lubben, Kathryn Atchison, and Stuart Schweitzer. 1997. "Sexual Activity and Satisfaction among Very Old Adults: Results from a Community-Dwelling Medicare Population." *The Gerontologist* 37(1): 6–14.

Maxwell, Stephanie, Marilyn Moon, and Misha Segal. 2000. "Growth in Medicare and Out-Of-Pocket Spending: Impact on Vulnerable Beneficiaries." Urban Institute Report. December. Accessed at www.urban.org/health/growth-in-medicare.html, Jan. 5, 2001.

May, Martha. 1987. "The Historical Problem of the Family Wage: The Ford Motor Company and the Five Dollar Day." Pp. 111–31 in *Families and Work*, ed. Naomi Gerstel and Harriet Engel Gross. Philadelphia: Temple University Press.

McCaughey, Martha. 1999. "Fleshing Out the Discomforts of Femininity: The Parallel Cases of Female Anorexia and Male Compulsive Bodybuilding." Pp. 133–55 in *Weighty Issues: Fatness and Thinness as Social Problems*, ed. Jeffrey Sobal and Donna Maurer. New York: Aldine De Gruyter.

McHugh, Kevin. 2000. "The 'Ageless Self'? Emplacement of Identities in Sun Belt Retirement Communities." *Journal of Aging Studies* 14(1): 103–15.

McKinlay, J., and H. Feldman. 1994. "Age-Related Variation in Sexual Activity and Interest in Normal Men: Results from the Massachusetts Male Aging Study." Pp. 261–86 in *Sexuality across the Life Course*, ed. Alice Ross. Chicago, Ill.: University of Chicago Press.

McMullin, Julie. 1995. "Theorising Age and Gender Relations." Pp. 30–41 in *Connecting Gender & Ageing: A Sociological Approach*, ed. Sara Arber and Jay Ginn. Buckingham, UK: Open University Press.

———. 2000. "Diversity and the State of Sociological Aging Theory." *The Gerontologist* 40(5): 517–30.

McNeil, John M. 1999. "Preliminary Estimates on Caregiving from Wave 7 of the 1996 Survey of Income and Program Participation." No. 231, U.S. Department of Commerce, Bureau of the Census. Located at www.census.gov/dusd/MAB/wp231.pdf. Accessed Jan. 4, 2000.

Millet, Kate. 1972. *Sexual Politics*. Garden City, N.Y: Doubleday.

Minichiello, Victor, David Plummer, and Anne Seal. 1996. "The 'Asexual' Older Person? Australian Evidence." *Venereology* 9: 180–88.

Minichiello, Victor, Jan Browne, and Hal Kendig. 2000. "Perceptions and Consequences of Ageism: Views of Older People." *Ageing and Society* 20(3): 253–78.

Minkler, Meredith. 1990. "Aging and Disability: Behind and beyond the Stereotypes." *Journal of Aging Studies* 4(3): 246–60.

———. 1996. "Critical Perspectives on Ageing: New Challenges for Gerontology." *Ageing and Society* 16(4): 467–87.

———. 1999. "Intergenerational Households Headed by Grandparents: Context, Realities, and Implications for Policy." *Journal of Aging Studies* 13(2): 199-218.

Minkler, Meredith, and Ann Robertson. 1991. "The Ideology of 'Age/Race Wars': Deconstructing a Social Problem." *Ageing and Society* 11(1): 1–22.

Mitchell, Olivia S., Phillip B. Levine, and John W. Phillips. 1999. "The Impact of Pay Inequality, Occupational Segregation, and Lifetime Work Experience on the Retirement Income of Women and Minorities." Public Policy Institute. AARP: Washington, D.C.

Moen, Phyllis, Julie Robeson, and Vivian Fields. 1994. "Women's Work and Caregiving Roles: A Life Course Approach." *Journal Of Gerontology: Social Sciences* 49(4): S176–S186.

Moody, H. 1989. "Toward a Critical Gerontology: The Contribution of the Humanities to Theories of Aging.' In *Emergent Theories of Aging*, ed. J. Birrin & V. Bengston. New York: Springer Publishing.

Moon, Marilyn, and Janemarie Mulvey. 1996. *Entitlements and the Elderly: Protecting Promises, Recognizing Reality*. Washington, D.C.: The Urban Institute Press.

Morgan, Kathryn P. 1998. "Women and the Knife: Cosmetic Surgery and the Colonization of Women's Bodies." Pp. 25–45 in *The Politics of Women's Bodies: Sexuality, Appearance, and Behavior*, ed. Rose Weitz. New York: Oxford University Press.

National Alliance for Caregiving and AARP. 1997. *Family Caregiving in the U.S.: Findings from a National Survey*. Washington, D.C.: National Alliance for Caregiving.

Neal, Margaret B., Berit Ingersoll-Dayton, and Marjorie E. Starrels. 1997. "Gender and Relationship Differences Among Employed Caregivers." *The Gerontologist* 37(6): 804–16.

Nelson, Margaret K. 1999. "Between Paid and Unpaid Work: Gender Patterns in Supplemental Economic Activities among White, Rural Families." *Gender & Society* 13(4): 518–39.

New York *Times*. 2000. Living Section, p. 1, Oct. 8.

Oberg, Peter. 1996. "The Absent Body—A Social Gerontological Paradox." *Ageing and Society* 16(6): 701–19.

Oberg, Peter, and Lars Tornstam. 1999. "Body Images among Men and Women of Different Ages." *Ageing and Society* 19(5): 629–44.

Oliver, Melvin, and Thomas Shapiro. 1995. *Black Wealth/White Wealth: A New Perspective on Racial Inequality*. New York: Routledge.

O'Rand, Angela M. 1996. "The Precious and the Precocious: Understanding Cumulative Disadvantage and Advantage over the Life Course." *The Gerontologist*, 36(3): 230–38.

Palmore, Erdman. 2000. "Guest Editorial: Ageism in Gerontological Language." *The Gerontologist*, 40(6): 645.

Pampel, Fred C. 1998. *Aging, Social Inequality, and Public Policy*. Thousand Oaks, Calif.: Sage.

Parker, Sheila, Mimi Nichter, Mark Nichter, Nancy Vuckovic, Colette Sims, and Cheryl Rittenbaugh. 1995. "Body Image and Weight Concerns among African American and White Adolescent Females: Differences that Make a Difference." *Human Organization* 54: 103–14.

Peek, Kristen, Raymond T. Coward, Chuck W. Peek, and Gary R. Lee. 1998. "Are Expectations for Care Related to the Receipt of Care: An Analysis of Parent Care among Disabled Elders." *Journal of Gerontology: Social Sciences*, 53B(3): S217–S136.

Peek, Kristen, Raymond T. Coward, and Chuck W. Peek. 2000. "Race, Aging, and Care: Can Differences in Family and Household Structure Account for Variations in Informal Care?" *Research on Aging* 22(2): 117–42.

Phillipson, Chris. 1998. *Reconstructing Old Age: New Agendas in Social Theory and*

Practice. Thousand Oaks, Calif.: Sage.

Pierce, Jennifer L. 1995. *Gender Trials: Emotional Lives in Contemporary Law Firms*. Berkeley, Calif.: University of California Press.

Pina, Darlene L., and Vern L. Bengtson. 1995. "Division of Household Labor and the Well-Being of Retirement-Aged Wives." *The Gerontologist* 35(3): 308–17.

Pliner, P., S. Chaiken, and G. L. Flett. 1990. "Gender Differences in Concern with Body Weight and Physical Appearance over the Life Span." *Personality and Social Psychology Bulletin* 16: 263–73.

Pogrebin, Letty Cottin. 1996. *Getting Over Getting Older*. Boston: Little, Brown and Company.

Pope, Mark, and Richard Schultz. 1996. "Sexual Attitudes and Behavior in Midlife and Aging Homosexual Males." Pp. 267–75 in *Gay and Gray: The Older Homosexual Man*, second edition, by Raymond M. Berger. New York: Harrington Park Press.

Press, Julie E., and Eleanor Townsley. 1998. "Wives' and Husbands' Housework Reporting: Gender, Class, and Social Desirability." *Gender & Society* 12(2): 188–218.

Pringle, Rosemary. 1992. "Absolute Sex? Unpacking the Sexuality/Gender Relationship." Pp. 76–101 in *Rethinking Sex: Social Theory and Sexuality Research*, ed. R. W. Connell and G. W. Dowsett. Melbourne: Melbourne University Press.

Pruchno, Rachel A. 1999. "Raising Grandchildren: The Experiences of Black and White Grandmothers." *The Gerontologist* 39(2): 209–21.

Pruchno, Rachel A., and Katrina W. Johnson. 1996. "Research on Grandparenting: Review of Current Studies and Future Needs." *Generations* 20(Spring): 65–70.

Quadagno, Jill S. 1988. "Women's Access to Pensions and the Structure of Eligibility Rules: Systems of Production and Reproduction." *The Sociological Quarterly* 29(4): 541–58.

———. 1996. "Social Security and the Myth of the Entitlement Crisis." *The Gerontologist* 36(3): 391–99.

———. 1999. *Aging and the Life Course*. Boston: McGraw-Hill.

Quadagno, Jill S., and Madonna Harrington Meyer. 1990. "Gender and Public Policy." *Generations* 14(2): 64–66.

Quam, Jean K., and Gary S. Whitford. 1992. "Adaptation and Age-Related Expectations of Older Gay and Lesbian Adults." *The Gerontologist* 32(3): 367–74.

Quinn, Joseph F., Joseph V. Burkhauser, and Daniel A. Myers. 1990. *Passing the Torch: The Influence of Economic Incentives on Work and Retirement*. Kalamazoo, Mich.: W. E. Upjohn Institute for Employment Search.

Radner, Hilary. 1995. *Shopping Around*. New York: Routledge.

Rank, Mark R., and Thomas A. Hirschl. 1999. "Estimating the Proportion of Americans Ever Experiencing Poverty During their Elderly Years." *Journal of Gerontology: Social Sciences* 54B(4): S184–S193.

Ray, Ruth E. 1996. "A Postmodern Perspective on Feminist Gerontology." *The Gerontologist* 36(5): 674–80.

Read, Jane. 1999. "ABC of Sexual Health: Sexual Problems Associated with Infertility, Pregnancy, and Ageing." *British Medical Journal* 318(February): 587–89.

Reiss, Ira. 1995. "Is This the Definitive Sexual Survey?" *Journal of Sex Research* 32: 77–85.

Reissman, Frank. 1990. "Restructuring Help: A Human Services Paradigm for the 1990s." *America Journal of Community Psychology* 18(2): 221–30.

Rexroat, Cynthia, and Constance Shehan. 1987. "The Family Life Cycle and Spouses' Time in Housework." *Journal of Marriage and the Family* 49(4): 737–50.

Rich, Cynthia. 1983a. "Aging, Ageism and Feminist Avoidance." Pp. 53–64 in *Look Me in the Eye: Old Women, Aging and Ageism*, by Barbara Macdonald (with Cynthia Rich). San Francisco: Spinsters, Ink.

————. 1983b. "Cynthia's Afterword." Pp. 102–6 in *Look Me in the Eye: Old Women, Aging and Ageism*, by Barbara Macdonald (with Cynthia Rich). San Francisco: Spinsters, Ink.

Richardson, Virginia, and Keith M. Kilty. 1992. "Retirement Intentions among Black Professionals: Implications for Practice with Older Black Adults." *The Gerontologist* 32(1): 7–16.

Risman, Barbara J. 1987. "Intimate Relationships from a Microstructural Perspective: Men Who Mother." *Gender & Society* 1(1): 6–32.

Rix, Sara E. 1993. "Women and Well-Being in Retirement: What Role for Public Policy?" *Journal of Women & Aging* 4(4): 37–56.

Rix, Sara E., and John B. Williamson. 1998. "Social Security Reform: How Might Women Fare?" Public Policy Institute, Issue Brief No. 31. Washington, D.C.: AARP.

Roberto, Karen A., Katherine R. Allen, and Rosemary Blieszner. 1999. "Older Women, Their Children, and Grandchildren: A Feminist Perspective on Family Relationships." *Journal of Women & Aging* 11(2/3): 67–84.

Roberts, Linda J., Deborah Salem, Julian Rappaport, Paul A. Toro, Douglas A. Luke, Edward Seidman. 1999. "Giving and Receiving Help: Interpersonal Transactions in Mutual-Help Meetings and Psychosocial Adjustment of Members." *American Journal of Community Psychology* 27(6): 841–68.

Robertson, Ann. 1991. "The Politics of Alzheimer's Disease: A Case Study in Apocalyptic Demography." Pp. 135–50 in *Critical Perspectives on Aging: The Political and Moral Economy of Growing Old*, ed. Meredith Minkler and Carroll L. Estes. New York: Baywood.

Rodeheaver, Dean. 1987. "When Old Age Became a Social Problem, Women Were Left Behind." *The Gerontologist* 27(6): 741–46.

————. 1990. "Labor Market Progeria." *Generations* 14(3): 53–58.

Rodeheaver, Dean, and Nancy Datan. 1985. "Gender and the Vicissitudes of Motivation in Adult Life." *Advances in Motivation and Achievement* 4: 169–87.

Rose, Hilary, and Errollyn Bruce. 1995. "Mutual Care but Differential Esteem: Caring between Older Couples." Pp. 114–28 in *Connecting Gender & Ageing: A Sociological Approach*, ed. Sara Arber and Jay Ginn. Buckingham, UK: Open University Press.

Rosenberg, Harriet G. 1997. "Complaint Discourse, Aging and Caregiving among the Ju/'hoansi of Botswana." Pp. 33–55 in *The Cultural Context of Aging: Worldwide Perspectives*, 2nd ed., ed. Jay Sokolovsky. Westport, Conn: Bergin & Garvey.

Rosenfeld, Dana. 1999. "Identity Work among Lesbian and Gay Elderly." *Journal of Aging Studies*, 13(2): 121–55.

Rozin, P., and A. Fallon. 1998. "Body Images, Attitudes to Weight, and Misperceptions of Figure Preferences of the Opposite Sex: A Comparison of Men and Women of Two Generations." *Journal of Abnormal Psychology* 97: 342–45.

Rothblum, E. 1990. "Women and Weight: Fad and Fiction." *The Journal of Psychology* 124: 5–24.

Rubin, Gayle S. 1993. "Thinking Sex: Notes for a Radical Theory of the Politics of Sexuality." Pp. 3–55 in *American Feminist Thought at Century's End: A Reader*, ed. Linda S. Kauffman. Cambridge: Blackwell.

Rubinstein, Robert L., Baine B. Alexander, Marcene Goodman, and Mark Luborsky. 1991. "Key Relationships of Never Married, Childless Older Women." *Journal of Gerontology* 46(5): 5270–77.

Safilios-Rothschild, Constantina. 1977. "Sexuality, Power, and Freedom among 'Older' Women." Pp. 162–66 in *Looking Ahead: A Woman's Guide to the Problems and Joys of Growing Older*, ed. L. Troll, J. Israel, and R. Israel. Englewood Cliffs, N.J.: Prentice-Hall, Inc.

Sandell, Steven H., Howard M. Iams, and Daniel Fanaras. 1999. "The Distributional Effects of Changing the Averaging Period and Minimum Benefit Provisions." *Social Security Bulletin* 62(2): 4–13.

Schaei, K. Warner. 1993. "Ageist Language in Psychological Research." *American Psychologist* 48(1): 49–51.

Schiavi, Raul C. 1996. "Sexuality and Male Aging: From Performance to Satisfaction." *Sexual and Marital Therapy* 11: 9–13.

Schiavi, R. C., J. Mandeli, and P. Schreiner-Engel. 1994. "Sexual Satisfaction in Healthy Aging Men." *Journal of Sex and Marital Therapy* 20: 3–13.

Schwalbe, Michael. 2001. "The Elements of Inequality." *Contemporary Sociology* 29(6): 775–81.

Schwartz, Pepper, and Virginia Rutter. 1998. *The Gender of Sexuality*. Thousand Oaks, Calif.: Pine Forge Press.

Scott, Charles G. 1999. "Identifying the Race or Ethnicity of SSI Recipients." *Social Security Bulletin* 62(4): 9–20.

Scott, Charles G. 1991. "Aged SSI Recipients: Income, Work History, and Social Security Benefits." *Social Security Bulletin* 54(8): 2–11.

Segraves, R. T., and K. B. Segraves. 1995. "Human Sexuality and Aging." *Journal of Sex Education and Therapy* 21: 88–102.

Shaw, Lois, Diane Zuckerman, and Heidi Hartmann. 1998. *The Impact of Social Security on Women*. Washington, D.C.: Institute for Women's Policy Research.

Shenk, Dena, and Elise M. Fullmer. 1996. "Significant Relationships Among Older Women: Cultural and Personal Constructions of Lesbianism." *Journal of Women & Aging* 8(3/4): 75–89.

Shirey, Lee, and Laura Summer. 2000. "Caregiving: Helping the Elderly with Activity Limitations." *Challenges for the Twenty-First Century: Chronic and Disabling Conditions*, no. 7. Washington, D.C.: National Academy on an Aging Society.

Sicker, Martin. 1994. "The Paradox of Productive Aging." *Ageing International* 11(2): 12–14.

Siegel, Jacob S. 1999. "Demographic Introduction to Racial/Hispanic Elderly Populations." Pp. 1–19 in *Full Color Aging: Facts, Goals, and Recommendations for America's Diverse Elders*, ed. Toni P. Miles. Washington, D.C.: The Gerontological Society of America.

Siever, Michael D. 1994. "Sexual Orientation and Gender as Factors in Socioculturally Acquired Vulnerability to Body Dissatisfaction and Eating

Disorders." *Journal of Consulting and Clinical Psychology* 62: 252–60.

Slevin, Kathleen F., and C. Ray Wingrove. 1998. *From Stumbling Blocks to Stepping Stones: The Life Experiences of Fifty Professional African American Women*. New York: New York University Press.

Smeeding, Timothy M. 1999. "Social Security Reform: Improving Benefit Adequacy and Economic Security for Women." Aging Studies Program Policy Brief no. 16, Center for Policy Research, Maxwell School of Citizenship and Public Affairs. Syracuse, N.Y.: Syracuse University.

Smeeding, Timothy M., Carroll L. Estes, and Lou Glasse. 1999. "Social Security Reform and Older Women: Improving the System." Income Security Policy Series Paper No. 22, Center for Policy Research, Maxwell School of Citizenship and Public Affairs. Syracuse, N.Y.: Syracuse University. Located at www.cpr.maxwell.syr.edu/incomsec/pdf/inc22.pdf. Accessed March 6, 2000.

Social Security Administration. 1998a. Annual Statistical Supplement, *Social Security Bulletin*. Washington, D.C.: U.S. Government Printing Office.

Social Security Administration, Office of Policy. 1998b. *Women and Retirement Security*. www.ssa.gov/policy/sswomen.pdf [prepared by the National Economic Council Interagency Working Group on Social Security, Oct. 27, 1998]. Accessed March 1, 1999.

Social Security Administration, Office of Research, Evaluation and Statistics. 1998c. *Income of the Population 55 or Older, 1996.* www.ssa.gov/statistics/incpop55toc.html. Accessed March 1, 1999.

Social Security Administration. 1999. Annual Statistical Supplement, *Social Security Bulletin*. Washington, D.C.: U.S. Government Printing Office.

———. 2000a. Annual Statistical Supplement, *Social Security Bulletin*. Washington, D.C.: U.S. Government Printing Office.

———. 2000b. *Fast Facts and Figures about Social Security*. Washington, D.C.: U.S. Government Printing Office.

Sokolovsky, Jay. 1993. "Images of Aging: A Cross-Cultural Perspective." *Generations* 17: 51–54.

———. 1997a. "Culture, Aging and Context." Pp. 1–15 in *The Cultural Context of Aging: Worldwide Perspectives*, 2nd ed., ed. Jay Sokolovsky. Westport, Conn.: Bergin & Garvey.

———. 1997b. "Bringing Culture Back Home: Aging, Ethnicity and Family Support." Pp. 263–75 in *The Cultural Context of Aging: Worldwide Perspectives*, 2nd ed., ed. Jay Sokolovsky. Westport, Conn.: Bergin & Garvey.

Sontag, Susan. 1979. "The Double Standard of Aging." Pp. 72–80 in *An Ageing Population: A Reader and Sourcebook*, ed. V. Carver and P. Liddiard. New York: Holmes and Meier.

South, Scott J., and Glenna Spitze. 1994. "Housework in Marital and Nonmarital Households." *American Sociological Review* 59(3): 327–47.

Spelman, Elizabeth V. 1988. *Inessential Woman: Problems of Exclusion in Feminist Thought*. Boston: Beacon Press.

Stoller, Eleanor Palo. 1993. "Gender and the Organization of Lay Health Care: A Socialist-Feminist Perspective." *Journal of Aging Studies* 7(2): 151–70.

Stoller, Eleanor P., and Rose C. Gibson. 2000. *Worlds of Difference*, 3rd ed. Thousand Oaks, Calif.: Pine Forge Press.

Storey, James. 1986. "Policy Changes Affecting Older Americans During the First

Reagan Administration." *The Gerontologist* 26(1): 27–31.

Szinovacz, Maximilliane E. 1980. "Female Retirement: Effects of Spousal Roles and Marital Adjustment." *Journal of Family Issues* 3: 423–38.

———. 2000. "Changes in Housework After Retirement: A Panel Analysis." *Journal of Marriage and the Family* 62(1): 78–92.

Szinovacz, Maximilliane E., Stanley DeViney, and Maxine P. Atkinson. 1999. "Effects of Surrogate Parenting on Grandparents' Well-Being." *Journal of Gerontology: Social Sciences* 54B(6): S376–S388.

Szinovacz, Maximilliane, and Paula Harpster. 1994. "Couples' Employment/Retirement Status and the Division of Household Tasks." *Journal of Gerontology: Social Sciences* 49(3): S125–S136.

Taylor, Robert Joseph, and Linda M. Chatters. 1991. "Extended Family Networks of Older Black Adults." *Journal of Gerontology: Social Sciences*, 46(4): S210–S217.

Thompson, Edward H. Jr. 2000. "Gendered Caregiving of Husbands and Sons." Pp. 333–44 in *Intersections of Aging: Readings in Social Gerontology*, ed. Elizabeth W. Markson and Lisa Ann Hollis-Sawyer. Los Angeles: Roxbury Publishing Company.

Thompson, J. Kevin, L. J. Heinberg, M. Altabe, and S. Tantleff-Dunn. 1999. *Exacting Beauty: Theory, Assessment and the Treatment of Body Image Disturbance.* Washington, D.C.: American Psychological Association.

Thornton Dill, Bonnie. 1983. "Race, Class, and Gender: Prospects for an All-Inclusive Sisterhood." *Feminist Studies* 9: 131–50.

Todd, Judith, Ariella Friedman, and Priscilla Wanjiru Kariuki. 1990. "Women Growing Stronger with Age: The Effect of Status in the United States and Kenya." *Psychology of Women Quarterly* 14: 567–77.

Tolman, Deborah L. 1994. "Doing Desire: Adolescent Girls' Struggles for/with Sexuality." *Gender & Society* 8(3): 324–42.

Tunaley, Jillian R., Susan Walsh, and Paula Nicolson. 1999. "'I'm Not Bad for My Age': The Meaning of Body Size and Eating in the Lives of Older Women." *Ageing and Society* 19(6): 741–59.

Turner, Bryan S. 1992. *Regulating Bodies: Essays in Medical Sociology.* London: Routledge.

Twiggs, Joan E., Julia McQuillan, and Myra Marx Ferree. 1999. "Meaning and Measurement: Reconceptualizing Measures of the Division of Household Labor." *Journal of Marriage and the Family* 61(3): 712–24.

Underwood, Nora. 2000. "Body Envy: Thin is in—And People Are Messing with Mother Nature as Never Before," *Maclean's* 14(August): 36.

Uotinen, Virpi. 1998. "Age Identification: A Comparison Between Finnish and North-American Cultures." *International Journal of Aging and Human Development* 46(2): 109–24.

U.S. Bureau of the Census. 1996. Sixty-Five Plus in the United States. Current Population Reports, Series P23–190. Washington, D.C.: U.S. Government Printing Office.

———. 1998a. "Married Women Joining Work Force Spur 150 Percent Family Income Increase, Census Bureau Finds in 50-Year Review." www.census.gov/Press-Release/cb98-181.html. Accessed March 13, 2000.

———. 1998b. Current Population Reports, P20–514. Marital Status and Living Arrangements: March 1998 (Update). Washington, D.C.: U.S. Government Printing Office.

———. 1999a. "Household Income at Record High; Poverty Declines in 1998, Census Bureau Reports." Economics and Statistics Division. www.census.gov/Press-Release/www/1999/cb99-188.html. Accessed March 14, 1999.

———. 1999b. "Census Bureau Publishes Compendium for Millennium: 1999 Statistical Abstract Highlights 20th Century Changes." www.census.gov/Press-Release/www/1999/cb99-238.html. Accessed March 13, 2000.

———. 2000. Statistical Abstract of the United States: 2000. Washington, D.C.: U.S. Government Printing Office.

Waehrer, Keith, and Stephan Crystal. 1995. "The Impact of Coresidence on Economic Well-Being of Elderly Widows." *Journal of Gerontology: Social Sciences* 50B(4): S250–S258.

Wagenbach, P. M. 1997. Relationship Between Body Image, Sexual Orientation and Gay Identity. Unpublished doctoral dissertation, Virginia Consortium Program in Clinical Psychology, Virginia Beach, Va.

Wallace, Steven P. 1991. "Political Economy of Health Care for Elderly Blacks." Pp. 253–69 in *Critical Perspectives on Aging: The Political and Moral Economy of Growing Old*, ed. Meredith Minkler and Carroll Estes. New York: Baywood.

Wallace, Steven P., and Elisa Linda Facio. 1992. "Moving Beyond Familism: Potential Contributions of Gerontological Theory to Studies of Chicano/Latino Aging." Pp. 207–24 in *Aging, Self, and Community: A Collection of Readings*, ed. Jaber R. Gubrium and Kathleen C. Charmaz. Stamford, Conn.: JAI Press Inc.

Walker, Alan. 1990. "The Economic 'Burden' of Ageing and the Prospects of Intergenerational Conflict." *Ageing and Society* 10(4): 377–96.

———. 1996. "The Relationship between the Family and the State in the Care of Older People." Pp. 269–85 in *Aging for the Twenty-First Century: Readings in Social Gerontology*, ed. Jill Quadagno and Debra Street. New York: St. Martin's Press.

Walker, Alexis. 1992. "Conceptual Perspectives on Gender and Family Caregiving." Pp. 34–46 in *Gender, Families, and Elder Care*, ed. Jeffrey W. Dwyer and Raymond T. Coward. Newbury Park, Calif.: Sage.

Walker, Bonnie, ed. 1997. *Sexuality and the Elderly: A Research Guide*. Westport, Conn.: Greenwood Press.

Wallace, Meredith. 1992. "Management of Sexual Relationships among Elderly Residents of Long-Term Care Facilities." *Geriatric Nursing* (November/December): 308–10.

Walsh, P., and J. Worthington. 1995. *The Prostate*. Baltimore, Md.: Johns Hopkins University Press.

Weeks, Jeffrey. 1994. "The Body and Sexuality." Pp. 363–93 in *The Polity Reader in Gender Studies*. Cambridge: Polity Press, in association with Blackwell Publishers.

———. 1996. *Sexuality*. London: Routledge.

Weg, Ruth. 1996. "Sexuality, Sensuality, and Intimacy." *Encyclopedia of Gerontology* 2: 479–88.

Weitz, Rose. 1998. "A History of Women's Bodies." Pp. 25–45 in *The Politics of Women's Bodies: Sexuality, Appearance, and Behavior*, ed. Rose Weitz. New York: Oxford University Press.

Weibel-Orlando, Joan. 1997. "Grandparenting Styles: The Contemporary American Experience." Pp. 139–55 in *The Cultural Context of Aging: Worldwide Per-*

spectives, 2nd ed., ed. Jay Sokolovsky. Westport, Conn.: Bergin & Garvey.

Wellin, E. 1999. Review of *Handbook of Theories of Aging*, edited by Vern L. Bengtson and K. Warner Schaei. *Choice*, June. Electronic Collection: BA1390462 (Books in Print with Book Reviews, accessed September 13, 2000).

Wilcox, Sara. 1997. "Age and Gender in Relation to Body Attitudes: Is There a Double Standard of Aging?" *Psychology of Women Quarterly* 21(4): 549–65.

Wiley, Diana, and Walter M. Bortz. 1996. "Sexuality and Aging—Usual and Successful." *Journal of Gerontology* 51A(3): M142–M146.

Wilkinson, Doris Y. 1995. "Gender and Social Inequality: The Prevailing Significance of Race." *Dædalus*, 124(1): 167–78.

Wingrove, C. Ray, and Kathleen F. Slevin. 1991. "A Sample of Professional and Managerial Women's Success in Work and Retirement." *Journal of Women and Aging* 3(2): 95–117.

Wiseman, C. V., F. M. Gunning, and J. J. Gray. 1993. "Increasing Pressure to Be Thin: 19 Years of Diet Products in Television Commercials." *Eating Disorders: The Journal of Treatment and Prevention* 1: 52–61.

Wiseman, M. A., J. J. Gray., J. E. Mosimann, and A. H. Ahrens. 1992. "Cultural Expectations of Thinness in Women: An Update." *International Journal of Eating Disorders* 11: 85–89.

Wolf, Naomi. 1991. *The Beauty Myth: How Images of Beauty are Used Against Women*. New York: Doubleday.

Woods, James. 1996. "Pension Benefits Among the Aged: Conflicting Measures, Unequal Distributions." *Social Security Bulletin* 59(3): 3–30.

Woodward, Kathleen, ed. 1999. *Figuring Age: Women, Bodies, Generations*. Bloomington: Indiana University Press.

Wu, Zheng, and Michael S. Pollard. 1998. "Social Support Among Unmarried Childless Elderly Persons." *Journal of Gerontology: Social Sciences* 53B(6): S324–S335.

Yee, Jennifer L., and Richard Schulz. 2000. "Gender Differences in Psychiatric Morbidity among Family Caregivers: A Review and Analysis." *The Gerontologist* 40(2): 147–64.

Zeiss, Antoinette M. 1997. "Sexuality and Aging: Normal Changes and Clinical Problems." *Topics in Geriatric Rehabilitation* 12: 11–27.

Zita, Jacquelyn N. 1997. "Hersey in the Female Body: The Rhetorics of Menopause." Pp. 95–112 in *The Other within Us: Feminist Explorations of Women and Aging*, ed. Marily Pearsall and Susan Sontag. Boulder, Colo.: Westview Press.

Zsembick, B. A., and A. Singer. 1990. "The Problem of Defining Retirement Among Minorities: The Mexican Americans." *The Gerontologist* 30(6): 749–57.

I N D E X

Toni Calasanti is Associate Professor of Sociology and a faculty affiliate of the Center for Gerontology at Virginia Tech, where she also teaches women's studies. Her articles on political economy, feminism, and aging have appeared in many journals, including *The Gerontologist, Journal of Gerontology: Social Sciences, Hallym International Journal of Aging, Journal of Aging Studies,* and *The Sociological Quarterly*. Current research projects focus on social inequalities in relation to (paid and unpaid) work and retirement; theorizing age relations; ageism and its intersections with other inequalities; and sexuality and gender in old age.

Kathleen F. Slevin is Chancellor Professor of Sociology at the College of William and Mary. In recent years, her research interests have focused on women in retirement. She is co-author (with C. Ray Wingrove) of a 1998 book on retired African American women, *From Stumbling Blocks to Stepping Stones*, published by New York University Press. Current research interests also center on gender and the aging body.

Intro, ch. 1, 3, 4, 5, 6